The Political Vindication of Radical Empiricism

with application to the
Global Systemic Crisis

VOLUME IX: TOWARD ECOLOGICAL CIVILIZATION SERIES
JEANYNE B. SLETTOM, GENERAL EDITOR

OTHER BOOKS IN THIS SERIES

An Axiological Process Ethics, Rem B. Edwards
Panentheism and Scientific Naturalism, David Ray Griffin
Organic Marxism, Philip Clayton and Justin Heinzekehr
Theological Reminiscences, John B. Cobb, Jr.
Integrative Process, Margaret Stout and Jeannine M. Love
Replanting Ourselves in Beauty, Jay McDaniel & Patricia Adams Farmer, eds.
For Our Common Home, John B. Cobb, Jr., & Ignacio Castuera, eds.
Whitehead Word Book, John B. Cobb, Jr.

The Political Vindication of Radical Empiricism

with application to the
Global Systemic Crisis

MICHEL WEBER

PROCESS
CENTURY
PRESS

The Political Vindication of Radical Empiricism: With Application to the Global Systemic Crisis

Process Century Press
RiverHouse LLC
802 River Lane
Anoka, MN 55303

Process Century Press books are published in association with the International Process Network

Cover Design: Susanna Mennicke
Cover Image: Adapted from Adobe Stock

Toward Ecological Civilization Series
Jeanyne B. Slettom, Series Editor

ISBN 978-1-940447-12-4
Printed in the United States of America

Series Preface: Toward Ecological Civilization

We live in the ending of an age. But the ending of the modern period differs from the ending of previous periods, such as the classical or the medieval. The amazing achievements of modernity make it possible, even likely, that its end will also be the end of civilization, of many species, or even of the human species. At the same time, we are living in an age of new beginnings that give promise of an ecological civilization. Its emergence is marked by a growing sense of urgency and deepening awareness that the changes must go to the roots of what has led to the current threat of catastrophe.

In June 2015, the 10th Whitehead International Conference was held in Claremont, CA. Called "Seizing an Alternative: Toward an Ecological Civilization," it claimed an organic, relational, integrated, nondual, and processive conceptuality is needed, and that Alfred North Whitehead provides this in a remarkably comprehensive and rigorous way. We proposed that he could be "the philosopher of ecological civilization." With the help of those who have come to an ecological vision in other ways, the conference explored this Whiteheadian alternative, showing how it can provide the shared vision so urgently needed.

The judgment underlying this effort is that contemporary research and scholarship is still enthralled by the 17th century view of nature articulated by Descartes and reinforced by Kant. Without freeing our minds of this objectifying and reductive understanding of the world, we are not likely to direct our actions wisely in response to the crisis to which this tradition has led us. Given the ambitious goal of replacing now dominant patterns of thought with one that would redirect us toward ecological civilization, clearly more is needed than a single conference. Fortunately, a larger platform is developing that includes the conference and looks beyond it. It is named Pando Populus (pandopopulus.com)in honor of the world's largest and oldest organism, an aspen grove.

As a continuation of the conference, and in support of the larger initiative of Pando Populus, we are publishing this series, appropriately named "Toward Ecological Civilization."

~John B. Cobb, Jr.

Table of Contents

III. Conclusion

Introduction

This philosophical essay is the product of the interplay of two streams of thought: one that seeks to revisit the foundations of James' radical empiricism and to generalize it to politics; and one that endeavors to think the current global systemic crisis as the last burst of international capitalism. Since our reflections are put under the dual patronage of William James (1842–1910) and Alfred North Whitehead (1861–1947),[1] they use as often as possible the process language of experience and events—instead of speaking about facts, things, reality, substance, and the like.

The essay is structured as follows: first, a theoretical part that proposes a political vindication of radical empiricism; second, a practical part providing some application to the global systemic crisis; and third, a conclusion exploring the pragmatics of political change. In this last part, we propose more a thorough programmatic argument than a detailed analysis simply because the future is open and it would be unwise to privilege a full understanding of past events—something that is impossible anyway (see the concept of opacity §3.2.1)—at a time when we need to create new political ventures.

I. The Political Vindication of Radical Empiricism

All the higher, more penetrating ideals are revolutionary. They present themselves far less in the guise of effects of past experience than in that of probable causes of future experience, factors to which the environment and the lessons it has so far taught us must learn to bend. (James, *Will to Believe*, 1897, 188–89)

The theoretical part of this essay argues for two complementary theses, one pertaining to epistemology and the other to politics.

First, unless philosophy adopts a radical empiricist standpoint and seeks the uttermost generalities, it cannot differentiate itself from yet another form of limited expertise, and it becomes remarkably useless. Hence two important requirements: on the one hand, no experience, no fact, can be excluded a priori from the philosophical agenda; on the other hand, philosophy has to pragmatically and imaginatively seek the broadest empirical truths; it should not to be satisfied with low-level abstractions.

Second, both radical empiricism and imaginative pragmatism lead the philosopher towards the left end of the political spectrum, i.e., to a radically progressive politics. In other words, the more you experience, the more you become acquainted with the world, the more concern you find for your fellow human beings, for other forms of life, and eventually for the entire biosphere. And, as you reflect imaginatively upon that growing experiential field, the more you are lured towards the concept of the common good. Conversely, if you shift to the right, you experience more of the same, and you get stuck with the same a priori enforcing self-centeredness, selfishness, and greed.

We can establish this thesis through the following steps. First, we revisit the question of the nature of the difference between philosophy and expertise. Second, some definition of the socio-political field is provided. Third, the philosophical gesture is specified with a focus on its epistemological dimension. Fourth, consequences are drawn in the political field. A short conclusion goes over the stakes again.

1. Expertise, Experience, and Philosophy

Although there is no agreement amongst philosophers on the definition of their discipline (think, for instance, about the distance that separates Hegelian idealism from logical positivism), it is possible to consider all philosophical discussions from a common perspective. For they all select certain *experiences* to deal with and, in order to achieve some systematic understanding of them or at least to obtain applicable *generalizations,* they apply some kind of *method.* In this chapter, we propose to look at philosophical discussions from the perspective of the *method* that is applied to the *experiences* they debate. There are three broad speculative possibilities that matter in the context of our argument: radical empiricism, empiricism per se, and rationalism. All three cast a different light on the *data/method/outcome* dialectic or cognitive string.

First, from what data do we start?

From all experiences whatsoever? If, one early morning, I see a pink elephant in my bathroom, this experience should then be taken *prima facie* and find an interpretation in my worldview, possibly under the tag "symptom." From some *outer* experiences? In this case, what is called "factual" concerns only what is disclosed in sense-perception and especially in sight; additionally, it is often claimed that facts ought to be measurable. Philosophy would thus be concerned with the same factual reservoir as empirical science. From some *inner* experiences? The factual here concerns only what is clear and distinct to my mind, and these "facts" do *not* spring from sense-perception, from memory, or from imagination (all three being notoriously unreliable) but from *some* ideas or even "Ideas." An introspection of sorts, probably fueled by an ad hoc *epokhê*, would be at the core of the philosophical exercise.

Second, what method do we apply to these data?

Since the exact same experience or event never recurs (we do not step twice in the same river), if all experiences are taken into account, only a pragmatic method can allow us to deal with their plurality (James). It is however advisable to enlarge the scope of pragmatism and to argue for some form of imaginative generalization in order to discuss all possible experiences and to obtain, so to speak tangentially, a Worldview worthy of that name (Whitehead's version of pragmatism). If only some *outer* experiences are to be dealt with, simple observation or a noncritical form of (scientific) experimentation seems appropriate (Locke). If only some *inner* experiences are worth the attention of the philosopher, a *mathesis universalis* of sorts will do (Descartes).

Third, what is the outcome of the procedure?

Radical empiricism's outcome is panpsychism, which involves two arguments. First, experience does not start from a conscious subject but from a network of preconscious experiences binding social actors and their environment. James carves out the concept of pure experience in order to name that primordial and pristine reality in which relations are given. Second, that vague, confused, complex, and neutral experience occasions phenomenal transparency through a triple genesis: our conscious experience emerges progressively as the process of individuation takes place (an *ontogenesis* such as the one Piaget argues for), together with socialization (a *koinogenesis* underlined by Stern or Bateson) and after a long biological evolution (*phylogenesis* championed by Spencer, Darwin, and their kin—see below, §3.3.1).

For their part, empiricism and rationalism bring forth similar ontologies. Empiricism's outcome is materialistic substantialism, which also involves two claims. First, experience consists of passively acquired simple (particular) ideas; second, these ideas are progressively associated to produce the state of consciousness of everyday life. That is, simple (atomic) impressions occasion simple ideas that are consequently associated to progressively obtain more and more complex ideas and eventually a unified, conscious experience. Rationalism's outcome is idealistic substantialism, which follows the exact same pattern; innate general ideas are organized by calculus to obtain conscious experience. In other words, a close reading of both rationalist and empiricist arguments reveals that both philosophical streams share the exact same substantialism, one rather pluralistic and the other rather monistic.

Accordingly, radical empiricism is designed to overcome *both* rationalism (with its innate general ideas formatted by *calculus*) and empiricism (with its acquired particular ideas put together by *association*). It claims that primitive experience is not equivalent to elementary experience; empiricists have mixed up the source or origin and the element. Experience *qua* experience—"pure experience" as James calls it—does not have at all the clarity, the simplicity, the atomicity, the individuality that is presupposed by rationalists and empiricists alike. It is vague, confused (neither clear nor distinct, and certainly not rational), and, above all, relational.[2]

This heuristic 3x3 matrix of speculative possibilities (the *data/method/outcome* string combined with empiricism, rationalism, and radical empiricism) requires three short specifications before we resume the main argument. First, there can be of course a circularity involved in the definition of the data: the outcome of a given train of thought typically serves as rationale for its refinement with the help of data *selected* for their compatibility. The only way to avoid this dogmatic limitation of scope is to adopt radical empiricism. Second, an additional argument would be needed in order to show that there is a conceptual necessity between (i) the three respective types of data, (ii) the three methods, and (iii) the three outcomes. Historically, the correlation is nevertheless plainly obvious. Furthermore, both materialistic and idealistic substantialism are degenerate forms of dualistic substantialism. Whitehead argues that ontological dualism is, by definition, totally incoherent. The only way to try to think two irreconcilable substances is to invoke a divine intervention. As soon as the "God hypothesis" is revoked,[3] dualism degenerates into a one-substance ontology: historically, (techno-scientific) materialism won. Third, this argument presupposes the triple opening of the world that defines postmodernity: spatial (Cues, Bruno), temporal (Spencer, Darwin), and consciential (Myers, Freud).[4]

The most relevant question is to define the cognitive string *data/method/outcome* that best matches the philosophical ideal—as it was defined, say, by Socrates—or at least to specify which one is the most inclusive. It seems to me that only the radical empiricist string both allows the fulfillment of the agenda of philosophy *and* provides an understanding of the other forms of philosophy that exist or have existed. From the radical empiricist standpoint, one can indeed make sense of the rational and of the empirical forms of substantialism— whereas substantialism cannot understand radical empiricism. The very same argument has been made since Heraclitus; the process approach allows us to understand both change and stability. The substance approach can barely suggest a rationale for the stability of *some* features of our experience.

In order to keep the argument tight, we will now develop only the first possibility of each of the three dimensions of our matrix and thereby seek to clarify James' and Whitehead's complementary standpoints.

It is actually easy to clarify the philosophical gesture they adopt. It is made of a very straightforward cognitive thread.

1.1. Data: Radical Empiricism

Philosophy starts from experience—but what part of it? According to process thinkers, all experiences should be taken at face value and find a proper assessment in the philosophical framework. No experience should be rejected a priori. It makes no philosophical sense to refuse to take into account an experience, even if it is an unusual one, such as a hallucination. As soon as the philosopher adopts a perspective that leads to the rejection of some parts of his or her experience, s/he leaves the philosophical field and adopts, willy nilly, the standpoint of *expertise*. (This sharp distinction is as old as Parmenides' poem *On Nature*.)

Jamesian scholars, lured by Perry's groundbreaking works, have always been tempted to read the philosopher's corpus only from the perspective of James' own blend of pragmatism. Sometimes, they have complemented this approach with the topic of pluralism. It is obvious to me, as it has been to John McDermott, Charlene Haddock Seigfried, and Eugene Taylor, that the very core of James' contribution actually lies in his radical empiricism.[5]

There are two main stages of the development of his concept of radical empiricism. First, a pre-systematic radical empiricism: James claims straightaway that psychology and philosophy should deal with all experiences. This is especially important in philosophy; experiences should not be filtered by an a priori judgment. The philosopher who chooses to do so builds her speculations on a Pandora's box always susceptible to release of its uncritical network of presuppositions. Second, a critical and systematized radical empiricism, springing when James adopts, in the years 1904–1905, the *all experiences and only experiences* motto and carves out the concept of pure experience.

Let us bracket the developmental issue to analyze solely this critical stage, which clearly presupposes pluralism:

> The difference between monism and pluralism is perhaps the most pregnant of all the differences in philosophy. *Prima facie* the world is a pluralism; as we find it, its unity seems to be that of any collection; and our higher thinking consists chiefly of an effort to redeem it from that first crude form. Postulating more unity than the first experiences yield, we also discover more. . . .

> He who takes for his hypothesis the notion that it is the per-
> manent form of the world is what I call a radical empiricist.
> For him the crudity of experience remains an eternal element
> thereof. There is no possible point of view from which the world
> can appear an absolutely single fact. (WB viii-ix)

Absolute unity is never to be discovered, either experientially or concep-
tually. We will come back to the issue of pluralism later.

To adopt radical empiricism amounts to two moves. On the one
hand, James argues that *only* experiences are worthy of philosophical
inquiry:

> Nothing shall be admitted as fact, it says, except what can be
> experienced at some definite time by some experient; and for
> every feature of fact ever so experienced, a definite place must be
> found somewhere in the final system of reality. In other words:
> Everything real must be experienceable somewhere, and every
> kind of thing experienced must somewhere be real. (ERE 160)

This, James writes, is the principle of pure experience *qua* methodical
postulate: "the postulate is that the only things that shall be debatable
among philosophers shall be things definable in terms from experience" (MTr xii). It corresponds to what Whitehead calls the ontological principle, which can be summarized by "no actual entity, then no
reason" (PR 19). Both James and Whitehead basically ask philosophers
to center their speculations on their own first-hand experiences, not on
somebody else's.

On the other hand, *all* experiences should be accepted as evidences:

> We feel things differently according as we are sleepy or awake,
> hungry or full, fresh or tired; differently at night and in the
> morning, differently in summer and in winter, and above all
> things differently in childhood, manhood, and old age. Yet we
> never doubt that our feelings reveal the same world, with the
> same sensible qualities and the same sensible things occupying
> it. The difference of the sensibility is shown best by the differ-
> ence of our emotion about the things from one age to another,
> or when we are in different organic moods. What was bright
> and exciting becomes weary, flat, and unprofitable. The bird's
> song is tedious, the breeze is mournful, the sky is sad. (PP I 232)

Experience differs according to one's mood, age, health, environment, and so forth and so on. As the late Aldous Huxley says "nothing short of everything will really do."[6] Whitehead is also very clear about this:

> In order to discover some of the major categories under which we can classify the infinitely various components of experience, we must appeal to evidence relating to every variety of occasion. Nothing can be omitted, experience drunk and experience sober, experience sleeping and experience waking, experience drowsy and experience wide-awake, experience self-conscious and experience self-forgetful, experience intellectual and experience physical, experience religious and experience sceptical, experience anxious and experience care-free, experience anticipatory and experience retrospective, experience happy and experience grieving, experience dominated by emotion and experience under self-restraint, experience in the light and experience in the dark, experience normal and experience abnormal. (AI 226; cf. FR 79; PR 161, 239; MTh 238)[7]

Taking into account all experiences means to open the field of *empirical* evidence as widely as possible. This requirement sweeps away most of Western philosophy, which has heavily relied upon sight to find evidences for and against its theses. Jonas, for one, has forcefully shown the impact of the metaphor of vision—a study that, interestingly enough, might have been directly spurred by Whitehead's own insistence on the issue.[8] The metaphor of vision imposes the idea of a *spectator-subject* factually unaffected by the scenery or by visceral awareness. The three essential characters of vision are: *simultaneity* of the data presented (an instant-like coordinated picture); *neutralization* of the causality of sense-affection (a frozen, non-relational, perspective); and *distantiation* in the spatial and mental senses (a totally passive onlooker independent of all mundane contingencies). From this perspective also, substance metaphysics is most definitively shortsighted.

Accordingly, simply accepting data from all senses would already constitute a tremendous improvement, but James has a far broader field in mind. Whereas sight suggests and enforces dualism, the mundane roots of the normal state of consciousness (that I call the "zero" state in order to avoid the derogatory aspect of the concept of "normality" and to suggest straightaway the existence of a local hierarchy of states)[9] gradually emerge as soon as the data coming from the other senses are brought into consideration: the spectator-subject discovers his or her embodiedness *and* embeddedeness. Three main types of experiential opening need to be taken systematically into account: coenesthesia, relations, and altered states of consciousness.

First, coenesthesia, i.e., the togetherness of exteroception, interoception, and proprioception, is of importance.

Taking exteroception—the five external senses that are commonly gathered under the heading "sense perception"—fully into account is the first step. Consciousness-zero is neither the product nor the producer of data disclosed solely in visual perception. Hearing, smell, touch, and taste are involved as well and each adds more depth to the extent to which we are fully part of a world that actually welcomes us and that is being transformed by our action.

Interoception names the internal sensitivity complementing the exteroceptive one. Its messages, coming from receptors housed by all organs and tissues, are, through reflex (i.e., nonconscious) action, the source of a harmonious bodily life. One can distinguish internal pains (cephalalgia, colic, etc.), internal taste (chemical sensitivity ruling various reflex activities), and internal touch (sensitivity to variations of pressure, like distension of the bladder or the rectum, stomach contractions, antiperistaltic contractions of the esophagus, determining the nausea feeling).[10]

Proprioception names the messages of position and movement allowing, with the help of the internal ear's semi-circular canals a spatialization—i.e., a full (ap)propriation—of the body. Proprioceptive perception grows from sensorial receptors[11] delivering data about the position and the relative movements of the different parts of our body. Through reflex action, it regulates the muscular tone and helps us to localize ourselves in space and to create a sense of depth (stereognosy). Proprioception also includes the muscular sensitivity that complements exteroceptive touch in offering estimates on the weight and volume of the prehended and/or moved object. The structuration of our proprioceptive field provides for the fundamental organic anchorage of our identity. Whitehead's *withness of the body* can be said to emerge out of the togetherness of all three of these perceptive modes, internal as well as external.

Second, relations deserve to be listed separately by reason of their historical and speculative importance. Because Western philosophers have traditionally accepted only a quite limited range of data (coming from sight), the very existence of relations has been sometimes denied (Bradley) or only internal relations have been acknowledged (Hegel) or only external relations have been reluctantly accepted (Hume). James takes internal and external relations as granted and furthermore hints that what was previously explained from the subject-object dualistic perspective requires a new understanding that got fully clarified by Whitehead twenty years later: relations are vectorial. They are *both* internal and external.

Third, altered states of consciousness also matter; they range from perceptual aberrations to abnormal psychology and spiritual intercourse. The above quotes from the *Principles of Psychology* (PP I 232) and *Adventures of Ideas* (AI 226) give us a good hint: all the experiences that are usually discarded need to fit somehow in the system. These experiences stretch from the very common states of dream, absentmindedness, hypnotism, nausea, automatism, hysteria, degeneration, genius, drunkenness and other intoxications, to less frequent "pathologies" such as neurosis, hallucinations, multiple personality, schizophrenic delusions, demoniacal possession, witchcraft, and religious visions.[12] All experiences that are at the edges of the zero state, i.e., that take place around the threshold of consciousness, in the fringes unplundered by substantialism, are of tremendous importance for two reasons. First, they bring to the fore data that cannot be ignored if one seeks to overcome the ever-present danger of limited expertise and dogmatism. Second, they display or advocate for the existence of relations and especially of causation.

This extended conception of data can be interpreted, from Whitehead's perspective, with the help of his distinction between causal efficacy and presentational immediacy or with the concepts of concrescence and transition. The two sets of concepts are correlated in the same way *Process and Reality's* macro and micro analyses are. In sum, one has to take seriously the withness of the body and common sense. The former concept underlines the coenesthesia we have just considered; it corresponds to what phenomenology has called the *lived body*. The latter emphasizes that the construction of the world through bodily perception is always a co-construction of a common world.

1.2. Method: Imaginative Pragmatism

Accepting all experiences leads of course the philosopher to be buried under data. And these data, which are representative only of past experiences, never entirely determine future experiences. New events happen all the time—indeed this is the most fundamental trait of our existence. James and Whitehead offer complementary standpoints as to how the philosopher should deal with this wealth of data. The former insists on the pragmatic methodology that should be adopted and that basically involves sorting out relevant experiences with the help of their known or expected consequences. The latter underlies the importance of imagination to cope with a process universe; he assumes the feasibility of critical systematization and consequently emphasizes the necessity of resorting to imagination.

To clarify: if one takes the idea of a process multiverse seriously, it becomes impossible for philosophy and science to work with the usual metaphor of the quest for the principle (or "archè"). There is no one single principle from which all processes come, and none of the many principles involved is fully rationalizable. Hence James' advocating of a pragmatic method. Whitehead agrees but nevertheless argues that philosophy can obtain a speculative system that is precise enough to spur conceptual and practical consequences *and* loose enough not to determine future events or to make past ones fully transparent.

It is well known that James attempted only at the very end of his life to work out his own philosophical system and hence tried to define what philosophy is, or ought to be. Although his endeavor to circumscribe the philosopher's attitude, purpose, and temperament (cf. SPP 6) was never completed, James points at a *central trait* that is likely to be accepted by all philosophical schools and at a *gesture* that is actually a bit more controversial.

James argued for pragmatism before he ventured into the field of speculative philosophy, i.e., before seeking for the ultimate generalities, the abstractions that would hold for every possible experience, perhaps even in every possible universe. The broadening of his inquiry involved the implicit expansion of pragmatism that Whitehead has since made explicit: the intrinsic chaosmotic[13] nature of experience can only be bypassed by creative imagination. In other words, Jamesian pragmatism has become imaginative pragmatism. It evolved from a local and neutral epistemological standpoint to a global and metaphysical one—hence axiologically orientated.

On the one hand, the philosopher seeks ideas of universal scope (SPP 5), a system of completely unified knowledge (SPP 27): coherent, logical, necessary, and applicable (PR 3).[14] Such a completely unified system is however unobtainable in a chaosmos, i.e., in a world that is in becoming. The philosopher can only create a system that happens to fit—but will never match—local contingencies. Whitehead circumscribed this theoretical doom with his concept of "cosmic epoch." Please note that launching such a systematic inquiry constitutes already a sophistication of the basic requirements ruling over the professional philosopher's life. Studying and teaching philosophy basically amounts nowadays to mastering some part of the history of Western ideas. The historical cursus that defines scholarship is, first, synoptic (its goal is to somehow grasp the entire philosophical territory, as it is spread through Western space and time); second, genealogical (to be able to identify conceptual and individual trajectories within that territory); and, third, ideological (to become aware of the existence of at least some implicit hermeneutical decisions[15]). In sum, the professional philosopher and the professional philosopher-in-the-making are supposed to obtain a degree (preferably from a first-world university), to have a reasonable publication record (with high-profile publishing houses and triple-A journals, *certified* for instance by the European Science Foundation), and some academic affiliation (again, the international rankings—such as the *Times Higher Education Supplement*'s—will give an immediate quantification of the value of the scholar). To make a case for the degradation of philosophy as expertise and impact-factor would not be complicated in such a context.

On the other hand, the philosopher's inquiry is also a personal quest: philosophy is not just a matter of theory but also of practice—in the most existential sense of the word. What existential difference does it make to use such and such concepts? Three criteria are relevant here: self-development or transfiguration, ironic dialogue, and destined vision.[16] They all point in the same direction: when it exists, the philosophical commitment bends the theoretical work because it seeks to transform the philosopher's own existence, social intercourse, and postmortem positioning. Philosophy has an ascetic dimension in the etymological sense of *askêsis*. It is an orthopraxis, not an orthodoxa.

Now, the philosopher who endorses the radical empiricist standpoint is very quickly drowned under innumerable experiences of various complexity, intensity, value, and frequency, some of them being firsthand, others secondhand or even imagined (the power of imagination to produce adequate *Gedankenexperimenten* is equally puzzling for Whitehead and Einstein). The problem is all the more acute in that these nebulae are not static objects at all. New experiences keep occurring, and they never repeat exactly the same pattern as their predecessors. We are not talking about *experiments* here. If the past is settled once and for all, its valuation, interpretation, and assessment varies according to the new situation. How should the philosopher deal with these experiential nebulae? Two stages can be distinguished: first, the solution offered by natural processes—pragmatic selection—and, second, the attitude required by philosophy—pragmatic deselection.

First, the zero-state allows a very sharp awareness of our contemporary world. This sharpness is basically achieved by cutting off as much data as possible—either because they are worthless (negative prehensions), or because they are redundant (transmutation)—and so are deemed irrelevant for survival: "Some narrow concentration on a limited set of effects is essential for depth. . . . Intensity is the reward of narrowness" (PR 111-12). This is very straightforward in the context of the biological theory of knowledge that sprang from Spencer's evolutionism and was later generalized by Peirce and James.

Herbert Spencer (1820–1903) founded, in his 1855 *Principles of Psychology* (four years before Darwin's *Origin of Species*) the *classical* "biological theory of knowledge"[17] with a dazzling claim: the structure of human intellect is "a priori for an individual" but "a posteriori for the whole species." Kant's thesis is refreshed on a new, empirical basis. Spencer's core argument is fairly simple: the original function of knowledge is purely utilitarian because our mental apparatus is the product of the struggle for life, i.e., of our continual adjustment to the sector of reality important for survival purposes. Since our cognitive functions are of empirical origin, they can have only limited applicability. *In illo tempore* there was not—but now is—a changeless a priori structure of human intelligence. It goes without saying that utilitarianism means here limited but *real* applicability. According to Spencer, and also such thinkers as Herman von Helmoltz (1821–1894), Hippolyte Taine (1828–1893), Ernst Mach (1838–1916), Alfred Fouillée (1838–1912), Théodule Ribot (1839–1916) (who translated Spencer's *Principles* in French), Richard Avenarius (1843–1886), and Henri Poincaré (1854–1912),[18] that evolutionary attunement is complete, simply because classical science provides the final truth. This position has been called Kantian "epistemological optimism." As Čapek wittingly says, adaptation actually culminates in the mind of a positivist philosopher of the 19th century.[19]

With the collapse of the classical worldview in the early 20th century, the "biological theory of knowledge" got more radical and argued that there cannot be a final and definitive picture of the Totality. Our sensory and cognitive apparatus are not settled, full stop. The three early actors are William James (who already criticized Spencer in 1878),[20] Charles Sanders Peirce ("in short, Spencer is not a philosophical evolutionist, but only a half-evolutionist—or, if you wish, only a semi-Spencerian. Now philosophy requires thoroughgoing evolutionism or none"[21]), and Henri Bergson, who severely condemns Spencerian "false evolutionism"[22] as well. In sum: considering that, on the one hand, evolution is incomplete; and that, on the other hand, the faculty of understanding is nothing but the appendage of the faculty of acting, theories of life and theories of knowledge become inseparable in their evolutive fluctuations.

Second, philosophers need both to become aware of this natural pragmatic selection process *and* to overcome it through a pragmatic deselection. Philosophers, like everybody else, usually enjoy a pretty limited experience of the world that is called consciousness-zero. Sense-data and behavioral patterns are selected and reinforced by habits according to our life contingencies—the shift to a technological society bringing, for instance, numerous changes to our ethos. Pragmatism acknowledges this is a process necessary for everyday purposes. But it is not because most experiences are ignored that they are philosophically irrelevant, on the contrary. They are not ignored randomly (this is the problem of *attention*, which comes later), but pragmatically:

> The difficulty has its seat in the empirical side of philosophy. Our datum is the actual world, including ourselves . . . The elucidation of immediate experience is the sole justification for any thought; and the starting point for thought is the analytic observation of components of this experience. But we are not conscious of any clear-cut complete analysis of immediate experience, in terms of the various details which comprise its definiteness. We habitually observe by the **method of difference**. Sometimes we see an elephant, and sometimes we do not. The result is that an elephant, when present, is noticed. (PR 4)

So, to make a long story short, "the task of philosophy is to recover the totality obscured by the selection" (PR 15). This means that beyond the contingencies of everyday life we find a nexus of experiences that actually secure the possibility of these contingencies *and* provide the conditions of possibility for a meaningful life. *Relations*—Whitehead would say *prehensions*—are decisive.

Process and Reality sketches the philosophical method with the help of the metaphor of the "flight of an aeroplane."

> The true method of discovery is like the **flight of an aeroplane**. It starts from the ground of particular observation; it makes a flight in the thin air of imaginative generalization; and it again lands for renewed observation rendered acute by rational interpretation. (PR 5)

Its point is not to reinforce the same selection as the natural one but to understand how the natural selection takes place and to provide a deeper comprehension of the selective process by digging data that are usually *not* selected or that are unconsciously selected. In sum, the pragmatic flight is the only method available for philosophy because of the pluralistic, chaosmotic nature of experience. But the late James and the equally late Whitehead point at the philosophical necessity of an imaginative form of pragmatism. Pragmatism is, in itself, a local method that allows the settling of local problems. As soon as the philosopher heads towards the big picture, a methodological update is required. In a nutshell, the problem is again cosmological. Looking for broader generalizations means reactivating the quest for the principle ("archè"), i.e., exactly what is forbidden by the chaosmos. Since the "Whole" is not conceived anymore as a *kosmos* or a *universus* but as a *chaosmos*, we never know exactly what comes next. Provided that we accept all experiences, we guarantee that our philosophical systematization will evolve accordingly. "Ever not quite" is definitively James' and Whitehead's motto.[23] Last but not least, it seems to me that the radical empiricist approach to philosophy is the sole one that prevents dogmatism. If one objects that defining philosophy amounts to, *ipso facto*, adopting a normative stance, one has not understood the radical opening that James' empiricism performs and the process context he works.

Of course, the exact epistemological—and more so, ontological— status to be given to nested sets of abstractions and systematic generalizations is notoriously difficult. Whitehead's solution, already spelled out in *Science and the Modern World,* is a halfway house between Plato and Aristotle, and it brings numerous additional systematic issues, such as the nature of the divine actuality. A pragmatic standpoint is helpful in these matters, and it can be spelled out with the help of the history of science. From the perspective of its everyday applicability, one can see Aristotle's physics as being a particular case of Newtonian physics, and Newtonian physics, as a local instance of special Relativity—one that actually provides only partial answers from the perspective of general Relativity. But the basic question remains: what exactly is lost when you abstract—and especially when you progress along the nested hierarchies of concepts? Plato would claim that the more you abstract, the closest you get to the very marrow of *Being*. According to Reichenbach, you don't lose anything when you abstract. Whitehead is ambiguous on the topic while James makes clear that the loss is tremendous. Concepts spring out of some stubborn facts and allow us to grasp other stubborn facts, but never fully so.

The basic requirement is thus experience—all of it. If thought starts from an embodied and embedded experience, i.e., if the very existence and significance of the body is not denied *and* that thoughts are rationally articulated in order to be able to be shared with fellows human beings, you are necessarily on the way towards the broadest generalities:

> Through feelings we become acquainted with things, but only by our thoughts do we know about them. Feelings are the germ and starting point of cognition, thoughts the developed tree. The minimum of grammatical subject, of objective presence, of reality known about, the mere beginning of knowledge, must be named by the word that says the least. Such a word is the interjection, as *lo! there! ecco! voilà!* or the article or demonstrative pronoun introducing the sentence, as the, it, that. (PP I, 222)

If thought does *not* start from an embodied and embedded experience, our argument does not apply but it is not falsified for all that. A madman does not think, neither does a politician, an economist, or a plumber, because their experience is limited to a certain section of the world and, moreover, because this experience goes in loops…

1.3. Outcome: Panpsychism

If one applies imaginative pragmatism to all experiences, one obtains a philosophical vision that amounts to panpsychism or, in the Whiteheadian lexicon, to panexperientialism. Conscious experience cannot indeed be segregated from its fringes, and these fringes are to be understood in continuity with our prehensions of the world. Sense-perception is only a refined form of sense-awareness, and it amply testifies to the reality of relations. There is thus a continuum of experiences, spreading from the very basic ones happening in the inanimate world ("low-grade experiences") to the sophisticated one of human consciousness ("high-grade experiences").

When the philosopher accepts all experiences and seeks to extract from them the broadest generalities, she is forced to adopt a *neutral monism* of sorts. The expression itself is not to be found in James' corpus because of its commitment to pluralism: James speaks only of a neutral and simple *pure experience* (ERE 26). But the tension between pure experience and pluralism is not pacified until the adoption of the *bud* theory of actuality, that Whitehead will call the *epochal* theory of time. Only then can we understand his mosaic philosophy (ERE 42 and 86).

This neutral monism actually constitutes a panpsychic worldview. Here also, the development of James' philosophy adumbrates White-head's. All experiences have to be taken into account, and the most significant of them are *not* the ones occurring in the normal state of consciousness (or consciousness-zero). This double mistake is typical of Modernity and prevalent in most contemporary philosophical schools. It is true that some scholars try to alleviate this blindness but the nosology they invoke is usually psychoanalytical and the patient dies uncured . . . In the same way that Locke improperly imported in psychology Boyle's corpuscular paradigm, Spencer wrongly used Laplace's cosmogenetic model of the solar system to understand psychogenesis. In the West, it is only in the process-pragmatic "school" that, thanks to the underground legacy of Myers and Ward, prophylaxis has substituted for the *analytical* cure.

The proper assessment of panpsychism involves *first* the precise definition of the incriminated concept, *second* the close study of its adequacy for James, and *third,* a close study of its adequacy for Whitehead. The two last quests further requiring the putting into perspective of the philosophical development of both thinkers and their possible interrelations. These points can only be sketched here.

First, we need to flesh out the meaning and significance of the concept of panpsychism. Like most philosophical concepts, it has been used in various ways and carries nowadays a wealth of meaning that often does not help clarify the debate.[24] The question that the concept seeks to answer is properly ontological: what can be predicated of *all* actualities? For the sake of the present short discussion, let us examine the two main sources of difficulties and thereby propose a 2 x 4 hermeneutical matrix.

On the one hand, the prefix "pan" can either refer to the Whole (*cf.* the concept of World-Soul) or to all parts (*cf.* the concept of hylozoism).

A complementary—Leibnizian—version of that basic contrast is the one between aggregates and individuals.[25] Please notice that this first partition makes no pretense of exhausting the set of possibilities (*tertium datur*); moreover it indicates the need to specify the relation(s) existing between the parts and the whole.

On the other hand, the root word "psychism" works at various *stages* or *levels* that can be heuristically identified and hierarchized in the following way. First, it stands for *psyche* or soul itself and, in conjunction with the prefix "pan," leads irresistibly in the direction of animism. Second, it stands for *subjectivity*, i.e., for consciousness or at least for an awareness of some sort: self-experience is its key word. Third, it stands for some *mental activity*, which means capacity of abstraction, of valuation, together with some freedom (or spontaneity, depending on how you define your variables). Fourth, it stands for *pure experience*, in the sense that everything that "is" either experiences or is experienced—full stop. This is what Whiteheadians call panexperientialism. This perspective discloses a developmental and abstractive progression: psychism/subjectivity/mentality/experience. As usual in philosophy, the use of abstractions is quite paradoxical. It means both the quest for ultimate generalities that are not necessarily obvious to common sense, i.e., there is a distantiation from immediate experience—*and* it claims that, by doing so, the very marrow of any experience whatsoever is revealed. A good example is Plato, whose argument leads him to claim that only the contemplation of *pure forms* is meaningful . . . because they are what is most *concrete!* This paradox, which stems from the disregard for sense perception inherited from the Greeks, should lead us to be exceedingly careful in the handling of daring generalities.

Second, the nature and extent of James' panpsychism needs to be assessed. At the very least, it is doubtful that his entire philosophical development belongs on the same panpsychic level. Secondary literature offers two complementary misleading examples. On the one hand, M. P. Ford has proposed an interesting analysis of the development of James' "panpsychism,"[26] but he offers no meta-criterion such as the one we have just suggested with the quadripartite hierarchy of stages. On the other hand, W. E. Cooper[27] proposes a minimal contrast of the semantic shades of the concept of panpsychism but factually ignores the intricate developmental side of the question. One could claim that the above abstractive progression is indeed at work in James, who first (already in the *Principles*) embraced a rather nontechnical (or gut) panpsychism. In 1909, he is actually still speaking of "mother-sea" or "common reservoir of consciousness."[28] Later (in the *Essays in Radical Empiricism*) Jame spelled out the (dry) basics of a panexperientialist framework.[29] The quest for higher generalities and the stripping of immediate (sometimes naive) experience of its "obvious" and "subjective" features are the two faces of the same coin. At any rate, these various conceptual stops do make sense from the perspective of the "infinite number of degrees of consciousness, following the degrees of complication and aggregation of the primordial mind-dust" (PP I 149).

Third, although there is no Whiteheadian panpsychism per se (the term cannot be found in his corpus and was rejected by word of mouth by Whitehead), it is now possible to understand how and why some commentators qualify his organic philosophy as panpsychism. The late Whitehead is actually proposing a vision made of the most abstract form of panpsychism: the panexperientialist one. He does not climb the quadripartite ladder but takes up residence straightaway (already in *Science and the Modern World*) at the last level. Since his concept of "feeling" is difficult to use in an intersystematic context, we can speak of "vectorial connexity" instead. Vectorial connexity highlights the theory of relations instrumental to Whitehead's panexperientialism. Internal (con-stitutive) and external (non-constitutive) relations are geared in a very powerful holistic gesture. As a result, we end up with a very moderate form of dualism. On the one hand, subject and object are *intrinsically* interconnected, both in their becoming and in their being; on the other hand, there is an important structural difference at work between true individuals and aggregates. Reality is through and through experiential.

2. The Socio-Political Axis

Now that the experiential nature of philosophy is clarified, we can turn to the social issue. What are the conditions of possibility for the authen-tic life and how are they bypassed in contemporary market democracies?

Social and political matters are intimately intertwined. For brevity's sake, one can claim that the political pole is nothing but the soul of the social body; the question being whether the soul imposes (or should impose) its will on a foreign body or whether the soul emerges out of a preexisting body. Historically, the very idea of participatory, or direct, democracy has provided evidence for the later alternative. So does, speculatively, contemporary process philosophy at large (but other possibilities could also be contemplated, such as the simultaneous co-development of both poles).

Dewey would argue that anyone who is blessed with a meaningful life is necessarily living in a democracy. This claim is not acceptable as such because representative democracy has proven to be a bankrupt concept while participatory democracy was historically built upon slavery. It is however possible to localize the conditions of possibility of authentic life in smaller structures: communities.[30] Three dimensions have to be taken into account in order to think the possible socio-political landscapes. They reflect the three characteristics of the creative advance of nature, Whitehead's core ideas—creativity, efficacy, and vision—are introduced contrapuntally. When James argues that "we live, as it were, upon the front edge of an advancing wave-crest" (ERE 69; cf. 86-87),[31] he means (i) that the world of humans as well as the natural world (there is only a difference of degree of complexity between them) is primarily a creative, eventful one; (ii) that these events take place in a context that usually bridles them and that is always modified by them; and (iii) that the interplay between creativity and contextual efficacy is oriented towards a better future because of the divine agency. There can be a creative advance only if these three conditions are fulfilled. How does this impact sociology?

2.1. Individuation

The individual is without doubt the basic social component—but it is neither a static nor an immortal one.[32] Human life, from birth to death, is a growth process that can be depicted with the concept of individuation: through life, each and every one of us seeks, willy-nilly, his or her own destiny. Autonomy or independence is the key word here; and it involves creativity and freedom (see §3.2.3.2).

Creativity means the irruption of the unheard, the unexpected, and the unforeseeable. When an event happens, it involves the ending of a past causal chain and the beginning of a new one. In common philosophical parlance, creativity refers to process and becoming, also to natality and birth. It necessitates the concepts of epochality; that is, the "epochal theory of time" that amounts to James' bud-like experience, and liberty. Difference necessarily involves discontinuity; and discontinuity is the signature of a free decision of sorts. Here dwells actuality per se and the present *qua* present that is worthy of one of the meanings of Bergson's concept of duration:

> reality appears as a ceaseless upspringing of something new, which has no sooner arisen to make the present than it has already fallen back into the past.[33]

Liberty, conceived broadly at the smallest scale, amounts more to spontaneity than to free choice. The point is to distinguish with Bergson liberty *qua* option-picking from liberty *qua* creation. We are free when we are creative. If freedom consists only of choosing between preexisting alternatives, we are actually not free at all since we are strictly bound by these options. (It would be perfectly fitting to exemplify this with the electoral game, during which we have to choose between twin candidates.) Freedom of the will is ultimately bondage of the will. (The liberium arbitrium is ultimately a servum arbitrium.) Here also, Abrahamic monotheism enforces the wrong categories.

The core of Whitehead's system thus radiates in numerous other works: those of Zeno, Plato, Suarez, Leibniz, Kant, Peirce, Ward, James, Arendt.[34] Let us mention two of these conceptual ties. Upstream, we find Kant, who has identified this conundrum. Freedom must break the law of nature, and yet freedom necessarily works within the laws of nature. To be free is to be able to depart from past causation and to create new causation—yet this is nonrational.[35] Downstream, Arendt's equation of the *principle of beginning* with the *principle of freedom* is straightforward. Hence truth *happens*; it is made true by events and can only be instrumentalized a posteriori—a reason why Bergson spoke of the *retrograde motion of truth*.[36] This is what Greeks called *archein*.[37]

Technically, the novel togetherness, called *concrescence,* is the outgrowth of mundane *prehensions.* It is the most important meaning Whitehead attributes to the concept of event. It is the event *qua* unique—but this unity is created by, and in turn creates, a multiplicity, a plurality, a multitude.

In market democracies, autonomy is replaced by conformism. Instead of seeking to individualize themselves, people nowadays have to content themselves with adopting a purely opinative worldview. Plato, as usual, identified the problem but it was left to La Boétie to pinpoint it (1574) and to Tocqueville to show the consequences of conformism (1835). The fact is that nobody sees the difference anymore between true individuals and clones.

2.2. Solidarity and Community

Although it makes sense to understand community from the perspective of the interactive aggregation of individuals in the making, the argument can be made that community always comes first; that no individual was ever born in a social vacuum (although s/he can die of course in a social void); and that most of them do not reach a social consciousness of any sort. There is no pre-social individual, but one can imagine a pre-contractual one. Solidarity or heteronomy is what matters here, i.e., some form of efficacy and determinism.

Efficacy basically means the power of the past, the stubborn reproduction of existing patterns either of previous events or of atemporal archetypes (*Process and Reality's* eternal objects). In common philosophical parlance, efficacy refers to being. It necessitates the concepts of continuity and determinism: the efficacy of the past fosters the same patterns forever. In other words, repetition involves blind continuity. It belongs to potentiality or virtuality,[38] i.e., to the pervasive past and its physical time—but also to the continuous transition towards an impending future.

Technically, the past togetherness that conditions the creative irruption of a new togetherness is called a *transition*: it is through transition that the "actual [evolves] to the merely real" (PR 214). To a certain extent, transition can be linked with the alternation of perchings and flights in James' *Principles of Psychology*. This second meaning of the concept of event was actually developed first by Whitehead, essentially in the *Principles of Natural Knowledge* (1919). It focuses on the *sense-perception* of objects rather than on the prehension of actual entities.

So objectification and superjection are two faces of the same Whiteheadian coin. Whitehead's concept of satisfaction names another type of praxis: to pass through one to get to the other;[39] that is, the achievement of the subjective process of concrescence and the toppling into mundane objective endurance and divine everlastingness.[40] Every subject becomes an object; all objects have been a subject. As *Process and Reality* claims: "there is a becoming of continuity, but no continuity of becoming" (35).

When solidarity breaks, it paves the way to atomism and individualism. The trick is to make sure that people love their individualistic servitude (La Boétie, Spinoza, Rousseau, Huxley . . .) and to blur the essential complementarity between individuation and community.

2.3. Culture

The double tension between the individual and the community, between independence and interdependence, is at the root of Jamesian pluralism. There are genuine individuals endowed with an existential trajectory incommensurable with any other and, yet, they all belong to the one same community that benefits from their idiosyncrasies, reinforces them, *and* bends them toward the common interest. In a nutshell:

> The community stagnates without the impulse of the individual. The impulse dies away without the sympathy of the community. (WB 231)

A strong community requires—and fosters—strong individuals. Dewey has seen this very clearly, e.g., in "Creative Democracy: The Task Before Us."[41] For his part, Cobb, together with Whitehead and Christian philosophers, speaks of "individuals-in-community."[42] The same dialectic can be found with Whitehead's actual entities and nexūs or with his mental and physical "poles." It is also at work at a deeper level: "The individuality of entities is just as important as their community. The topic of religion is individuality in community" (RM 86).

Culture *qua* imaginary institution of society conditions personal growth so that it is likely to contribute to social growth—while the imaginary institution of individuals seeks to bring social progress. (Growth and progress are used here in their original existential meaning as inspired by their biological meaning. Econometrics is totally irrelevant.) There is, in other words, a *common sense* that inspires the best definition of culture: culture embodies the grand narrative that allows the merging of the conditions of possibility of individuation *and* of socialization. When a philosophical school demands renunciation of common sense, it undermines solidarity. When it doubts sense-perception, it puts a damper on individuation. When it claims scientificity by rejecting all forms of political concern, it paves the way to the unquestioned acceptance of a big narrative that is not worthy of that name anymore. Taken together, the three requirements seal the divorce between philosophy and life and lead the philosopher to compartmentalize his professional activities.

As a result, in a community where a genuine culture prevails, all citizens are animated with a sense of social duty that takes the form of a sacerdotal citizenship; the personal spiritual quest and the enforcement of the common good do coincide. This was, at the very least, plain in Athenian participatory democracy, and the Judeo-Christian creation narrative constitutes probably the best recent historical exemplification of Western culture. But France's Third Republic motto—*liberté, égalité et fraternité*—and the *Bildungsroman* offer, respectively, a global and a local instance that seems more likely to be universally adopted. Culture is thus more than an antique form of leisure—although leisure was neither idleness or acedia.[43]

Here again anthropological expertise could lead us to relativize this claim, but it does not falsify it. Granted, the non-Western world shelters numerous examples of successful societies minimizing the individual's idiosyncrasies and maximizing the solidarity of the community, but each and every one of its members receives some particular social attention and some elbow room. Let us remember the socialization process that takes place during the rite of passage. So when the Western imaginary contemplates, for instance, the depressing homogeneous Asian masses, it basically looks at itself through a mirror but without the ability to recognize itself (remember the mirror test, which gauges whether non-human animals "recognize" themselves). Technoscience has produced the exact same social patterns worldwide, made of conformism, atomicity, and fear.

Vision basically designates an eschatological horizon, a melioristic open trend, not a teleological one. To offer an anthropomorphic exemplification: creativity refers to natural novelty; cultural invention; efficacy to causation, i.e., the repercussion of past actions; and vision to horizon and the projection of oneself in a more or less imaginary future. If we refine these conceptual milestones, we come to the concepts of, respectively, event (or accident, in the Aristotelian sense of *sumbebekos*), plastic structure, and divine eschaton. The structure is plastic because it is both a condition of possibility of eventfulness and a consequence of it. The history of philosophy offers three interesting complementary instantiations of these functors: (i) Heraclitus, who insists on becoming, seemingly refusing any speculative worth to being; (ii) Parmenides, who attempts on the contrary to think exclusively the Absolute Being; and (iii) Plotinus' hierarchy of beings (or, alternatively, Teilhard, with his noodynamics and omega-point). In Arendt's interpretation of the Greeks, vision is, of course, *theorein*,[44] but a *theorein* that is a *contact* rather than a contemplation per se. Jonas could be evoked again in order to show the relevance of a critical interpretation of the metaphor of sight.[45]

Traditionally, the political "right" insists on the individual and the necessity to give as much elbow room to free will as possible, whereas the "left" argues that community values should come first. This simplistic stance has not lost its validity, but it gains applicability when it is properly defined with the help of the concept of social horizon that is used in §3.2 below in order to refresh the concepts of class, class consciousness, and class struggle. To sum up, culture allows individuals to be in unison within the society. It allows everyone to engage fully and responsibly with oneself and the world. To use a metaphor that has become quite common: culture factually acts in communities just as the so-called invisible hand is supposed to act in markets (Adam Smith).

Technically, culture refers, in common Whiteheadian parlance, to God's luring of all existences. It necessitates the concepts of (hierarchies of) universals (or eternal objects) and of (the primordial nature of) god. In a purely metaphorical way, it can be attached to the future.[46] Here are the stakes:

> The fact of the religious vision, and its history of persistent expansion, is our one ground for optimism. Apart from it, human life is a flash of occasional enjoyments lighting up a mass of pain and misery, a bagatelle of transient experience. (SMW 193)

We have seen that creativity is wild and efficacy is blind. Only some vision can orient the gearing of creativity and efficacy towards the best possible world. In Peirce's lexicon: *firstness* governs qualities; *secondness*, forces; and *thirdness*, mediation. It is important to notice here that Whitehead does not offer any demonstration of the existence of God. Since God belongs to *Process and Reality's* "Derivative Notions," not to its "Categoreal Scheme," it could even be argued that God is not a metaphysical necessity, only a contingent cosmological feature of our "cosmic epoch." Gnosticism would not be far.

In market democracies, the complementarity between individuation and community is replaced by a synergy between, respectively, conformism and atomization. Furthermore, denizens mistake their atomization for individuation and their conformism for solidarity. This is the sure sign that culture is gone, that only a "small" narrative is at work—the one of fear, hate, terror . . . Instead of communal growth, market democracies foster a clone war; all denizens seek the same consumption goods through interpersonal conflict. Of special interest is that chiasm or inversion between the two main poles. Individuation is replaced by atomism whereas solidarity is replaced by conformity. In other words, while people think they have some individuality, they are simply crippled by atomism and loneliness. They also believe they still enjoy some solidarity, but they are actually only soaked in conformal patterns of thought and behavior.

3. On Epistemological Blindness

Now that the general background of our discussion is settled, a more specific argument can be provided. This section is directly inspired by James' "On a Certain Blindness in Human Beings," a lecture delivered in

1892 and originally published in *Talks to Teachers on Psychology* (1899). It provides the bridge between the epistemological issues lying at the core of the philosophical enterprise and the political consequences that will be drawn from them in the next chapter.

3.1. Historical Context

The historical context in which James delivers this lecture is itself quite eloquent. Three points deserve to be mentioned, starting with the most general one.

3.1.1. Monroe Doctrine, 1823

The broadest background of James' political stance is the Monroe Doctrine. According to Carlos Pereyra, author of *La doctrina de Monroe: El destino manifiesto y el imperialismo* (1908) and *El mito de Monroe* (1914), the doctrine developed in three stages.

The first one is the presidential message delivered by Monroe in 1823, directly inspired by his Secretary of State John Quincy Adams. The address was meant to reply, on the one hand, to France's intention to dispatch troops in Hispanic America in order to support and foster Spanish monarchies and, on the other, to Russia, which was ogling Oregon after Alaska. Monroe made two claims. On the one hand, the U.S. will not tolerate any European intervention in the Americas; and, on the other, the U.S. will not intervene in European politics.

The second stage consists of the nebulous and dogmatic glorification of the U.S. written for Ulysses Grant by his Secretary of State Hamilton Fish in 1870. Its rationale is the following: the U.S. will not support the Cuban revolution against the Spanish colonists if the U.K. agrees to pay war damages for the support they granted to the Confederates during the Civil War. The British agreed and paid in 1872, but the U.S. nevertheless invaded Cuba in 1898.

The third stage occurs with the affirmative biblical imperialism of McKinley, Roosevelt, Lodge, Taft, and Wilson, that the U.S. take South America under its wing to protect it against European colonialism, full stop. Hence the possibility of preemptive wars and the shameless affirmation of imperialism thereafter.

3.1.2. Cuban war and Philippines wars, 1898

The year 1898 sees the start of two important conflicts: the Cuban war (April 21), seemingly a direct consequence of the unexplained explosion of the USS Maine (Feb. 15), and the Philippine war (May 1st), resulting from the annexation of the Philippines by the United States.

3.1.3. The American Anti-Imperialist League, 1898

The war was welcomed by the intelligentsia. Some intellectuals disagreed, however, with the warmongers. On June 15th, the American Anti-Imperialist League is established to battle the annexation of the Philippines. James becomes a dedicated member of the League from 1899 until 1910, the year of his death. So did Mark Twain and a couple of atypical figures.

3.2. Basic Claims: Pluralism and Common Sense

Here is how James introduced his lecture "On a Certain Blindness in Human Beings" in *Talks to Teachers*:

> In 1892 I was asked by the Harvard Corporation to give a few public lectures on psychology to the Cambridge teachers. . . . Those who have done me the honor of reading my volume of philosophic essays [*The Will to Believe*, 1897] will recognize that I mean the pluralistic or individualistic philosophy. According to that philosophy, the truth is too great for any one actual mind, even though that mind be dubbed 'the Absolute,' to know the whole of it. The facts and worths of life need many cognizers to take them in. There is no point of view absolutely public and universal. Private and uncommunicable perceptions always remain over, and the worst of it is that those who look for them from the outside never know *where*. (Pref. to TT, iii-v)

James gives us two main hints here. Whatever "truth" is and whatever/whoever "God" is, they are different, i.e., there is some ontological surplus, some experiential opacity. The individual perceiver can never properly communicate his or her experience, which itself is intrinsically limited to local past events, which in turn means that language and rationality break down at some point. God is not truth insofar as God does not prehend the truth of created and ontologically dependent beings and insofar as no being prehends the truth of God.

However, a closer look reveals that three complementary claims are made in James' enduring pluralistic argument: (i) the opacity of facts, (ii) the privacy of minds, and (iii) the existence of a "common sense."

3.2.1. Opacity of facts

James' epistemological pluralism manifests itself first of all in his advocacy of the opacity of factual experiences. This opacity basically means that we experience more than what we are conscious of and more than we can conceive or rationalize. According to James, it is undeniable that

> any number of impressions, from *any number of sensory sources, falling simultaneously on a mind* WHICH HAS NOT YET EXPERIENCED THEM SEPARATELY, *will fuse into a single undivided object for that mind.* The law is that all things fuse that can fuse, and nothing separates except what must. . . . The baby, assailed by eyes, ears, nose, skin, and entrails at once, feels it all as one great blooming, buzzing confusion. (PP I 488)

This can be read as an early expression of the concept of *pure experience*. Please notice that James presupposes here the plurality of experiences; all experiences fuse that can fuse. (The question of the continuity of experience per se is raised below in §3.2.3.2.)

Needless to say, this opacity cannot be clarified, but only partially circumscribed. To do so we propose two stages or filters.

3.2.1.1. Experiential wealth

First, the opacity is due to the fact that we experience more than what we are *conscious* of. The data available in consciousness-zero constitute only the tip of the experiential iceberg; they are neither the sole data available, directly or indirectly, nor the most relevant ones for philosophy.

The fact that what we consciously experience is only a part of our total experience is usually not welcomed by professional philosophers unless they are under the spell of psychoanalysis. The following exchange between Russell and Whitehead exemplifies this perfectly:

I began to develop a philosophy of my own during the year 1898 . . . It was Whitehead who was the serpent in this paradise of Mediterranean beauty. He said to me once: "You think the world is what it looks in fine weather at noon day; I think it is what it seems like in the early morning when one first wakes from deep sleep." I thought this remark horrid, but could not see how to prove that my bias was any better than his. At last he showed me how to apply the technique of mathematical logic to his vague and higgledy-piggledy world, and dress it up in Sunday clothes that the mathematician could view without being shocked.[47]

As a matter of interest, Russell never really took into account Whitehead's radical empiricist argument. He merely used the lineaments of the method of extensive abstraction (in *Our Knowledge of the External World as a Field for Scientific Method in Philosophy*, Lowell Lectures, 1914), to fulfil his own logical and atomistic agenda.

3.2.1.2. Nonrationality

Second, we experience more than we can *conceive* or rationalize: what we consciously experience is only partially rational and what we unconsciously experience is largely—but not entirely—symbolical. Whitehead's definition of symbolic reference is eloquent:

The human mind is functioning symbolically when some components of its experience elicit consciousness, beliefs, emotions, and usages, respecting other components of its experience. The former set of components are the 'symbols,' and the latter set constitute the 'meaning' of the symbols. (S 7-8)

This symbolic reference is the active synthetic element contributed by the percipient. Of course the two issues blend into one another: experiential wealth induces nonrationality and nonrationality manifests itself in the buzzing confusion. Rationalization per se takes place in consciousness-zero.

If you should liken the universe of absolute idealism to an aquarium, a crystal globe in which goldfish are swimming, you would have to compare the empiricist universe to something more like one of those dried human heads with which the Dyaks of Borneo deck their lodges. The skull forms a solid

> nucleus; but innumerable feathers, leaves, strings, beads, and
> loose appendices of every description float and dangle from it,
> and, save that they terminate in it, seem to have nothing to do
> with one another. (ERE 46)

In other words, idealists understand the universe as purely transparent to reason (that is, what is rational is real and what is real is rational). Radical empiricists understand the universe as made of elements that should be seen as asymptotic experiences and variegated relations, or, in the Jamesian lexicon, as the privacy of the skulls and the innumerableness of their binding appendices.

3.2.2. Privacy of minds

Pluralism does not manifest itself only in factual opacity but also in mental privacy. Whether we are awake or asleep, we mysteriously keep our identity:

> When Paul and Peter wake up in the same bed, and recognize
> that they have been asleep, each one of them mentally reaches
> back and makes connection with but one of the two streams of
> thought which were broken by the sleeping hours. (PP I 238)

For Whitehead also, the individual immediacy of an occasion of experience is the final unity of subjective form (AI 177).

Here again we can distinguish two complementary issues: first, we are not fully transparent to ourselves, and second, neither are our fellow human beings transparent to us.

3.2.2.1. Who am I?

First, we are not fully transparent to ourselves:

> My present field of consciousness is a centre surrounded by a
> fringe that shades insensibly into a subconscious more. I use
> three separate terms here to describe this fact; but I might as
> well use three hundred, for the fact is all shades and no boundaries. (PU 288)

Even if I am an experienced radical empiricist (no pun intended), I still cannot comprehend all of my immediate experience and even less all of my entire terrestrial journey. Perhaps I will intuit in a glimpse what really matters and act accordingly, but this will remain to a large extent a pre-rational and private insight. Some of us have an intense introspective life; others accumulate experiences through social intercourse, reading, travel; and some have a talent to envisage the universal interconnectedness of events. Yet others have an intense religious faith or even have enjoyed natural or drug-induced altered states. But no one is able to answer this simple question: *who am I?*

3.2.2.2. Who is s/he?

Second, this privacy also applies to others. James has often emphasized this, for instance quoting Josiah Royce (*The Religious Aspect of Philosophy*, 1885, 157–62):

> What, then, is our neighbor? . . .Thou hast regarded his thought, his feeling, as somehow different from thine. Thou hast said, "A pain in him is not like a pain in me, but something far easier to bear." He seems to thee a little less living than thou; his life is dim, it is cold, it is a pale fire beside thy own desires. (TT 241)

This is plain common sense unless you are endowed with the spurious behavioristic faith—in that case, although you cannot access your own experience, you are fully able to elucidate someone else's.

Overall, we are all haunted by a sense of intrinsic difference and peculiar destiny. In contemporary massified societies, where people are made to conform *even in their dissent*, all still cling to their presupposed difference and are willing to fuse with the first heroic archetype fed to them.

3.2.3. Common sense

In sum, factual opacity and mental privacy are not only due to the complexity of our world (that could be understood statically with the help of canonical substantialism) or the limitation of our faculties, intuitions, and/or linguistic skills (a very old theme), but also to the world's process character. Opacity and privacy are basically experiential and experience *happens*; it does neither last nor recur as such. Please notice that this means each new experience is incommensurable with all past experiences. Even if it somehow repeats a past event, taking place in the exact same spatial standpoint and reproducing the exact same experiential pattern, it is not the same event for the simple reason that it cannot take place in the same spot of the extensive continuum, which is, in the Whiteheadian lexicon, the matrix of solidarity that underlies all events. Events happen, and then they are gone forever.

However, pointing at experiential opacity and privacy constitutes only half of the story. The argument needs to be pushed in two additional directions. On the one hand, despite the nebulous aspects of inner and outer experiences, we all share a common world; on the other hand, the basic reason for this lies in the panpsychic nature of experience.

3.2.3.1. Consensual interobjectivity

Despite the cultural tensions that exist between, say, a forest settler and a Boston Brahmin, and the natural differences the latter experiences with the animal and vegetal kingdoms, a common world is shared within, or even without, a given culture.

> Now, as I have already insisted, few of us are tender-foot Bostonians pure and simple, and few are typical Rocky Mountain toughs, in philosophy. Most of us have a hankering for the good things on both sides of the line. (P 13)

You are a cosmopolitan philosophical aristocrat living in buzzing cities surrounded by sophisticated intellectuals and multiple contraptions. When you meet a simple fellow, poorly if at all educated, dwelling in the woods and enjoying voluntary simplicity, you cannot but acknowledge that the factual opacity that is his existence, however remote from your own, somehow reaches the universal nexus of experiences that classical philosophers called "reality." His vision is not yours, but it makes sense and could become yours. His feelings are different but not foreign. His mental privacy thus manifests itself in such a way that you will not doubt of his humanity and perhaps that you will even look forward to his company. Such is the mystery of friendship, as it already stood out in Aristotle and Augustinus. Whether you are a tough-minded accepter of facts or a tender-minded respecter of principles does not matter here. Moreover, this existential proximity extends to animals, with whom we are—or used to be—in severe competition. (The Umwelt-like reality of the construction of the world can be bypassed for the time being; see §4.2.1.)

3.2.3.2. Panpsychism

That sympathetic intercultural *experience* can be extended to other forms of life. Granted, we feel particularly close to mammals, and especially to those that share our everyday life. However, it is not difficult to recover or to build, even in our day and age, our sense of sympathy for all life forms and, gradually, for the entire biosphere. James and Whitehead came to believe, especially in their late years, that no valid argument can be made to break the proximity between types of existence and forms of being. To establish an ontological gap between types or grades of experience would amount to renewing the mistake of substantialism.

The technicalities of this claim are not always easy to work out in detail, but the basics are straightforward enough. As soon as you acknowledge the humanity of *some* of your fellow humans, you are necessarily led to acknowledge the community of *feeling*[48] that exists with all other humans, and, step by step, you become aware of the unity of the pluriverse. The concept of pure experience is the heir of one epiphany, namely, opacity is privacy and privacy is opacity. What matters is the standpoint that one seeks to express. The opacity of facts is the late sign of the privacy of minds in the Whiteheadian sense. Events are subjective before toppling into objectivity, while that subjectivity is itself the consequence of the togetherness of "objects" (transitional or satisfied actual entities and eternal objects).

A subsidiary issue needs to be settled before we shift to our next section: does panpsychism involve a continuous or a discontinuous ontology? Atomic experiences per se are ruled out by radical empiricism since this would lead us to renounce relations, as did substantialism. We thus have to decide between continuity and contiguity. Continuity can be defined by infinite divisibility and contiguity by the strict consecution of spatio-temporal slabs or durations: it is the "concept of temporalization as a successive realisation of epochal durations."[49] From the perspective of psychology, it amounts to a renunciation both of Hume's bundle theory and of Freud's atomic unconscious. How did the concept develop?

Until *Some Problems of Psychology*, James remained unclear on the issue of the continuity of experience. *Principles of Psychology* is supposed to foster a *continuist* perspective, but it still houses traces of pluralism.[50] *A Pluralistic Universe* is supposed to have shifted to epochality—

> [Radical empiricism] stands or falls with the notion I have taken such pains to defend, of the through-and-through union of adjacent minima of experience, of the confluence of every passing moment of concretely felt experience with its immediately next neighbors. (PU 326)[51]

—but it still insists on the all shades and no boundaries axiom (PU 288). In a letter James wrote to Bowne in 1908, after reading his *Personalism*, James insisted on his Bergsonian debt and remarked: "my 'radical' empiricism denies the flux's discontinuity, making conjunctive relations essential members of it as given, and charging the conceptual function with being the creator of factitious incoherencies."[52]

The discrimination between these two possibilities is immediate in the context of our Jamesian discussion. Although various forms of panpsychism are possible (see §1.3), we have to pick a bud-like understanding of panpsychism in order to secure pluralism. The evidence comes from our *physical* experience, and the rationale is offered by our *mental* experience. On the one hand, as *Problems of Psychology* (488) claimed, all experiences fuse that can fuse and, as we have just underlined, each individual does not find him/herself in continuity with others. On the other hand, there is a conceptual necessity. The fundamental argument for such a *bud* or *epochal* theory involves the discussion of Zeno's paradoxes.

> If we admit that 'something becomes,' it is easy, by employing Zeno's method, to prove that there can be no continuity of becoming. ... There is a creation of continuity (PR 35 citing SPP 155 sq.)

Thus writes Whitehead, who concludes:

> In substance I agree with [James'] argument from Zeno; though I do not think that he allows sufficiently for those elements in Zeno's paradoxes which are the product of inadequate mathematical

knowledge. But I agree that a valid argument remains after the removal of the invalid parts. (PR 68)

But Whitehead is not always that categorical. He is clearly convinced that Achilles' paradox is based upon a mathematical fallacy (PR 69). He also considers that the fate of Zeno is to be again and again refuted or proven useless.[53] Actually, the assessment could work in both ways, depending on your own presuppositions. On the one hand, Zeno's paradoxes hold only in the Greek context of a closed *kosmos* in which being is the sole ontological value. As soon as you accept the primacy of becoming over being and open up the *kosmos* to a chaosmos,[54] the paradoxes fade away and become simple contradictions. On the other hand, Zeno could be seen as the forerunner of the postmodern movements. In that case, his paradoxes aim at showing the inadequacy of the *kosmic* presupposition. From that perspective, Whitehead makes the bold claim that will later be endorsed for instance by K.-O. Apel: logic presupposes a metaphysics. Therefore, what is paradoxical from a substantialistic standpoint, making sense within some historical worldview, is not necessarily so from a more processual standpoint belonging to another culture.

There is, however, a broader argument implicit in the works of process philosophers. As far as I know, the matter is nowhere clearly settled, but it can be systematized as follows: (i) a meaningful life is impossible unless humans can exert some liberty and (ii) that exercise involves breaking past causal chains and installing new ones, which means that (iii) at least some events involve discontinuing the ontological flow, whereas (iv) continuous features of our experience can be understood if one acknowledges the priority of discontinuity. In sum, without creativity, without an open future, life is not worth living.[55] If we unfold these steps we obtain the following argument:

(i) **Meaning** and **liberty** are co-extensive. Of course this does not mean that we can and actually do pose free acts all the time. It suffices that in all deep existential matters a choice is available. Notice that such a choice should not be understood as taking place between preexisting possibilities but between preexisting possibilities and *created* possibilities. This is the fundamental distinction that springs from Kant—and especially from Bergson—and that was promptly echoed by

James, Whitehead, and Dewey. Real freedom is *creative freedom*, not optative freedom. The possibilities created by the free or spontaneous action can only be identified *ex post*.

(ii) Liberty manifests itself in **creativity**, i.e., in new habits of nature and novel patterns of thought which involve the overcoming of causation. Here the trick is *both* to think physical and mental causation together *and* their subordination to the creative act. On the one hand, free acts or spontaneous events (there is no need to discriminate between them here) break past patterns. On the other hand, they buttress themselves against past causation. This gearing has been traditionally thought with the help of teleological categories that do not have real applicability in a process ontology, although they can be reconstructed from a mesocosmic perspective. Some authors, such as Ricoeur and Ladrière, have championed the concept of *eschaton* in order to alleviate the correlation that exists between teleology, substantialism, and *kosmos*. Their argument does not go far enough. It could be claimed of course that meaning actually springs from the acceptance of our fate, from a life lived in harmony with the Whole—whatever its name is. This makes sense if you are blessed with the experience of such a unison of becoming, but what happens if you are not? Actually, there is always some dissatisfaction involved in consciousness-zero, and this can be traced precisely to the dualism the zero state fosters. How to understand the shift from one state of consciousness to another? How to comprehend that some psychological pathologies break out while others suddenly fade "because" the individual has opted for meaning instead of accepting to sink in melancholia? Without the epochal theory, no proper answer can be given.

(iii) James speaks of "abrupt increment of novelty" (SPP 187), but if novelty requires a **discontinuity** in the chain of events, it nevertheless does not nullify continuity. Now, thinking discontinuity amounts to thinking nonrationality, a limit concept—in the sense of *Schranke* (an excluding limit), not *Grenze* (a terminating limit)—that has been introduced above precisely in order to debate the opacity and the privacy of experience. Hence two consequences: we have a tool to specify what is at stake in human existence. But this notorious conundrum is not rationally solvable, and epochality, together with nonrationality, are often and unsurprisingly rejected as nonsense. It is however tempting to reply to these scholars that no fully rational account of our terrestrial initiation will ever be available—unless, as James remarks, one resigns to invoke "God," the "great solvent of absurdities" (SPP 195). In that case the question bounces back, of course: what/who is "God"? Either you have some answer because of a firsthand experience—which cannot be adequately, rationally, and even less, linguistically expressed—or you rely more or less uncritically upon secondhand experience. *Varieties of Religious Experiences'* working hypotheses are stated clearly and early in the book. It would profit us very little to study "secondhand religious life," i.e., the life of the "ordinary religious believer," who follows the conventional observances imposed upon him/her by local social contingencies. Says James: "His religion has been made for him by others, communicated to him by tradition, determined to fixed forms by imitation, and retained by habit" (VRE 6). He knows as much of religion as a Welsh farmer knows of the tigers in India. In any case, James remarks that "the classic obstacle to pluralism has always been what is known as the 'principle of causality'" (SPP 189). If the effect in some way already exists in the cause, "the effect cannot be absolutely novel" and "in no radical sense can pluralism be true" (SPP 190).

(iv) If the occurrence of discontinuous events is granted, one can explain the **continuity** of experience with the help of the concept of contiguity. If it is rejected, one cannot explain discontinuity, or novelty, or liberty—and meaning eludes us. But of course, one cannot demonstrate that life has a meaning in the first place . . .

The basic argument is thus straightforward, and it moreover belongs to a long historical series of speculations, as Skrbina has shown.[56] By means of conclusion, it is expedient to mention three problems that panpsychism seems to have difficulties coping with. First, if a mind well-trained in imaginative generalizations eventually envisions the forcefulness of the concept of atomic events, it remains difficult to intuit the conceptual bridge that needs to be established between these eventful drops or actual occasions and mesocosmic phenomena. Granted, Whitehead's concepts of nexus and society offer tools to conceptualize the smooth transition between the microscopic level of concrescence and the macroscopic level of transition. However, the intuition usually leaves the philosopher in demand. Second, although the concept of a ladder or scale of events, spreading from the simplest ones—such as an electronic occasion—to the most complex ones— such as what Whitehead names the consequent nature of God—is very elegant, it is not easy to conceptualize the grades of complexity, intensity, and especially of value. Third, the argument framed by process philosophers does not amount to a complete rejection of substantialism. Substantialism and subject-predicate grammar carve a worldview that is adequate to everyday life but not to all possible experiences. Substantialism has only a very limited scope, and it can be reconstructed from a wider process perspective.

3.3. Three Cases of Epistemological Blindness

Finally, let us mention three topics that are assumed by our analysis and that have important parallelism in politics, which is the subject of our next chapter.

3.3.1. Opacity presupposes factual selection

Our analysis presupposes the genesis of consciousness-zero through the selection of data. Awareness becomes sense-perception through a triple genesis. Experience is not *amalgamated* by calculus or by association from simple to complex, but its intersubjectively *emerges* from complex to simple. The reader interested in developmental psychology will find here an approach akin to the one championed by Stern's *Interpersonal World of the Infant* (1985).

First, the cognitive functions of the human mind are not static operators at all. They are the transient *phylogenetical* result of a long adaptive process (see Spencer, *Principles of Psychology*, 1855). Under the pressure of environmental adjustment (better knowledge allows a better chance for survival), the human intellect has become a master in the kinetics of solid bodies and in "Aristotelian" logic. However, this is just an evolutionary adjustment to a limited—perceived—segment of a throbbing and coalescing world. In sum: the categories that are *a priori* for the individual are *a posteriori* for the species. This process is nothing but the very root of pragmatism.

Second, these functions result furthermore from an *ontogenetical* process. Individuals are not born fully equipped with the rational apparatus embodied in adult consciousness-zero (see Piaget's groundbreaking work *La représentation du monde chez l'enfant*, 1926, or Wallon's or Stern's processualization thereof). According to Piaget, four temporally and logically sequenced stages can be distinguished: (i) the sensorimotor stage (ages 0–2) during which sense perception and spatial movement are tuning-in to explore the world; (ii) the preoperational stage (ages 2–7) which coordinates motor skills with little significant mental actions on objects; (iii) the concrete operational stage (ages 7–11) which exhibits logical thinking only about concrete operations directed at objects and events; and (iv) the formal operational stage (ages 11–adult) which exhibits the ability to think and reason abstractly on a representation of the world.[57]

Third, the evolutionary success of humans also lies in the fortunate oversimplifications the species has achieved and perpetuates through cultural endeavors (see Bateson, *Naven*, 1936). *Koinogenesis*[58] is the process of socialization *qua* convergence of individual consciousnesses through learning. It is a process of integrative synchronic tuning that can be contrasted with schismogenesis—or progressive and pathological differentiation.[59]

Last but not least, not all the data produced by triple genesis are actually entertained: *attention* provides yet another filter. In sum: the transition from factual opacity to perceptive transparency takes place through a triple genesis. *Factual selection* means the creation of facts from experiences. Strictly speaking, infants do not live in the same world as adults; neither did Australopithecus enjoy life as we do or Italians habit the world as Chinese do. Additionally, you have the depressed, the borderline, and, e.g., the psychotic individuals, who go around in a rather peculiar manner . . .

3.3.2. Privacy presupposes a mental blind spot

Triple genesis explains how the past "objective" world brings about the contemporary "subjective" one. It is only by metaphor that James writes about how "mind brings things together."[60] As Whitehead claimed, well-tempered process philosophy "is a recurrence to pre-Kantian modes of thought" (PR xi). The idea of the construction of phenomena and of the importance of subjectivity is kept in process philosophy. However, the categorical work is replaced by triple genesis, and anthropocentrism is gone. The *reformed* subjectivism that is advocated works within a panpsychic worldview. According to Kant, subjects bring objects into phenomenality; according to Whitehead, past subjects bring contemporary subjects into existence.

The blind spot is not another name for the transcendental ego but a metaphor for the inadequacy of consciousness-zero. Experience in the making cannot be fully rationalized: it can only be fully experienced, felt, enjoyed, writes Whitehead. Consciousness-zero, strictly speaking, is a consciousness of the past; reason works with data that are not actual, only past. As soon as we are fully immersed in the experience, rationality is bypassed.

Interestingly enough, this contrast between immersion in experience (or awareness) and emersion in consciousness is at work whether you interpret it from the perspective of a pure flux (i.e., of continuity) or from the perspective of a sequenced flux (i.e., of epochal contiguity). In the former, there is simply no spot at all but dark fluxes; in the later, the spot is embodied in the contemporary duration defining the concrescent experience.

3.3.3. Common sense presupposes cultural bias

The common sense that binds private and public aspects of experience is always, in its concreteness, culturally determined—and this brings to the fore precisely the topic of our next chapter. Each individual belongs to a certain social horizon or *Umwelt,* and only a few core experiences actually overlap with all horizons. These are what Griffin called the hardcore common sense beliefs that are inevitably presupposed in practice, even if denied in theory. The main ones belong to ontological realism: there is a world lying outside of our experience and mentation; this world is structured by physical causality; our volition can bend this causality; freedom thus constitutes an important dimension (however fleeting and rarely actualized) of our existences.[61] As adumbrated above:

either you subscribe, implicitly or explicitly, to the postulate of human freedom, or you renounce finding meaning in life. Of course, the case could be made that life has no meaning or that the question is irrelevant.

4. Blindness in Political Matters

Let us now repeat our argument in a political atmosphere.

4.1. War and Peace

First of all, what is the broad context as provided by Whitehead's and by James' respective legacies?

Whitehead has unfortunately left very few indications with regard to his personal political stance and the political consequences of his organic philosophy.[62] We basically know (i) that in the 1880s, he served as the Secretary of the Cambridge General Committee of the Toynbee Association, which oversaw Cambridge's activities in the poverty stricken areas of East London; (ii) that he participated in political meetings in Grantchester at the time he was living in the Old Mill House, i.e., *circa* 1899–1907, and (iii) that he had been chairman of the Cambridge branch of the *Men's League for Women's Suffrage* in the years 1907–1910, i.e., until he resigned his Lectureship and moved unexpectedly to London.[63] In 1888, Whitehead was promoted to the position of Lecturer at Trinity College and hired as a (probably unpaid) tutor at Girton College, England's first women's college, founded in 1867 by Emily Davies, a feminist and suffragist.

Dorothy Emmet (1904-2000) told James Bradley (1947–2012) that she heard Whitehead say of *Process and Reality*, probably in the years 1929–30, when she was on a Fellowship at Radcliffe, "It's a defence of liberalism!"[64] But where do we go from there? Concerned with the proletarization of English society and the emancipation of women in society as well as in universities, he was a liberal in the old sense of the word, but not a pacifist (this trait being one of the bones of contention with Russell):

> My political opinions were, and are, on the liberal side, as against the conservatives. I am now writing in terms of English

party divisions. The Liberal party has now (1941) practically vanished; and in England my vote would be given for the moderate side of the Labour party. (ESP 13)

Here is one of Whitehead's most "liberal" claims:

The political, liberal faith of the nineteenth century was a compromise between the individualistic, competitive doctrine of strife and the optimistic doctrine of harmony. It was believed that the laws of the Universe were such that the strife of individuals issued in the progressive realization of a harmonious society. In this way, it was possible to cherish the emotional belief in the Brotherhood of Man, while engaging in relentless competition with all individual men. Theoretically, it seemed possible to conciliate the belief with the practice without the intrusion of contradiction. Unfortunately, while this liberalism was winning triumph after triumph as a political force in Europe and America, the foundations of its doctrine were receiving shock after shock. . . . The mere doctrines of freedom, individualism, and competition, had produced a resurgence of something very like industrial slavery at the base of society. (AI 33-34)

How strife can lead to harmony is a pretty obscure concept (indeed contradictory) when it is generalized—a move that Whitehead would not advocate, although Heraclitus and Hegel did of course advocate it before Adam Smith. Two main ideas can be drawn from this excerpt: (i) liberalism *qua* humanitarian ideal is Whitehead's main concern; (ii) he is afraid that this ideal has been betrayed by the industrial revolution. This would mean that liberalism has actually initiated, not a civilizational advance, such as Hayek's shift from servitude to freedom, but decadence from one limited form of freedom to a more complete servitude.

Whitehead's standpoint is well known. The basic conceptual tool the philosopher manipulates in the adjacent field of the history of ideas and of civilizations is actually borrowed from Plato's onto-theological speculations, perhaps augmented by Ferrero's.[65] The rise and fall of cultures would exemplify the struggle of two antagonistic forces: persuasion towards common Adventure versus coercion leading to individual and social sclerosis. The creation of the world is "the victory of persuasion over force" (AI 25, 42, 83—citing *Timaeus* 48a), the outcome of "the persuasion towards Adventure beyond achieved perfection" (AI 294-95, cf. 296). This struggle between persuasion and coercion has usually been interpreted naively, as if, for instance, the meaning and significance of Plato's own claim were themselves fully transparent.

Let us now peruse Whitehead's two main texts that address directly the issues at stake.

4.1.1. Whitehead's study of the past, 1933

We have seen that Whitehead expressed his concern for the betrayal of liberalism *qua* humanitarianism by the industrial revolution. The *Adventures of Ideas* passage (33-34) quoted above is excerpted from one of his four Mary Flexner Lectures, delivered at Bryn Mawr College in 1929-30, and reprinted in *Adventures of Ideas*, published in 1933. The same year *Adventures* is published, Whitehead goes back to these sensitive questions in "The Study of the Past—Its Uses and Its Dangers," an interesting—but not totally coherent—historical overview that articulates three stages: Feudalism, Individualism, and Ugliness.[66] In order to complement some sketchy remarks made in this "Study of the Past," I will systematically evoke arguments made in *Adventures of Ideas*.

First, the *ecclesiastical-feudal* system—which must not be confused with slavery (AI 27)—coordinated the intimate structure of society (AI 30) and provided some limited form of liberty for all its actors. Whitehead insists on the "Stoic-Christian ideal of democratic brotherhood" (AI 36) and on one of its main exemplifications, craftsmanship. With regard to brotherhood, he writes:

> For two thousand years, Platonic philosophic theories and Christian intuitions had furnished the intellectual justification for the slow growth in Western Europe of emotions of respect and friendliness between man and man—the notion of brotherhood. These emotions are at the basis of all social groups. As relatively blind emotions they must pervade animal society, namely, the urge to coöperate, to help, to feed, to cherish, to play together, to express affection. Among mankind these fundamental feelings reign with great strength within limited societies. But the range of human intelligence,—its very foresight as to dangers and opportunities, the power of the imaginative

entertaining of differences between group and group, of their divergencies of habit and sentiment—this range of intelligence has produced a ferocity of inversion of this very sentiment of inter racial benevolence. Mankind is distinguished by its strength of tribal feeling, and conversely it is also distinguished by far reaching malign exploitation and inter tribal warfare. Also the tribal feeling is apt to be chequered by limitations of benevolence to special sections within the boundary of the same community. (AI 37)

Notice that Whitehead submits that democratic brotherhood is a propensity that manifests itself naturally in small communities, implying that a "grand narrative," such as the Christian one, is needed to secure it in bigger communities. Also, his very last remark points at class issues as they will be introduced (see §4.2). In practice, Whitehead cultivates the idea that craftsmanship allows the freedom of the individual in a tightly knit social tissue; this at least seems to have happened in the Europe of the fifteenth, sixteenth, and seventeenth centuries that cultivated the "trend to free, unfettered, individual activity in craftsmanship, in agriculture, and in all mercantile transactions" (ESP 153). Of special relevance is the liberty in aesthetic appreciations, "the cultivation of fine sensibility" (ESP 164), as he calls it.

Second, the *Gospel of Individualism* spread its influence in the sixteenth century, culminating in the mythical American Far (or Wild) West. If feudalism is distinctively European, individualism is U.S.-American, claims Whitehead, who seems to uncritically adopt the colonialist idea of "a land without a people for a people without a land:"[67]

In America very special conditions for human life were at that time in full operation. An empty continent, peculiarly well suited for European races, was in process of occupation. Also that section of these races which felt the urge towards that type of human adventure had freely selected itself to constitute the American population devoted to this enterprise. Accordingly, in America this epoch exhibits a wonderful development of sturdy independence, with the individual members of the population freely carving out their own destinies. This is the Epic Epoch of American life, and after the initial struggles of small beginnings it had a wonderful central period of about a hundred and fifty to two hundred years. It was a triumph of individual freedom, for those who liked that sort of opportunity. And the population was largely selected by its own or its ancestral urge towards exactly that sort of life. Indeed the evil side of the survivals of feudalism in European life is illustrated by the bitter feelings which lingered amid the recollections and traditions of the American population. This episode in human existence, when individualism dominated American life, cannot be too closely studied by sociologists. It is the only instance where large masses of civilized mankind have enjoyed a regime of unqualified individualism, unfettered by law or custom. (ESP 155-56)

There are two distinct and significant problems here: (i) the negation of the existence of Natives and (ii) the apparent praise of anarchistic individualism. First, according to Zinn, there were probably 25 million Indians when Columbus arrived[68] and, by the time Whitehead began to work at Harvard, only a couple hundred thousand were parked in "Indian reservations," the civilized version of the concentration camps that were created in 1836 by President Andrew Jackson to dispose of these barbarians (hence far before their use during the Ten Years' War with Cuba and their rediscovery by Kichener during the second Boer war, 1899–1902).[69] In the meantime, a few hundred treaties had been signed with the Indians, and *all of them* had been reneged by the Whites. Is Whitehead simply poorly informed of the whereabouts of U.S.-American colonial beginnings, preferring to fancy its philosophical greatness?[70] Instead of seeking historical data, did he prefer to turn a blind eye on genocidal evidences? Or did he simply refuse to think about the consequences of his chronic optimism?

We reach here one of the troubling incoherences of the article. Although Whitehead seems to praise the unqualified individualism of the mythic Far West and sees it probably as the ultimate form of freedom at work—not the Greek concept but the anarchic one—he hints at the isolation of the "citizens" and at the loss of coordination. Atomism has replaced individualism. Instead of seeking individuation in a community, people are now concerned only by their own well-being, independently of the existence of any society. Did he read Tocqueville?

Third, *ugliness* was the brutal outcome of the industrial revolution in the nineteenth century. The introduction of this critical stage leads Whitehead to express new incoherent statements *and* to acknowledge by-the-by that some contradictions seem insuperable. On the one hand, we obtain "the first stage of a new and beneficent social structure." Great corporations and financial magnates are nothing less than a necessity for modern civilization (ESP 157-59). The progress of the race is obvious: "a slow, imperceptible change is always in progress" (ESP 105). On the other hand, the ugliness of this neo-feudalism constitutes the sure sign of decadence: "Of this trilogy, Feudalism, Individualism, Ugliness, today the Ugliness alone survives, a living threat to the values of life" (ESP 156). There are two main traits of the new "civilization," and both are equally problematic: (i) mass production and (ii) mass distribution or mass consumption. First, citizens *qua* producers suffer from "iron-bound conditions of employment" (ESP 157); they are forced into machine-like habitus in order to cope with mass production techniques. So much so that "the modern evolution of big business involves a closer analogy to feudalism, than does feudalism to slavery." (AI 27) Second, citizens *qua* consumers are a public with feeble—if not trivial—individual tastes" (ESP 157-60), both in their everyday consumption and for their amusement. In sum, conformism reigns, and this aggravates the destruction of the social tissue already compromised by atomism.

Whitehead's historical analysis is interesting insofar as it hints at the synergy between social atomism and conformism as they negate the independence and interdependence found in cultures worthy of that name:

> Routine is the god of every social system; it is the seventh heaven of business, the essential component in the success of every factory, the ideal of every statesman. The social machine should run like clockwork. . . . In such a routine everyone from the humblest miner to the august president is exactly trained for his special job. Every action of miner or president is the product of conditioned reflexes, according to current physiological phraseology. When the routine is perfect, understanding can be eliminated, except such minor flashes of intelligence as are required to deal with familiar accidents, such as a flooded mine,

a prolonged drought, or an epidemic of influenza. A system will be the product of intelligence. But when the adequate routine is established, intelligence vanishes, and the system is maintained by a coördination of conditioned reflexes. . . . Unless society is permeated, through and through, with routine, civilization vanishes. So many sociological doctrines, the products of acute intellects, are wrecked by obliviousness to this fundamental sociological truth. Society requires stability, foresight itself presupposes stability, and stability is the product of routine. But there are limits to routine, and it is for the discernment of these limits, and for the provision of the consequent action, that foresight is required. (AI 90)

Citizens do not need to understand the system as a whole; they should only be able to adapt, through a special training, to a routine and to foster its maintenance. Atomism has allowed the shift to the massification of production and of consumption which, in turn, has fostered conformism. According to Günther Anders and Vance Packard, it is undoubtedly through the consumption of mass commodities that mass men are produced.

This general configuration brings immediately two major issues to the fore. First, does it still make any sense to pretend that the citizens are "free"? Sadly no:

In any large city, almost everyone is an employee, employing his working hours in exact ways predetermined by others. Even his manners may be prescribed. So far as sheer individual freedom is concerned, there was more diffused freedom in the City of London in the year 1633, when Charles the First was King, than there is today in any industrial city of the world. (ESP 157)

Neo-feudalism might be worse than feudalism per se. Second, technological progress necessarily brings gains in productivity, and this makes it impossible to preserve full employment:

The combination of mass production and of technological improvement secures that more and more standardized goods can be produced by fewer and fewer workers. Here and there there are mitigating causes. But the general fact remains, ever advancing in importance. The issue is unemployment. The

proper phrase is "technological unemployment." But you do
not get rid of a grim fact by the use of a technical term. The
result is that a portion of the population can supply the standardized necessaries of life, and the first luxuries, for the whole
population. A portion of the population will be idle, and as time
goes on, this portion will grow larger. (ESP 159)

Whitehead touches here the very core of the capitalistic problem but
does not seem to realize it, so much so that he envisages an impossible
merging between mass production and craftsmanship:

> any blending of a machine age with a vigorous craftsmanship will
> require a large cooperation between schools and universities and
> the great business interests concerned with production and distri-
> bution. . . . If it can be accomplished it will add to the happiness
> of mankind, notably so by stabilizing the popular requirements
> and widening the area of useful occupations. (ESP 164-65)

It should be clear, indeed, that mass production and craftsmanship are
intrinsically contradictory—a fact that Whitehead actually acknowledges
during a parallel discussion:

> it was possible to cherish the emotional belief in the Brother-
> hood of Man, while engaging in relentless competition with all
> individual men. Theoretically, it seemed possible to conciliate the
> belief with the practice without the intrusion of contradiction.
> Unfortunately, while this liberalism was winning triumph after
> triumph as a political force in Europe and America, the foun-
> dations of its doctrine were receiving shock after shock. (AI 33)

The sole argument that Whitehead evokes in favor of such a merging
consists in pointing at the French economy, which allegedly preserved
craftsmanship in her industrial era. But he cannot demonstrate his thesis
by simply referring the reader to the French fashion business—which
is hardly representative—while not acknowledging that in 1933 France
was still largely a rural country and that industry's massification and
craftsmanship's individualism are simply living side by side.

This being said, his advocation of a reconciliation of technical
production and craftsmanship is consistent with earlier claims, such
as the following:

The life of man is founded on Technology, Science, Art and Religion. All four are inter-connected and issue from his total mentality. But there are particular intimacies between Science and Technology, and between Art and Religion. No social organization can be understood without reference to these four underlying factors. (AE 72)

The Aims of Education chooses to underline the plainly obvious: technoscience has become culturally as pervasive as religious art had been in previous stages of Western civilization. But the fourfold has to be interpreted with all possible combinations. In *Religion in the Making*, Whitehead contends that religious dogmas and scientific dogmas are correlated and that their development should follow similar empirical-critical routes. In the "Study of the Past," he points at the synergy that should be brought to life between technique and art, i.e., between mass production and craftsmanship. Each time there is a different emphasis on a particular correlation. Each time the equifinality of the fourfold is forgotten. In sum, two stages are needed to assess the applicability of the fourfold: first, to express all the possible synergies between science, technology, religion, and art *and* to weave these synergies together in order to obtain the full cultural picture; second, to question the presuppositions that led to the selection of these four fields to pace all possible culture.

Johnson summarizes pretty well Whitehead's discussion of the feedback loops existing between the increase in labor productivity, unemployment, loss of freedom, and the eventual decrease of sales:

in a very real sense, there is less freedom in England in the twentieth century than there was under the tyrant Charles I. The level of subsistence may be higher, and political restrictions are less obvious. But there are massive restrictions in many areas of experience. These restrictions are extremely serious. In all parts of the Western world, modern man is immersed in some vast commercial enterprise. He is required to carry out some relatively simple routine task. In many cases it is meaningless drudgery. There is no opportunity for creative initiative. He does as he is told or loses his job. Generally speaking, his amusements are also restricted non-creative and reflect, either directly or indirectly, the profit motive. He is amused only when others are amused. He is amused only when someone else provides the stimulus. His aesthetic *appreciation*, for example, is also inhibited.[71]

No doubt Whitehead came up very short from acknowledging the cultural devastation of consumerism and especially the fact that individuals matter only insofar as they are consumers. Even citizens *qua* workers are not indispensable anymore. Do Marxists realize this?

4.1.2. Whitehead's appeal to sanity, 1939

A short historical reminder is not pointless to show the extent to which Whitehead has failed to pay attention to *contemporary* political issues. Here are some key events with, between brackets, the book or article Whitehead published that year. In 1911, Sun Yat-Sen overthrows the Chinese emperor [*An Introduction to Mathematics*]. The Bolshevik Revolution took place in 1917 [*The Organization of Thought, Educational and Scientific*]. It was shortly followed by the creation of the *Spartakusbund* by Karl Liebknecht and Rosa Luxemburg (1918). The reaction of the well-born "conservatives" is prompt: the *Fasci italiani di combattimento* is created in 1919 [*An Enquiry Concerning the Principles of Natural Knowledge*], the *Nationalsozialistische Deutsche Arbeiterpartei* in 1920 [*The Concept of Nature*] and the French *Synarchie* in 1921 ["Report to Committee Appointed by the Prime Minister to Inquire into the Position of Classics in the Educational System of the United Kingdom"]. Mussolini becomes Prime Minister in 1922 [*Principles of Relativity*], Hitler writes *Mein Kampf* in 1924 and publishes it in 1925 [*Science and the Modern World*]. Then comes the 1929 October Crash [*Aims of Education, Process and Reality, The Function of Reason*], Salazar is Prime Minister of Portugal in 1932 ["Objects and Subjects"], and Roosevelt's New Deal is implemented the same year the Reichstag's arson takes place: 1933 [*Adventures of Ideas*—with the notable exception of "The Study of the Past"]. Franco starts suppressing the republican insurgency in 1934 ["Indication, Classes, Numbers, Validation"]; the *Anschluß* is performed in 1938 [*Modes of Thought*] and Poland invaded in September 1939.

In March 1939, however, Whitehead seems to briefly wake up from his political slumber when he publishes in Boston's *Atlantic Monthly* his "Appeal to Sanity." His analysis is rather dispassionate even though it claims to assess its topic with the concept of emotion:

> To-day the world is plunged in this second phase of contagious emotion. . . . The point to notice is that war, even if successful, can only increase the malignant excitement. The remedy is peace, fostering the slow growth of civilized feelings. War may be necessary to guard world civilization. But for Central Europe the effective remedy is peace. (ESP 53-56)

Strangely, he further invokes the possibility of a *miracle* to solve the crisis.[72] No account of the apocalypse in the making occurs in either of his late papers [1941: "Autobiographical Notes," "Immortality," "Mathematics and the Good"]. The year 1941 is actually neither the year of the battle of Tobruk, of the end of the London Blitz, or of Operation Barbarossa, but of the twelve-hundredth anniversary of his beloved boarding school Sherborne (ESP 5; cf. 31)!

In his "Appeal to Sanity," Whitehead insists again on the "supreme duty" of the "fostering of certain types of civilization" (ESP 53-54), on the "duty to the future" (ESP 56). Already in "The Aims of Education," the 1916 Presidential Address to the Mathematical Association of England that was first reprinted in *The Organisation of Thought, Educational and Scientific* (1917) and later in the eponymous book (AE, 1929), he points at the "religious" essence of education:

> A religious education is an education which inculcates duty and reverence. Duty arises from our potential control over the course of events. Where attainable knowledge could have changed the issue, ignorance has the guilt of vice. And the foundation of reverence is this perception, that the present holds within itself the complete sum of existence, backwards and forwards, that whole amplitude of time, which is eternity. (AE 14)

On the one hand, education should impart a Roycean sense of world-loyalty.[73] We have to become conscious of the historical roots of present events in order to anticipate the consequences of our decisions. On the other hand, education should bestow the awareness of the deep interconnectivity of the world, as it generates the present experience. In sum, education is the mastering of temporality, i.e., of its own rhythms.

The real issue here is that Whitehead chooses to ignore, or does not write about, the major socio-political events of his time. All the scholars who have known him have testified to his encyclopedic mind, so the argument cannot even be made that before his Harvard epoch (1924– 1947) he had no time or no interest in socio-political—and certainly not historical—matters. As Russell testified, he had been for instance perusing Paolo Sarpi's *History of the Council of Trent* (1619).

Under the hypothesis that socio-political issues were of no real *scholarly* concern to him until he drafted *Adventures of Ideas*, we still wonder why Whitehead failed to realize the immense suffering of the U.S.-American people (as it has for example been made plain by Zinn[74]). Interestingly, an ontological argument and an historiographical one can be put forward to explain his reluctance. The ontological argument springs from the epochal theory itself; i.e., all contemporary events take place independently of each other; one can neither know nor influence what happens in the contemporary world (this can be approximated by the concept of simultaneity). The historiographical argument springs from the fact that the asymptotical ideal of scientific objectivity could be activated only if one has access to all the archives and firsthand testimonies of the debated event. In practice, the criteria imposed by scientific objectivity can be contradictory: since most archives are not made available before 50 years, scientific research has to wait for the death of the main actors to start its work. Moreover, even in the case of research fulfilling the scientific criteria, the historian really has to mobilize all her will to summon the relevant data. For instance, as we speak, access is being granted to all the archives covering one of the most troubled epochs of human history: the Russian communist revolution and the consequent rise of Nazi totalitarianism. We now have the possibility to reassess the propaganda of the Second World War and of the Cold War in light of tangible sources . . . and the exact opposite is happening. Save for the seminal work of courageous historians such as Annie Lacroix-Riz, Reinhold Billstein, Jacques Pauwels, James Stewart Martin, Charles Higham, Gabriel Kolko, or Howard Zinn, the blackout on the cultural and scientific advances of communist Russia and on the intrinsic link existing between international capitalism and the rise of fascistic regimes not only remains complete, but is getting worse since the eighties with the shift of all political agendas to the right. One should know, for instance, that until the morning of 17 March 1939 (the Munich Agreement took place in September 1938), much of Chamberlain's hopes for peace rested on *encouraging* Germany to go to war . . . against the Soviet Union. That evening, Chamberlain realized Hitler had put on hold plans to attack the Soviet Union and was most likely looking West, threatening the Empire's interests: Hitler had decided to give Ruthenia to Hungary instead of using it against Russia.[75] The social tension was, however, palatable, as the hysterical reaction to Orson Wells' program broadcast on 30 October 1938, the evening before Halloween, testifies (a radio adaptation of H. G. Wells' novel *The War of the Worlds*, 1898).

But neither of these arguments constitutes a fair reply to Klemperer's condemnation, and Whitehead remains accused of *not* applying the broader criteria he had himself insisted upon: duty and reverence. Klemperer, a German Jew who survived the Nazi regime because of his marriage with an Aryan, has described in detail how the German people had been lured into Nazi totalitarianism by the manipulation of words, propositions, symbols, patterns of thought, and the like. In a nutshell, his interpretation is quite straightforward. On the one hand, Klemperer is full of commiseration for the suffering of the German *people* and does not condemn them, not even for the fate of the Jews after 1933. On the other hand, he has a deep grudge against the German *intelligentsia*, that had all the data in hand and all the intellectual tools to understand the storm ahead . . . If often they simply did nothing, sometimes they welcomed it warmly. According to his experience, academics, scholars, and other intellectuals are the ones actually responsible for the cultural collapse orchestrated by Goebbels.[76]

So the very first meaning of the title of our section refers to Whitehead's political blindness and to the chronic weakness of Whiteheadian political studies.[77] Intellectuals—and especially academics—totally fail their mission when they lack political commitment, full stop.

4.1.3. James' "Remarks at the Peace Banquet,"1904

As a result, to assess the political significance of Whiteheadian process philosophy, it is advisable to use James' and Dewey's respective historical commitments. Here primary and secondary literatures are burgeoning, but, as far as I know, no political argument has ever succeeded to sail close to the radical empiricist wind itself. Pragmatist approaches are championed, sometimes assisted with pluralistic premises.

First of all, it is easy to identify James' stance. "How does the state of the world strike you?," asks James to Grace Norton in 1900 to introduce his own diagnosis:

> Our children and perhaps their children are evidently bound to live through another great epoch of savagery. It seems to be that we ought to let China alone, too thankful that she is contented to cork herself up. When once she grows inoculated with restlessness and progress and machinery she is much likely to pauperize us by her labor, than enrich us by her purchases.[78]

For the Bostonian philosopher, duty and reverence are more anchored in political experience than in pedagogical and metaphysical speculations. James sees that scholarship and commitment are intertwined—a point Pierre Bourdieu (1930–2002) repeatedly made only a few decades later.

The first lecture that is worth citing in this context is James' 1904 "Remarks at the Peace Banquet," made the year he became Vice-President of the national Anti-Imperialist League:

> Our permanent enemy is the noted bellicosity of human nature. Man, biologically considered . . . is simply the most formidable of all beasts of prey, and, indeed, the only one that preys systematically on its own species. We are once for all adapted to the military status. A millennium of peace would not breed the fighting disposition out of our bone and marrow, and a function so ingrained and vital will never consent to die without resistance, and will always find impassioned apologists and idealizers. . . . This is the constitution of human nature which we have to work against. The plain truth is that people *want* war. (MS 300-04)

Really, there is "something wrong about us as we naturally stand" (VRE 508)—but how could we be saved from this wrongness?

> We do ill . . . to talk much of universal peace or of a general disarmament. We must go in for preventive medicine, not for radical cure. We must cheat our foe, circumvent him in detail, not try to change his nature. (MS 304)

James remains nevertheless evasive on the *preventive cure* of sorts that is needed. One cannot dispose of martial virtues, "man lives *by* habits indeed, but what he lives *for* is thrills and excitements" (MS 303). Would a bit of educative work make individuals, and especially political "leaders" and other economic "movers and shakers" more responsible? Actually not.

4.1.4. James' "Moral Equivalent of War," 1906

Let us face it: "History is a bath of blood" (MS 269). "The Moral Equivalent of War" (1910) claims that pacifists need to proactively invent substitute outlets and sublimated forms of the military life:

> Martial virtues must be the enduring cement; intrepidity, contempt of softness, surrender of private interest, obedience to command, must still remain the rock upon which states are built. . . . The martial virtues, although originally gained by the race through war, are absolute and permanent human goods. Patriotic pride and ambition in their military form are, after all, only specifications of a more general competitive passion. (MS 287-88)

"New outlets for heroic energy" (MS 306) are needed. Therefore James proposes to replace military service by a civil service in order to inflame the civic temper just as "past history has inflamed the military temper" (MS 293).

The Jamesian pragmatic trick is very seductive, but how practical is it? It irresistibly suggests the idea of transforming the entire society into a scout camp, a gigantic sandpit to raise soldiers in the making without actually letting them become soldiers. They would get a pitchfork instead of a submachine gun, and the spirit that goes with it. James' intuition is different insofar as it insists on individual heroism rather than on the morale *qua esprit de corps*. It brings to mind the utopia that the late Huxley wrote: *Island* (1962). Community should foster individuation, and this process benefits from some physical, mental, and spiritual training indeed. Initiation is its experiential keystone.

4.2. Basic Claims: Pluralism and Common Praxis

Whitehead provided an alternative formulation of the radical empiricist axiom when he argued that

> [t]he chief danger to philosophy is narrowness in the selection of evidence. This narrowness arises from the idiosyncrasies and timidities of particular authors, of particular social groups, of particular schools of thought, of particular epochs in the history of civilization. The evidence relied upon is arbitrarily biased by the temperaments of individuals, by the provincialities of groups, and by the limitations of schemes of thought. (PR 337)

Hence, the task of philosophy is *to recover the totality obscured by the selection*—never ever to add an extra process of exclusion. The very same holds for political philosophy.

How can we avert the chief danger of narrowness? In order not to repeat the exact same argument as the one unfolded in the previous chapter, it is necessary to introduce a new type of experience, one specific to socio-political issues, and to proceed from there. Here is how the argument is adjusted: (i) factual opacity is embodied in the opacity of class awareness; (ii) mental privacy becomes the privacy of class consciousness; (iii) common sense is replaced by a common praxis that binds *and* separates citizens: the class struggle. When that general process standpoint is applied to politics, a new form of radicalism is disclosed. The basic idea is simple: the more you experience, the more you imagine and the more you think, the more you expand your social horizon, and the more you shift to the left of the political spectrum. In order to arouse a different vision, I suggest using Orwell's terminology rather than the usual political lexicon.

It is often claimed that our heart dictates compassion and a socialist outlook of sorts whereas reason leads us to realize, sooner or later and whether one likes it or not, that only a healthy individualism allows us to reach the best possible common world. Actually the exact opposite is the case: all human beings are born with a purely selfish drive towards self-preservation and self-enjoyment, i.e., with the smallest social horizon—themselves—that actually includes their mother (see especially Wallon and Stern on this). It is only very slowly that the social horizon grows and that concern for other forms of life becomes actual. This maturation process takes place through direct experience, imagination, and thought.

Direct *experience* basically involves meeting other human beings. It is difficult to deny that cultural boundaries are promptly overcome when you meet people in a proper context. We all share the same humanity, and only "inner party" members and other sociopaths seek to make us believe that some human beings "hate us."

Imagination provides the link between past factual experiences and possible future ones. Imagination is crucial when we seek broader generalizations in a world that is everlastingly in the making. We do not need to meet all Iranians to realize that they are as peaceful as Luxemburgians are. To claim the contrary would amount to plain racism anyway.

The activity of *thinking* involves the quest for the highest generalities. Here also, it amounts to reaching the "universals" that apply to most, if not all, of us and thus to bridge social and cultural gaps.

In sum, we obtain the following claim: the process of individual maturation necessarily leads us from selfishness to altruism. It takes a fair amount of ideology and propaganda to interrupt that process and to scare (actually, to infantilize) people enough that they eventually accept waging useless wars against their fellow humans. This process is however never fully completed and it requires a continuous escalation of lies. Some fellow human are portrayed as the ultimate evil and an imminent threat to our survival (see Arthur Ponsonby or Noam Chomsky[79]). In light of the poor success of recent imperial wars and especially in light of the psychological problems that occur in these armies, it is nevertheless doubtful that soldiers can be, in the long run, fooled so easily.

The main tool to think through these issues is the concept of class, which unfolds in three stages.

4.2.1. Opacity of classes

The first thing to do is to define the concept of class to be put to work in our argument. I will not directly rely upon Marx for two, only apparently contradictory, reasons. First, we need a broader argument, independent of the question of the relations of production *(Produktionsverhältnisse)*. If there is such a thing as social classes, they mold the social tissue in a deeper way. In other words, everything should be done to avoid reading Marx as reducing all that matters in human experience to economics and, by the same token, adopting a blind materialism. Economic materialism can aptly describe the ideological core of the 20th and 21st centuries. It has had only nefarious consequences, both in capitalist and in communist societies. Moreover, in light of Whitehead's remarks on the vacuity of materialism,[80] it is clear that Marx could—and should—be rescued from such a short-sighted vision of cosmic evolution. Second, we should not seek the same universality of the concept of class per se. Class struggle is a praxis that has only fairly recently replaced *another* form of social polarization; namely, cast alliances. This also means that the concept of private property has to be relativized. With the enclosures, aristocrats shifted from a community-oriented stewardship of their land to a bourgeois ownership that made possible the start of ecological and environmental abuses.

Needless to say, the starting point of our radical empiricist overhaul should be experiential. There is a very concrete experience that is usually ignored outside ethology and sociology; that is, the existence of a sociological horizon that corresponds to what Whitehead calls our "actual world" and to von Uexküll's "Umwelt" (named after von Baer's studies but independently of Peirce's).[81] The *Umwelt* of a living organism is similar to a soap bubble or a cobweb that would be animated by two virtues. On the one hand, the organism in question is largely defined by its relational tissue. On the other hand, the horizon itself incorporates interferences between different *Umwelten* and accounts for the relativity of the perceptual community. Scale effects do of course matter; the world of the ant is not the one of the mole. The *Welt* is a mosaic of *Umwelten*. Humans are born with the smallest experiential and social horizon possible—themselves. It is only very slowly that the interpersonal world of the infant grows and that her horizon expands. Slowly, gently, the infant appropriates movements, spaces, forms of mentation, temporalities, abstractions. . . . and her surrounding world grows accordingly.

Interestingly, that idea is also adumbrated by Huxley:

> An Alpha-decanted, Alpha-conditioned man would go mad if he had to do Epsilon Semi-Moron work—go mad, or start smashing things up. Alphas can be completely socialized—but only on condition that you make them do Alpha work. Only an Epsilon can be expected to make Epsilon sacrifices, for the good reason that for him they aren't sacrifices; they're the line of least resistance. His conditioning has laid down rails along which he's got to run. He can't help himself; he's foredoomed. Even after decanting, he's still inside a bottle—an invisible bottle of infantile and embryonic fixations. Each one of us, of course . . . goes through life inside a bottle. But if we happen to be Alphas, our bottles are, relatively speaking, enormous. We should suffer acutely if we were confined in a narrower space. You cannot pour upper-caste champagne-surrogate into lower-caste bottles. It's obvious theoretically. But it has also been proved in actual practice. The result of the Cyprus experiment was convincing.[82]

That bottling process is similar to the magic cap that we wear down over eyes and ears to make-believe there are no social monsters.[83] It is only within one's class that our fellows' behaviors, expectations, and arguments make sense. Outside this class, one can only extrapolate from one's own experience.

Freely inspired by Uexküll's ethological work on the *Umwelt*, here is how I propose to define and to refine the concept of class.[84] A *class* is an unconsciously lived, experiential territory. For simplicity's sake, we could arbitrarily reduce its dimensions to three: a lived space, a lived duration, and lived values. However, a more shaded approach adds considerable weight to this concept. *Qua* unconscious, the lived territory involves an internal boundary and an external boundary, which were, *mutatis mutandis*, also foreseen by James. I mention Uexküll's relevant concepts in parentheses.

4.2.1.1. Internal boundary

The *internal* boundary is embodied in the physical standpoint of the subject considered. It is from that existential nucleus that the horizon itself is outlined.

> The knower is not simply a mirror floating with no foot-hold anywhere, and passively reflecting an order that he comes upon and finds simply existing. The knower is an actor, and coefficient of the truth on one side, while on the other he registers the truth which he helps to create.[85]

There is no unembodied standpoint. The "lived body"[86] can be analyzed in two complementary worlds: first, the presented world *(Gegenwelt)*, i.e., the environment as apprehended (constructed) by the central nervous system; second, the innerworld *(Innenwelt)*, made of affectivity, interoception, proprioception, and imaginative projections.

4.2.1.2. External boundary

The *external* boundary is constituted by the social horizon itself *(Umwelt)*. The fringes or "surrounding-world" can be analyzed in two steps: first, the perceived world *(Merkwelt)* woven by education, values, (over-)consumption, etc.; second, the operational world *(Wirkwelt)* which is the sociographical area defined by the subject's actions in space and time. Bourdieu's cardinal concepts of habitus, field, and capital (economical, cultural, social, and symbolic) can be interpreted from this standpoint. Symbolic violence requires only one further step.

In order to delineate how exactly do the internal and external boundaries relate to the opacity of classes, we need to shift to the next stage.

4.2.2. Privacy of class consciousness

The existence of social classes is a given, a *presentation* that is not necessarily *represented*. To use a metaphor: all human beings live in a bubble that is more or less extended, more or less transparent, and more or less pervious to her fellows' whereabouts. However, because of personal circumstances not always purposely sought, some individuals become conscious of the existence of their own class and therefore pave the way for a new understanding of social intercourse. This is one of the main issues of the 1848 *Manifesto*.

The class *qua* consciously represented territory involves the boundaries mentioned in the previous section: it mobilizes either nuclear or liminal perspectives, or both.

4.2.2.1. Nuclear representation

From the perspective of the *internal* boundary, the nuclear standpoint becomes conscious when it is contrasted with other standpoints. This involves three main fluid characteristics: age, gender, and race. More subtle cultural categories could be evoked to further specify the nuclear representation, but these three mark out adequately the territory at stake.

4.2.2.2. Liminal representation

From the perspective of the *external* boundary, the horizon itself gets, so to speak, fleshed out when one realizes that there is, if not actually, at least potentially, an overlap of horizons.[87] This step of the argument introduces a presupposition: the existence of a *local* form of social hierarchy. Some people have more family and friends than others, some have friends from various social *horizons*, some pick them only within their neighbors or their colleagues, while others have a far broader sample of social personalities. In brief, some citizens simply have access to a *richer* experience than others. The old metaphor of the social pyramid is thus useful to fuel the discussion. What is presupposed is then made explicit by the analysis. Please notice that no *global* hierarchy is either presupposed or demonstrated. Precisely because we are condemned to speak from a certain sociological standpoint, the opacity of our horizon prevents an all-embracing vision. At the global level, the social circumstance could equally be depicted as a coral rather than a tree. This is, *mutatis mutandis*, the same question as Darwin's.[88]

To understand the different possible overlappings, three criteria matter.

First, the horizontal **size**. Some individuals have a far bigger horizon than others. This is really an experiential matter. Physical, mental, and spiritual growths, that are supposed to be enforced together by a proper upbringing and an adequate education, should, by definition, amount to increasing the size of the experiential horizon of the members of the community. However, size matters only insofar as it increases the probability of the awareness of *qualitatively* different experiences. Hence the two following dual characteristics.

Second, the **elongation** of the horizon and its **direction**. What is the shape of the horizon and how is that shape orientated in the social power field? A very wide horizon that includes only experiences of the same type does not really prepare the subject to become conscious of the social stakes; it defines a shallow horizon covering similar experiences. Another way of putting it is to speak of a *horizontal* horizon within the social pyramid or field. A *vertical* horizon is an elongated horizon that runs through multiple levels of the local pyramid. Although both types of horizon could have the same size, their significance is completely different. In sum, every citizen belongs to a social horizon that is defined by its size and orientated shape. A big horizon is always preferable but a horizontally elongated horizon does not have the same impact on social consciousness as a vertically elongated one.

Third, the **centration** of the subject and her **projection** clarify how the subject values her position within her horizon. First, the subject is rarely centered within her horizon. Usually she has a better knowledge of some areas encompassed by the horizon than others. Second, the subject is never statically (de)centered. There is always a tropism that brings her towards some parts of the horizon. Most of the time, the subject is attracted by the lifestyle of the upper classes. But sometimes, the ideal of voluntary simplicity scales down her social agenda.

In conclusion, the opacity of classes can be partially made conscious within a private subjectivity, but this does not necessarily awaken the subject to the ethos that drives other social actors.

4.2.3. Common praxis

Once the private class consciousness is actualized through the consideration of overlapping horizons or territories, the subject becomes able to rationalize its meaning and significance. When, additionally, different private class consciousnesses are shared, i.e., rationally discussed, another step is crossed, and the meta-concept of class struggle can be obtained.

We actually get this straight from the horse's mouth: "There's class warfare, all right—Mr. Buffett said—but it's my class, the rich class, that's making war, and we're winning."[89] Two reasons are commonly given: (i) there is a natural law that leads the more capable to manage the destinies of all citizens; the "elite" rules because no one else can or even wishes to rule; and (ii) furthermore it rules for the common good. This question bounces back in section 8.

So far we have dealt with the statics of the system. We must now understand its dynamics. Currently, Western and Westernized societies (the reality behind the *politics* of "globalization" and its fancy literature) are ruled by the class struggle, but this hasn't been always the case, and one can hope it will not continue to be the case. One of the oldest examples of a social ethos is the hierarchically differentiated caste-based communities.[90] Their basic *modus operandi* is the caste alliance that provides a rigid social organization, which means less opportunities for the subject to change his social status but also more cohesion and, overall, more meaning. An individual born into slavery is likely to die a slave, but his owner has a direct interest in keeping him alive and well. Proletarians are unlikely to raise above their ill-birth, and the capitalist should only worry about paying the minimum wage. The reproduction of their stock is not always a concern since foreign work power is available; that is, before plants were actually delocalized. This is the most common example provided in comparative discussions, but it involves putting on the hot seat forms of "civilization" that are quite recent. The same holds, *mutatis mutandis*, for feudal times, but feudal caste systems are not necessarily slave based. The first, second, and third estates (respectively *oratores*, *bellatores*, and *laboratores*) were living in a symbiosis. One should cast an inquisitive eye on smaller and older communities; before social differences were used in order to bring *more* differences to the benefit of the dominant caste, i.e., when communities were self-perpetuating like a clockwork without an escape mechanism.

4.2.3.1. From caste entente to class struggle

The current ethos is the class struggle. It was brought to the fore by a triple opening or deterritorialization *circa* 1516, 1855, and 1900.

First, the spatial opening that started in the 15th century with the enclosures (mentioned already by Thomas More in 1516), was carried on with Columbus' "discovery" (1492), and crowned with the works of Cusa (*De Docta ignorantia*, 1440), Copernicus (*De Revolutionibus orbium cœlestium*, 1543), and Bruno (*La Cena de le ceneri*, 1584). The Greek-given *kosmos*, which offered its premises to the Christian-created universe, was about to become a pluriverse and its finite hierarchy, infinite.

Second, the temporal opening originating in the transformation of the concepts of growth and progress, which used to be private matters, into public realities by the works spreading from Herder (1764) to Condorcet (1793). It was then carried on by the speculation around the biological theory of evolution by Spencer (*Principles of Psychology,* 1855), Wallace ("On the Tendency of Varieties to Depart Indefinitely From the Original Type," 1858), and Darwin (*The Origin of Species by Means of Natural Selection,* 1859). Last but not least, numerous technical innovations materialized these ideological openings: the steam locomotive (1784), the dynamo (1869), the electric engine (1873), and the marketing of the "Ford T" (1908).[91]

Third, the consciential openings. Usually scholars mention only Freud's *Traumdeutung* (1900), but Freud dogmatized a broader (and deeper) conceptual and therapeutic revolution that goes back to Leibniz and Mesmer, the Nancy and Salpêtrière schools, and psychophysics (Herbart, Weber, Helmoltz). Political openings have to be mentioned as well (the Republiek der Zeven Verenigde Nederlanden, 1579–1632; the Bloodless Revolution, 1688; the Boston Tea Party, 1773; the French revolution, 1789), alongside the Reformation (Luther, 1517).

As a result of all these openings, the social model shifted from perpetual clockwork (Claude Lévi-Strauss' "société-horloge") to steam locomotive ("société-vapeur").[92] The Renaissance-created universe is an engineered machine tool of sorts (spatially infinite; without hierarchy).

How, as deterritorializations, do the three openings relate to class struggle? The caste entente, and, broadly speaking, communities, require a clockwork world. Culture has been destroyed insofar as there is no big narrative providing the conditions of possibility of both independence and interdependence. There is no more culture, only some cultivated people often cherishing outmoded ways of living. Culture is now something that one *has*, possibly alone and certainly in very limited circles. No one *is* cultivated anymore.

4.2.3.2. Fascistic terror or reterritorialization?

In light of the current state of affairs, especially since 2008 but 1968 constitutes a watershed, the next stage is likely to be fascistic terror. The key is the political apathy that has ruled over the last two decades, basically since the failure of the 1968 movements. As Bourdieu kept repeating: there is nothing worse than a failed revolution because in such a case the counter insurrection forces see their powers unleashed. What does observation teach?

First, terror is already the contemporary motto and its enforcement factually cancels class struggles. In order to have a class struggle per se you need individuals endowed with a sharp class consciousness and organized into unions or similar entities. On the one hand, class consciousness relies indeed upon the existence of reasonably sized social horizons and especially upon *overlapping* horizons. On the other hand we have to ask how is terror possible? Aristotle (and Tocqueville later) knew it already. To allow the rule of a tyrant, the City should not be composed of citizens seeking individuation (independence, autonomy) and keen to secure solidarity (interdependence, heteronomy)—but should be composed of conforming and atomized consumers of sorts.[93] The description of the current state of the world and the blueprint of what comes next is written down in black and white in *Nineteen Eighty-Four*. Only two technoscientific possibilities seem to have escaped Orwell: (i) the forthcoming bio-nano robotics and (ii) the extensive use of geolocalized RFID chips . . . Chapter 4 of Part II seeks precisely to close this loophole.

Second, the common praxis would become an alliance if the actors could recover their respective sense of duty and reverence. Since we are now in the antechamber of a fascistic implosion of unknown magnitude, the reversion to a feudal mentality could, alas, constitute an improvement.

Third, only the irruption of the ideal of participatory democracy could really obtain a decisive improvement in the life of all the actors.

It would involve scaling down the social tissue in order to nurture again the compassion that keeps communities alive. Sacerdotal citizenship would be back.

Of course, a process perspective cannot rule out the possibility of a reterritorialization with a return to an alliance system or the creation of compassionate communities, but its likelihood seems low.

4.3. Three Cases of Political Blindness

Overall, the topological definition of classes presupposes two pluralistic facts: one, there are social differences and they are systematically enforced and inherited; two, these social differences are largely pre-conscious and opaque.

First, social differences are a qualitative matter, not a quantitative one. For instance, most people tend to believe nowadays that all individuals consume the exact same goods with the exact same enjoyment. The only difference between lower and higher wages is the size of their car(s), the amount of garages attached to their house(s), or the rate at which they can replenish their fridges. Besides sharp differences in sex, gender, and race, there is no social structure to worry about and certainly no class logic surreptitiously at work. We have shown that this is a very superficial understanding, first noticeable in U.S.-American society under the name of "the parable of the Democracy of Goods."[94] Democracy is defined in terms of equal access to (some) consumer products . . . hence antagonistic envy of the rich becomes unseemly and programs to redistribute wealth are unnecessary.

Second, these systematic differences are not obvious, either experientially or rationally, for citizens in their everyday life. Depending on your whereabouts, you may, or may not, become conscious of them, and your perspective will forever remain short-sighted unless you adopt a working hypothesis on the common praxis—but here also you can argue only for a limited clarification, both because of the finitude of your horizon and its cultural localization (its position in space and time). Let us further clarify this issue in light of the contemporary state of affairs.

4.3.1. Deselection of class membership

Applied to politics, radical empiricism requires not only that we accept all social experiences but that we look for new experiences at the edges of our customized territory. We need to adopt the widest social horizon possible, and this in turn leads to a broadening of our concern for our fellow human beings and to the enjoyment of a corresponding drift towards the far left of the political spectrum.

The first type of blindness that should be cured is the one touching the opacity of the class membership. So far, we have introduced the concept of class from the perspective of a personal, positive, experience. Complementarily, one can define classes by what is negated in or rejected by these experiences. Class membership is then the product of a process of selection that could be deactivated. When one reads the opacity of class membership as the ground for conformism, it becomes clear that, just like in epistemological matters, the selection process needs to be deactivated in order to allow for genuine individuation.

4.3.2. Lucidity of class consciousness

The deselection of class membership is not the sole key. The privacy of class consciousness, when it succeeds in overcoming the selective process, often leads to atomism.

Social lucidity requires the abandonment of atomic seclusion—at work even in class consciousness—to implement solidarity. The subject needs to focus on the overlappings between her horizons and other's and to enter in dialogue with her peers in order to break alienation.

4.3.3. The return of culture

Nowadays, the all-embracing reality of class struggle is doubtful because of the disintegration of the social tissue. Classes are not easy to identify anymore since each individual's horizon has tremendously shrunk and since the residual horizon *conforms* most of the time to one single pattern, that is, to the immediate satisfaction of a blind consumer's will. Even in the rare cases when a choice is rationally made, the instrumental rationality at work remains uncritical, and the data are valued through advertising. The question remains: could culture be a culture of struggle, war, and colonial predation? Social life should be woven out of sacerdotal citizenship; it cannot result from massified consumerism and warmongerism. Once the recent common praxis (class struggle) and its likely outcome (fascistic terror) are identified, it becomes possible to aim at a broadened rationality that transfigures class struggle into a compassionate lifestyle. The incipient terror is to be replaced by culture, and, to repeat, this leads to the inflation of our social horizon and therefore to a far left political standpoint.

In sum, the three forms of political blindness are best seen through the lens of the three necessary conditions of participative democracy, themselves reflecting the three guises of authentic life. The selection of class membership is detrimental to individuation. The blind spot of class consciousness needs to be lit by the requirement of solidarity; class struggle loses its nefarious impetus as soon as culture is activated. The difficulty is to think this threefold dialectic in a time of *crisis*, when past patterns are drifting and haven't settled yet. Orwell can help us think the possibilities. In his masterpiece, he puts these words in the mind of his anti-hero Winston:

> From the age of uniformity, from the age of solitude, from the age of Big Brother, from the age of doublethink—greetings!" (BNW 32)

Orwell's lexicon precisely reflects the three conditions of authenticity as we have spelled them out. Uniformity is conformism as it prevents individuation; solitude refers to atomicity[95] as it negates solidarity; Big Brother or DoubleThink embodies the Terror that crushes all forms of culture and hence all possible subversion.

Of extreme relevance is the inversion of the private and the public spheres. Individuation is, of course, essentially a private matter while solidarity is most obviously a public one. The destruction of individuation by conformism and the obliteration of solidarity by atomism are all the more damaging and discrete, now that private and public spheres are misplaced. On the one hand, the consumer who conforms to the late fashionable ethos thinks that s/he is taking part in a contemporary form of solidarity. On the other hand, the atomic consumer is made to believe that her isolation allows individuation. Not only are the conditions of possibility of authenticity replaced by their opposite, but they work as red-herrings—and this is possible because culture itself has been destroyed. Most people now seem to think that culture refers to old-fashioned intellectual taste and patterns of thought, only entertained by upper classes or at least by people who think they are different, who pretend to be different. The *Iliad* and the *Odyssey* have nothing to do with our contemporary circumstances, neither does *Die Zauberflöte* or *Finnegans Wake*. But *Mein Kampf* could be part of European culture, just like soccer or the *Tour de France*. From the perspective adopted in this essay, it is easy to discriminate between these claims. Culture is that which seeks to foster *both* individuation and solidarity. The towering cultural events possess a very broad relevance; minor cultural events are bound to local circumstances.

We have now entered the epoch of total disorientation. There is no self-identity (independence), no communal identity (togetherness), and no historical identity (Grand Narrative, i.e., *paideia* or *Bildung*) any-more. Crises are by definition times of opportunities, but when the social horizon has shrunk so much, it becomes difficult to remain optimistic. Citizens have basically the choice between the right and the extreme right, and this choice does not amount to the subtle difference that exists between neoliberals (Hayek, Friedman, Giddens) and neoconservatives (Strauss, Bloom, Wolfowitz).

II. Application to the Global Systemic Crisis

A false notion which is clear and precise will always meet with a greater number of adherents in the world than a true principle which is obscure or involved. ~Alexis de Tocqueville, *Democracy in America*, 1835, I, 251[96]

The practical part of this essay argues for two main complementary theses, one pertaining to politics and the other to psychology.

The global systemic crisis is first and foremost a political crisis, that is, the crisis of capitalist ideology and of its universal dogmatization under the name "globalization." Hence no solution to the crises (energetic, biospheric, demographic, social) will be provided unless the demotic (i.e., popular) decision is made to overcome capitalism.

Second, this political conundrum has to be examined with a psychologically informed gaze. Capitalism is not simply a very powerful enslavement tool among others; it provides the best framework for the blossoming of sociopaths.

In sum, the main steps of the argument are the following. In order to provide an assessment, from the standpoint of Whiteheadian optimism, of the current global systemic crisis (which amounts to a world economic depression with an ecological collapse in the background), it is advisable to proceed with simple questions. What is capitalism? When did it start? Who runs it? On whom is it imposed? How does it operate? Why? What are the likely outcomes of the present crisis? Are there any reasons to hope?

5. General Context

Let us contextualize the application of the radical empiricist standpoint to the contemporary state of affairs. First, we sketch that polymorphic crisis. Second, we use the works of Ellul, Gross, and Wolin to provide the context in which the global systemic crisis takes place. Third, we summarize the specificity of Whiteheadian political optimism. This optimism is not gratuitous. On the one hand, each of us can make a difference and *create* a better world. On the other hand, all the aspects of the global crisis being metastatic diseases of the same capitalistic cancer, they could be cured together by a bold political program.

5.1. The Global Systemic Crisis

The general contemporary state of affairs is properly depicted with the well-known U.S. military slang acronym (here sanitized): "Fouled Up Beyond All Recognition" (FUBAR). Five main critical areas can be identified, but their evolution should be understood together. The fact that experts and mainstream media shift their focus from one to the other, apparently randomly, or according to an agenda that is not transparent, is irrelevant.

5.1.1. Energetic and biospheric

First, the energy crisis is palpable since M. King Hubbert created the "peak oil" model in 1956 and accurately predicted that the United States oil production would peak between 1965 and 1970. In 2009, an expert of the *International Energy Agency* claimed that the production of conventional crude oil peaked in 2006, and this was stated in the *Agency's* annual report *World Energy Outlook 2010*. Whether this is the case or not (there is no consensus) does not really matter as international politics makes plain that all major actors are already behaving as if it had happened and are thus seeking to control the remaining resources (oil, of course, but also rare minerals and water). They most definitively act as if peak oil was *behind* us.

Second, the biospheric crisis is equally contemporary. The exhaustion of natural resources (water, biodiversity, minerals, etc.) is not the only biospheric issue. *Abrupt* climate change—and its correlate: chronic pollution—constitute also a major concern. So much so that scientists probe now the adequacy of the concept of "sixth mass extinction" that would include a near-term human extinction; a two-degree increase of the global temperature by 2030 would lock our fate with the breaking of the food chain.

5.1.2. Demographic crisis and social unrest

Third, the demographic crisis: in such a critical context, the Malthusian pressure is more problematic than ever. The human population is expected to surpass nine billion by 2050—a fifty percent increase, largely in developing nations, the U.N. predicts. From the perspective of Western imperialism, this also means that Whites will see their demographic weight plunge below 10 percent.

Fourth, pandemics and social unrest are expected, especially in countries without social security systems. Riots, famine, and overpopulation wars are likely, all the more so since speculation keeps an iron hand on the price of cereals while meat consumption is not discouraged in first-world countries.

5.1.3. Economic imperium and political vacuum

Last but not least, the political vacuum in which all these crises take place is staggering. Since politicians do not represent the citizens anymore (or the proles or the denizens) but only themselves and the corporatocracy (or inner party), each and every one of these issues is aggravated by their complete lack of *common sense* and of visionary management.

In sum, all these crises represent various sides of one single catastrophe: capitalism *qua* political system; i.e., the oxymoronic "market democracy." It is because of the greed and lust for power of a few thousand individuals worldwide that the social tissue (now being globalized) is corrupted and that the entire biosphere—starting with ourselves—will continue to be exploited until exhaustion and collapse.

Interestingly, although there is *in the civil society and in academia* no consensus on these crises—let alone on their intrinsic correlation—if you read the literature leaking (purposively or not) from *military and intelligence circles*, you find that all these issues—minus the political vacuum—have been a major concern for more than a dozen years.[97] Please also note that "terrorism," which seems the sole interest of politicians, is basically of no real relevance for the intelligence community.

The next step is self-evident: fill the political vacuum with *prismatic* "military intelligence." None of these crises is indeed really problematic for the inner party. Each crisis represents a call to deepen neoliberalism, and, as a matter of fact, each embodies new commercial opportunities. Whatever the threat, some commodity or some service will be provided for those who can afford it.

There is, however, a strong alternative trajectory that is called degrowth and involves voluntary simplicity. Cuba, for instance, has showed until recently a remarkable economic resilience. The collapse of the Soviet Union led Cuba abruptly to embrace a post-carbon era. It should be underlined that, from the perspective of the comparison of the Human Development Index with the Ecological Footprint, Cuba's achievements are nothing less than amazing.

5.2. Managed Democracy or Inverted Totalitarianism?

In which ground does this global crisis plant its roots? This section provides a quick overview of the available criteria. The historical depth of the crisis is introduced in §6.2.

The basic assessment tool we have at our disposal is the one that has been sketched above (chapter 2). Empowered citizenry requires individuation, solidarity, and culture. The West, and most of the "civilized world," lives now in massified societies in which individuation has been replaced by conformism, solidarity by atomism, and culture by fear if not by terror. Phobos and Deimos are its deities.

The ideal of direct democracy was created during the Age of Pericles, also known as the Golden Age of Athens; i.e., circa 462–429 BCE.[98] Citizens were required to argue in order find agreement on policies fostering the common good. Power was shared by the citizenry. By definition, culture (*païdeia*) leads to individuation and solidarity. Unfortunately, Greek direct democracy incoherently relied upon a slave system of labor.

Representative democracy sprang from the *Bloodless Revolution* (1688) and especially the U.S. and French revolutions (1776 and 1789). The electorate does not argue anymore; it is only supposed to vote in order to delegate its citizenship. Power is exercised by proxy, and those who hold the power usually are professionals. Theoretically, individuation, solidarity, and culture are still nurturing the social tissue, but, practically, atomization reigns while the system relies upon the prole tarization of labor.

In today's market democracy, the vote has no relevance anymore in the political arena. Consumers really "vote" in the supermarket: they neither argue nor vote but buy. This is not a figure of speech; this is how the system was carved out in the twenties when "public relations" and "planned obsolescence" were put in synergy.[99] Political apathy—which was considered by the Greeks to be one of the biggest political dangers—is the rule.[100] Inner and outer party members are busily ignoring facts, burying facts that should not be ignored under heaps of useless information, and, of course, telling lies—the more extravagant, the merrier.[101] We live, as it were, in a *pankatalepticon*. Very few seem aware of the clear and present danger, and those who are aware of the crises to come do not react; they are cataleptic.[102] The priests of power have no interest in culture, individuation, or solidarity; what matters is the infantilization of the population. We are at a turning point in Western history. The pre-totalitarian inversions that basically amount to the chiasma between the private and the public spheres are complemented by a properly totalitarian inversion between the roles of the police and the army. On the one hand, the police are more and more militarized and no longer seek to prevent crime but to punish it brutally. Additionally, infiltration and false-flag operations are more and more common. Social movements are criminalized. On the other hand, the army is used for policing foreign territories and getting ready to perform the same duties at home, with the *Posse Comitatus Act* (1878) being factually ignored.

All this was foreseen by authors such as Alexis de Tocqueville (*De la démocratie en Amérique*, 1835), C. Virgil Gheorghiu (*Ora 25*, 1949), Jacques Ellul (*La Technique ou l'Enjeu du siècle*, 1954), Günther Anders (*Die Antiquiertheit des Menschen*, 1956), William Burroughs (*The Naked Lunch*, 1959) and Guy Debord (*La Société du spectacle*, 1967). But the actual diagnosis of the neoliberal meltdown could of course be given only after the metastatic development of capitalism. Here, the work of Bertram Gross (*Friendly Fascism*, 1980) and Sheldon S. Wolin

(*Democracy Incorporated*, 2008) stand out.[103] In a nutshell, neoliberalism was born with Friedrich August von Hayek's (1899–1992) lampoon *The Road to Serfdom* (written in the years 1940–43 and published in 1944) at a time when it was completely inapplicable to the *Zeitgeist*. It would take nothing less than thirty years of networking and the opportunities provided by the crises of the seventies to obtain its implementation, first with Pinochet's coup in 1973.[104]

The point Gross makes is straightforward: fascism arises as soon as a partnership is established between "big government" and "big business." In a sense, as long as "big government" independently enforces policies aiming at (not necessarily achieving) social justice, it is a defensible entity. But when the private interest of faceless oligarchs rule not only the economy but also the politics of a country, this country can no longer claim to be democratic.

Wolin proposes a more sophisticated analysis but does not bring a new or better insight. The terms "managed democracy" and "inverted totalitarianism" are equivalent. The former emphasizes the technologies of corporate control, intimidation, and mass manipulation, which far surpass those employed by previous totalitarian states and, furthermore, are effectively masked by the glitter, noise, and abundance of a consumer society. The latter emphasizes both the inversion of democratic common sense and of totalitarian policies. We are no longer in a democracy because (i) the economy is piloting the politics, (ii) because the citizens have become apathetic "denizens," (iii) because of the fragmentation of the social tissue, and (iv) because all disensual forms are neutralized, e.g., by the private media's censorship.

However, still according to Wolin, we are not (yet) in a totalitarian regime, precisely (i) because bare political ideology is not piloting the economy, (ii) because social mobilization and solidarity are negated, (iii) because politization is denied, and (iv) because the opposition is not abolished, e.g., by the public media.

In sum, "inverted totalitarianism" points at that no-man's land in which the basic conditions of possibility of democracy are negated while the historical traits of totalitarianism are absent. Interestingly enough, an important characteristic of democracies is present, but subverted, in totalitarian regimes; that is, politics is the soul of society and individuals are heavily politicized. But the political mobilization does not take the form of the togetherness of independent individuals; massification operates in a way that negates individuation and solidarity. Politics should be a bottom-up process, not a top-down one.

Wolin is particularly good at emphasizing the correlation that exists between inverted totalitarianism and imperialism: Western countries—and especially the U.S., of course—have recently launched a new wave of colonial wars under the pretext of promoting democracy *abroad*. Now the fact is that such politics demand a totalitarian ideology at *home*. The tail is, yet again, wagging the dog.

5.3. Ellulian Criterion and Whiteheadian Optimism

Although this state of affairs leads all critical observers to be radically pessimistic in their assessment of the future of (Western) civilization, the duty of Whiteheadian philosophers is to remain optimistic, to bring out reasons to cultivate that optimism, and to show practical ways of implementing it. Why so? Basically because the future is not written and because the problem is, so to speak, *only* political. On the one hand, each of us can make a difference, can *create* a better world. On the other hand, all the crises mentioned, being metastatic diseases of the same capitalistic cancer, could be cured by a bold political program. Chapter 10 will suggest possible policies in that regard.

This vision basically strengthens the well-known Gramscian urge to cultivate the pessimism of the intelligence *and* the optimism of the will. The nature of the process from the Whiteheadian standpoint was the topic of the first part of this monograph and especially of its first chapter. How it impacts politics and culture is the topic of this second part. An additional criterion is however needed in order to screen the data and to provide workable alternatives. In order to pragmatically sort the relevant data, I argue that we especially need to consider the current trends in technoscience. This is Jacques Ellul's intuition regarding the question of futuribles (or "possible futures"[105]), but also the way think tanks address it. If we peruse the general tendency in R&D, we obtain indeed a fairly good idea of what the future should look like. There are basically two reasons for this. On the one hand, technoscientific possibilities have the stubborn tendency to be somehow implemented. Everything that is technically possible becomes actual, claims Ellul.[106] On the other hand, there is no ideological brake anymore. (Christianity used to work that way.) The only pilot of the technoscientific system is economical, i.e., greed and lust for power.

> The end of our foundation is the knowledge of causes, and secret motions of things; and the enlarging of the bounds of human empire, to the effecting of all things possible. [...] We have also parks, and enclosures of all sorts, of beasts and birds; which we use not only for view or rareness, but likewise for dissections and trials, that thereby we may take light what may be wrought upon the body of man.[107]

That general Ellulian criterion of technoscientific possibilities needs nevertheless to be specified in order to obtain a proper heuristic tool. It seems wise here to follow the intuition of the French group *Pièce et main d'œuvre* that has repeatedly directed our attention to RFID tags or chips and on their future use. (More on them in §6.2.3.[108])

From that perspective, it is likely that managed democracies, or pankatalepticons, will drift towards a "big mother" type of totalitarianism (or panopticon) before a implementing a "big brother" type of totalitarianism (or pancraticon). Bentham's important concept of *panopticon*[109] was actually inconspicuous in utilitarianism. It acquired visibility only with Foucault's *Discipline and Punish*.[110] Since the seventies, programs such as the codenamed "echelon" were put into motion and, at the moment, the numerical age allows even more massive surveillance programs that target not only individuals, States, and international organizations but also corporations in order to steal all information that might benefit the U.S. The recent Snowden scandal perfectly exemplifies this.

Of course such prospective analysis and studies have to be carried out critically. First, they only work with current R&D trends, extrapolating from what is already known. "Discoveries" are, by definition, out of reach. Moreover, even if an argument can be made for the likelihood or even the imminence of a given breakthrough, it does not say much about the actual event. For instance, Vernor Vinge and Ray Kurzweil insist that we are rapidly approaching a tipping point ("the singularity"), where the accelerating pace of smarter and smarter machines will soon outrun all human capabilities (perhaps as early as 2045). But it is impossible to predict its actual date and out of the question to guess how the human future might unfold after this point.

Second, research in the "defense" industry is difficult to assess. This is a more embarrassing fact since military Keynesianism is not a vain concept in contemporary capitalism (see §7.3).

Third, the greatest caution is needed when relying upon studies commissioned by the most reactionary foundations on the globe. It is never easy to determine their meaning and significance. Sometimes their claims should be turned inside out like a glove, either because they are short-sighted or because they seek disinformation. Two main arguments are possible here, and both have been made by Chomsky. On the one hand, information has to circulate in order to tune into the agenda of the inner and outer parties. On the other hand, the manufacture of dissent is becoming as important as the manufacture of consent. Even apparently subversive agendas can be piloted by specialized agencies.

Let us introduce the topic with a quick overview of three actors in the field: the Rockefeller Foundation, the RAND Corporation, and the Group on Ethics in Science and New Technologies.

In a recent study (2010), the Rockefeller Foundation adopts the pragmatic-Ellulian standpoint in order to assess the way technological innovation will determine, not merely impact, international economic development, i.e., growth.[111] Their conceptual oversimplification is the following: technological progress is the only factor allowing growth and employment and, as a consequence, also determining the viability if not the sustainability of politics, starting with social policies. This fundamental standpoint is made explicit in all Western circles and is supported at least implicitly by most other governments. The only ones who express a slight disagreement belong to the "axis of evil."

In order to keep the argument straightforward, we will not debate here at length either the fact that technological innovation has always, in the long run, destroyed employment, or the historical evidence that the concept of growth was born in colonial times and has been since quantified with incoherent methods. The gross domestic product has been used as an indicator of the economic health of a country since 1945, at a time when it was factually impossible to compare total revenue with total expenditures—a ratio that would make sense to assess macropolitics.

A purely ideological perspective on economical issues now defines what politics is about. The Rockefeller study does not conceptualize the phagocytation, or absorption, of politics by the economy; it simply defines the heuristics its authors have chosen. The study argues that technology is without doubt going to pilot economical development at the international level, acknowledging however the important indeterminations that subsist. Will technological innovation be Western or Eastern? How will the political climate influence the rhythm of innovations? Moreover, the study does not judge or anticipate the nature of the technological breakthroughs to come, but it identifies general trends in order to suggest prospective arguments.

The study is based on two sources of evidence: geopolitically, a multi-polar global system is emerging; demographically, global population growth will continue and will put pressure on food and water resources and especially on energy. Two criteria are used together in order to screen the futuribles: (i) the global political and economic alignment (i.e., the integration of politics and economics) and (ii) the adaptive capacity of individuals and communities. In other words, the questions are the following: first, will there be a deepening of globalization, i.e., a forced U.S.-Americanization of the planet, or a political fragmentation accompanied by a return of protectionism? Second, how will societies and communities adapt themselves to the variation of international integration and the social pressure occasioned by technological innovation? Hence the following grid:

	weak adaptive capacity	strong adaptive capacity
weak alignment	hack attack	smart scramble
strong alignment	lock step	clever together

Each alternative aims at depicting the world around the year 2030. It is introduced through an imaginary scenario in a rather playful manner. But are they really alternatives? All technological innovations seem interchangeable between scenarios . . . starting with the omnipresent, but never named, RFID chips.

If integration and adaptability are low, the international community would be the victim of all sorts of "**hack** attacks." Technological innovation would not prevent, or could even create,chaos. Containment measures would be needed to prevent crime and terror. Hence "identity-verification technologies become a staple of daily life."[112] If integration is weak and adaptability high, there would be a "technological **scramble**" of some communities at the expense of others. The humanity of tomorrow would exploit the civilizations of yesterday. If integration is strong and adaptability is low, some form of totalitarianism or "**lock** step" is expected. Technology would be more rudimentary and hostile to freedom. If integration and adaptability are high, some form of techno-harmony would ensue ("**clever** together"). International coordination would be maximal but not politically unified in the traditional top/down sense. It would be achieved by a consortium of nations, NGO's, and multinationals working from the bottom up. Technology would be a tool of good governance, of urbanization, and industrialization, especially thanks to data mining with the help of nanosensors and smart networks. It would be less a matter of surveillance than of *sousveillance* (or "inverse surveillance").[113]

The Rockefeller 2010 study quotes a RAND report on the *global technology revolution* (2006). The RAND Corporation, a think tank of the U.S. Air Force, provides here a more technical account of the futuribles in which RFID chips play an important role.[114] It analyzes how all the aspects of human and animal life will be impacted by biotechnologies, nanotechnologies, and information technologies. A worldwide accelerated technological development is expected.

The work of the *Group on Ethics in Science and New Technologies* also testifies to European activities in the field.[115] Here the diagnosis seems even simpler. Beyond the conceptual fog, one can distinguish a scarring lack of vision: "ethics will always lag behind."

6. Capitalism: the Human-Machine System

6.1. What Is Capitalism?

Now that the general background of our discussion has been specified, it is necessary to circumscribe capitalism itself and to cast some light on the input it requires and the output it generates.

6.1.1. Total exploitation

Capitalism necessarily involves *total exploitation* in order to maximize *private* profit. (Alternative models, such as Scitovsky's, Baumol's, or Marris' can be ignored here.) What does it mean in practice? On the one hand, private profit is the key to all economical processes; on the other hand, it is generated by exploitation and alienation of all phenomena.

6.1.1.1. Everything and everyone are commodities

First, everything and everyone are but commodities, i.e., available resources. They have no intrinsic value in their natural environment. All individuals are thus means—especially proles, of course. Utility is the keyword.

6.1.1.2. Everywhere: public and private; home and abroad

Second, this 360° commodification takes place everywhere, in public as well as private spheres. Total exploitation starts in the homeland but should be geographically expanded as much as possible. Globalization is a matter of principle.[116]

6.1.1.3. Everytime: synchronic and diachronic (past & future)

Third, this nefarious process is synchronic as well as diachronic. All contemporarily available resources qualify for total exploitation, but past and future resources should not be sheltered from insatiable greed. Oil and minerals, for instance, that took millions of years to settle, can be, without any doubt, exhausted in a couple of generations. Similarly, there is no need to try to preserve resources that would be essential for future generations. Whereas pre-Industrial Revolution common sense used to require that all decisions take into account at least two future generations, simply because it was a graspable reality—that is, an adult could get to know her children's children—and an existential imperative, in that there was inter-generational support. Nowadays the life of his children and of his children's children do not seem to be of any interest to most denizens! Perhaps here we get a clear glimpse of what deculturation—if not plain evil—is. When very few really care about children anymore, the end is near.[117]

Total exploitation thus fosters nothing less than two biocides. A genocidal capitalism would leave nature untouched—something that is obviously not the case. Even positive externalities are usually ignored.[118]

6.1.2. Upstream biocide

Upstream, we find the instrumentalization of all forms of life, which generally amounts to their destruction. For the "business class," nature is just a big reservoir to plunder *and* a huge dustbin. As Huxley remarked, the love of nature keeps no factory busy. There is so much pollution in some areas that life expectancy starts now to decline while health is more and more handicapped by pathologies such as asthma, diabetes, cancer, mental disorders, and genetic disorders.[119]

6.1.3. Downstream biocide

Downstream, the transformation of nature into technical commodities also means the substitution of artificial life for natural life. Nature is outmoded, sometimes even criminal; nothing should be free. Animals or plants reproducing themselves without any human intervention whatsoever is the nightmare of the corporate world. According to Berlan, the biotechnology industry seeks the sterilization of all forms of life in order to substitute *production* for *reproduction*.[120]

The conjunction of bio-technology with nanotechnology and information technology irresistibly leads in the direction of the disappearance of the natural realm, all for the entire benefit of multinationals. Interestingly, the existential consequences for human beings of technological innovations are only debated within techno-optimist circles such as the transhumanists. In other circles, ethicists are hired in order to sanction policies decided by technicians, something they happily do for only a small additional fee.

This is of tremendous philosophical relevance since it amounts to the obliteration of the contrast between nature ("physis") and art or artifice ("techne") which is at the root of the entire Western culture. As far as I know, only Jean-Pierre Dupuy has worked on this philosophical conundrum foreseen by Heidegger and Anders.[121] Here is the surest sign of a total cultural—hence civilizational—collapse.

6.2. When Did It Start?

Three watersheds are essential to grasp the nature of contemporary capitalism—(i) a technoscientific, (ii) an economical, and (iii) a data-processing innovation. They are, so to speak, the late thunder after three lightnings: 1784, 1929, and 1984. All presuppose the shift from caste stewardship to class property. Before the enclosures, the landed gentry saw itself as the warden of a certain vision of the world in which they were the elected people in charge of the land, the population, and the religion. They actually belonged to their land and people, securing the reproduction of caste structure. After the enclosures, ownership basically meant an endless power quest through the dematerialization of value. Land had no more intrinsic value but only extrinsic value, quantity substituted for quantity. Previously one could only crave for so much mundane wardenship; now money made possible a never-ending quest. Plus, the dematerialization secured by monetarization of exchanges introduced a financial logic. Money acquired an existence of its own, requiring, like a demon of sorts, to be fed by interest rates. A very tragic exemplification of misplaced concreteness indeed. Early bourgeois were still pretending to foster aristocratic values; later, aristocrats who survived revolutionary turmoil adopted the new bourgeois religion of money.

6.2.1. Industrial revolution: technoscience, 1784

The most important technological innovation that allowed the transformation of an agrarian society into an industrial one is without a doubt the discovery of the steam engine and more particularly the creation of the steam locomotive by James Watt (1736–1819) in 1784. The shift to oil production and to the combustion-engine is just a refinement of this process that later also involved other forms of production of electricity.

In a nutshell: without proper fuel, none of the new industrial contraptions would be of any use. Windmill, watermill, and horsepower were slowly abandoned; and the entry into the "carbon age" was progressive. Abraham Darby substituted coke for charcoal in 1709, allowing the industrial production of cast iron with high-quality coke and the birth of the iron industry itself (1749). Later, productivity was significantly increased with the adoption of puddling (1784). The production of coal skyrockets from 1830 on; then it is supplemented with the production of coke and eventually by oil.

Zénobe Gramme (1826–1901) invents the dynamo in 1869 and the electric engine in 1873. Thomas Edison (1847–1931) establishes the Edison Electric Light Co. (New York) in 1878. The electrification of the industrial West was about to begin, but not in the decentralized way imagined by Edison, who argued for the use of direct current (DC), far safer for users but inadequate for the creation of a distribution grid. His rival Westinghouse was keen to impose the use of alternating current (AC), essential to create monopolies of production and distribution.

The use of the explosion engine spread with the automobile industry, especially after the commercialization of the Ford Model T in 1908.

Oil exploitation had grown since 1850, but it was the development of new weapons prior to WWI—airplanes in 1912; armored divisions in 1916—that revealed the full military potential of oil. Petro addiction was then complete until the nuclear power industry painted its advantages in glowing colors. Enrico Fermi built the first experimental nuclear reactor in Chicago; it entered criticality in 1942. The first civilian reactor was Russian (AM-1 Obninsk, 1954), and the first portable one was U.S. (Alco PM-2A, 1960).

6.2.2. Economical revolution: consumerism, 1929

The question of the totalitarian nature of technique, and especially of technology, should be addressed straightforwardly but. However, in the context of the present claim of Whitehead's optimism and technophilia to the global systemic crisis, it is heuristically possible to sever technoscience from its managerial pole and to critically cultivate a romantic vision of technology.

According to Ellul, tehnique, and all the more so technology, is intrinsically totalitarian. It seeks to embrace everything. Still, for Ellul, capitalism actually constitutes an impediment to this all-embracing progress. Nothing should interfere with technique. It is criminal and antisocial to slow down this trend.[122] The destruction of organic and vital links and their replacement by technical links constitutes progress.

As stated by Mumford, technique and capitalism are intrinsically correlated, but technique could be made more organic. Writing in 1934, Mumford obviously tries to salvage the techno-optimism of *Adventures of Ideas* (1933). Giving the presumption of innocence to technoscience amounts to accepting the possibility that technoscience could be piloted by a genuine political vision instead of an economic-speculative one and hence contribute to the common good instead of the wealth of the 0-1 percent of the population. According to the late Huxley, it is not impossible, after all, that what Illich calls a convivial society (*Tools for Conviviality*, 1973) could be obtained through a synergy between technoscience and spirituality (*Island*, 1962). Huxley argued for a Buddhist vision while Whiteheadians are used to reading about a Christian vision (Hartshorne, Cobb, Griffin, etc.).

From the perspective of Whiteheadian scholarship, the emergence of consumerism can be sketched in the following way. There is first an economic problem that is essentially nebulous for all actors; namely, how to cope with overproduction. Then second, two new techniques emerge— planned obsolescence and public relations. They prove themselves useful in managing all the concerns of the oligarchy. Third, the implementation of these techniques grants the expressibility of the economic dilemmas and the connection is made between the economic crisis and the social and political crises. Consumerism constitutes, beginning in the 20th century, the apparent core of the capitalist agenda for the simple reason that it seemed to be the only solution to its chronic cycle of crises. Three main points should thus be underlined: (i) recurrent crises, (ii) programmed obsolescence, and (iii) public relations.

6.2.2.1. Capitalism is always already in crisis

First, capitalism has always already been in crisis. Economists did not have to wait for Jean de Sismondi (1773–1842) or Karl Marx (1818–1883) to become aware of the following iron law: seeking profit at all costs periodically creates crises of overproduction (sometimes called "necessary market corrections"), usually aggravated by shameless speculation. To concentrate on the period that is relevant to our argument, remember that the Great Depression of 1929–1939 was actually preceded by another crisis: the Depression of 1920–1921. Interestingly enough, the successions of recessions and recoveries remained a nebulous problem if not a simple taboo . . . until the existence of a solution *respectful of the interests of the business class* allowed them to formulate the issue clearly. This solution—forced consumption—has two poles: programmed obsolescence and advertising campaigns. Later the generalization of credit would compensate for the lack of buying power within the growing number of unemployed.

6.2.2.2. Planned obsolescence and public relations

Second, the first manifestation of the politics of planned obsolescence seems to be the Phoebus cartel (1924–1939), created to control the manufacture and sale of light bulbs and especially aimed at limiting their life expectancy. The issue was clearly identified by Huxley in his *Brave New World* (1932), but the term itself, apparently coined by Bernard London (*Ending the Depression Through Planned Obsolescence*, 1932), got some public visibility only in the sixties with the work of Vance Packard (especially *Waste Makers*, 1960). He argued that planned obsolescence can be divided into three subcategories: obsolescence of quality, obsolescence of function, and obsolescence of desirability. Sometimes an existing product breaks down or wears out; sometimes a new product that performs the function better is introduced; and sometimes the existing product simply becomes less attractive ("psychological obsolescence").[123]

Third, in the years 1912–1929 the new field of psychology emerged, and a new market sprang from it in the U.S.A.: public relations, or "PR." Here lies the missing link between the unexpressed problem and its clarification.

Psychological *science* comes out of Wundt's psychophysics and is essentially Pavlovian.[124] It developed with Watson's (1878–1958), Tolman's (1886–1959) and Skinner's (1904–1990) behaviorism.[125] Psychology had been taught at universities, as a discipline distinct from philosophy, since James and Wundt,[126] but psychology departments were created far later. Kuklick gives 1912 as the cut-off date between philosophy and psychology in the U.S. For instance, Harvard's department of psychology was fully autonomous only in 1936 while the first British department was created in 1928 by Charles Spearman (1863–1945) at University College, London.[127]

The market of "public relations" sprang from the hybridization of behaviorism and psychoanalysis; the mind can be controlled by tireless repetition of the same stimulus, especially if it targets some unconscious (read: sexual) drive. Of course, behaviorism is theoretically at daggers drawn with Freudian psychoanalysis, but both views actually share many materialistic and deterministic presuppositions that make them twin children of their time. Five stages are remarkable.

(i) Public relations was raised into prominence in 1914 when Ivy Ledbetter Lee (1877–1934) was hired by John D. Rockefeller Jr to represent his family and company, initially the "Colorado Fuel & Iron Company" and later "Standard Oil," after the "Ludlow Massacre." Ludlow basically saw strikers being machine-gunned by private militias in order to cure their lack of morality. It was not the first time that hundreds of armed guards were hired to break a strike (remember, e.g., the 1892 Homestead Strike), but this time the bloodbath was too obvious. Lee promptly demonstrated that public opinion could be controlled through the press.

(ii) The second feat of PR aficionados took place in the context of the work of the "Committee on Public Information" or "Creel Committee." This was created by Woodrow Wilson in 1917, just after the declaration of war, in order to introduce to the public the idea of a U.S. military intervention in Europe. Its main craftsmen were Edward Bernays (1891–1995), who had opened an office as Public Relations Counselor in New York in 1919 and was bragging of his familial ties with Freud,[128] and Walter Lippmann (1889–1974), who had already carved out the expression "engineering of consent" in 1922.

(iii) To the point: the first U.S. departments of psychology were created in the years 1914–1917 in order to provide assessment protocols for the army, now recruiting for continental operations, and to develop psychological warfare and other propaganda tools. Congress declared war on 6 April 1917, but the matter had been in the air since at least 1915, when the *Lusitania* was conveniently torpedoed.

(iv) Goebbels had been a shrewd spectator of these developments (he kept copies of Bernays' writings in his own personal library). He enters the public scene around 1927 with the christening of *Der Angriff* newspaper. One knows how much he contributed to securing the Nazi grasp on German minds.

(v) One last important milestone is Bernays' "torches of freedom" campaign of 1929 that successfully transformed a habit associated with the life of a *lost* woman, usually prostitutes, artists at best, into the public sign of a *liberated* woman. The exact same pattern is used nowadays to urge "new Europe" to smoke . . . At any rate, if you wonder what public relations can do, and if you are tired of the recent fuss about spin doctors and nonexistent Weapons of Mass Destruction, it is easy to remember that the biggest known crime against humanity, Hiroshima, was promptly advertised as the bare outcome of the necessities of modern warfare. Hardly anyone remembers that the Japanese were not only on their knees *before* August the 6th but also trying to reach a peace agreement months before the bombs were dropped.[129]

6.2.2.3. Consumerism or the Gulag

To sum up: while economic crises were seemingly more and more frequent and appeared to have more lasting effects (1920–1921, then 1929–1939), a new market quickly imposed itself as the *sine qua non* condition of profitable business and smooth (profitable) politics (1912–1939). The epiphany took place in the years 1927–1929, when it occurred to the business class that the solution to overproduction does not have to be communism but can be *consumerism* instead. The idea was simply to create a "superb consumer" who is restless, wasteful, conforming, debt-ridden, permanently discontented (with a "hunger for hard goods"[130]). The argument is brilliant. Since technoscientific capitalism grows osmotically with gains in productivity, sooner or later, these gains in productivity allow an industry to saturate the market. As the *New York Times* wrote in 1927, "it may be that the world's needs ultimately will be produced by three days' work a week."[131] Decadence, indulgence, materialism, cynicism, irresponsibility, selfishness, and the like are either accidental or irrelevant to the forced consumption system (Packard).

It seems then unavoidable to pare down the work week or at least to slow production down, but this would have two equally totally unacceptable results. First, profits would decrease; second, workers would have more time for themselves, for the pursuit of happiness and the creation of a dense tissue of solidarity. But why are these consequences scandalously unacceptable? Well, to advocate lower profits and degrowth is equivalent to stabbing capitalism in the heart. As a matter of principle, nothing should prevent the betterment of profits. Fair enough, but what about the pursuit of happiness? We find here the exact same rationale as the one that is behind military Keynesianism, which *de facto* constitutes the necessary condition of the contemporary blend of capitalism (cf. §6.3.3). That is, if citizens are urged to cultivate themselves, if they are given the time and the means to become genuine individuals and to foster a solidarity worthy of that name—i.e., to fulfil the Greek ideal of direct democracy—they simply become ungovernable by the oligarchy. But if we spend all our money, and more, on weapons that are socially totally useless, we keep people at work, ignorant, and in fear. How do you achieve that? How do you scare people to death? More prosaically, how do you keep them dissatisfied with their life and the goods that they already own and consume? Advertising, supposedly a mild form of propaganda but actually its quintessential substance, allows this quite easily, as the last hundred years amply demonstrate.

The capitalist mantra "keep the consumer dissatisfied"[132] is the addiction imperative. This is what Burroughs called "The Algebra of Need:"

> the addict needs more and more junk to maintain a human form . . . Junk is the mold of monopoly and possession. . . . The more junk you use the less you have and the more you have the more you use. . . . Junk is the ideal product. . . . the ultimate merchandise. No sales talk necessary. The client will crawl

through a sewer and beg to buy. . . . The junk merchant does not sell his product to the consumer, he sells the consumer to his product. He does not improve and simplify his merchandise. He degrades and simplifies the client. He pays his staff in junk.[133]

What matters is that the link between gains in productivity and need saturation is not a recent epiphany that took place in post-1968 radical thinking: *the business class was itself fully conscious of the stakes as early as 1926.* John E. Edgerton, president of the National Association of Manufacturers, declared for instance: "I am for everything that will make work happier but against everything that will further subordinate its importance. The emphasis should be put on work—more work and better work." "Nothing," he claimed, "breeds radicalism more than unhappiness unless it is leisure."[134]

More leisure and less production could foster citizenry but also radicalism. More production and less leisure guarantees conformism and atomism. The very terms of the debate are not new at all. Some radical thinkers simply rediscover nowadays what the inner party has buried under layers of useless information one hundred years ago.

A contemporary example makes this contrast striking. Every single known and unknown politician claims nowadays that the demographic evolution in Western countries requires that citizens work longer to finance social security. There is no other alternative, and this is considered common sense! But expected improvements in productivity alone could cover the alleged deficit, which is aggravated by financialization *aka* speculation. Plus it is obvious that production should be slowed down in the context of the global systemic crisis. And it is perhaps also clear that it is about time to redistribute wealth and leisure in a way that allows, finally, for the implementation of the democratic program lauded by the very same politicians.

The discovery of the solution to a liminal, i.e., almost conscious, problem has thus allowed a rephrasing of the alternatives. There is no need to renounce the accumulation of property and wealth by the happy few; there is no need to fear communism. Productivity will continue to soar. People will be kept at work 8 hours a day 5 days a week to try to buy the life they cannot afford. Massification will secure a carnivalesque democracy, itself allowing capitalism's endurance. Now that the danger can be safely averted, we can name the alternatives: (i) either the gulag or consumerism; (ii) either communist enslavement or capitalistic enslavement; (iii) either a vast prison for loosely connected individuals, who are perhaps still free in their heads, or (iv) an infinite desert populated by bodies free to go where they have nothing to do and to shout what they don't think, while their minds are firmly locked up by the current newspeak. Spinoza is perhaps the first one to have understood the possibilities that were actualized only in the 20th century and depicted by Huxley:

> But if, in despotic statecraft, the supreme and essential mystery be to hoodwink the subjects, and to mask the fear, which keeps them down, with the specious garb of religion, so that men may fight as bravely for slavery as for safety, and count it not shame but highest honour to risk their blood and their lives for the vainglory of a tyrant; yet in a free state no more mischievous expedient could be planned or attempted.[135]

Huxley did not mince his words either:

> There is, of course, no reason why the new totalitarianisms should resemble the old. Government by clubs and firing squads, by artificial famine, mass imprisonment and mass deportation, is not merely inhumane (nobody cares much about that nowadays); it is demonstrably inefficient—and in an age of advanced technology, inefficiency is the sin against the Holy Ghost. A really efficient totalitarian state would be one in which the all-powerful executive of political bosses and their army of managers control a population of slaves who do not have to be coerced, because they love their servitude. To make them love it is the task assigned, in present-day totalitarian states, to ministries of propaganda, newspaper editors and schoolteachers. But their methods are still crude and unscientific.[136]

It is after all easier to control minds rather than bodies.

All this brings us back to Lovejoy's contrast and its actualization in environmentalism and ecology. The recent craze for Mother Earth makes some people think that we are now confronted by a new state of affairs and that new alternatives are lurking within it. It should be absolutely clear that what the unwashed masses discover in 2014 was actually fully realized in 1927, if not earlier, by leading capitalists. The alternative is indeed between more genocidal capitalism and a form of communism. The decision is not negotiable.

The consumer has been substituted for the citizen. There are no more—if there ever were—individual members of an organic community. There are customers, clients, patients, students, fans, shoppers. Life is no more balanced between clearly defined private and public territories but wanders in blurred worlds, basically a society of the spectacle. Family, neighborhood, communities have been dissolved in gender issues, fear, and anxiety.

6.2.3. The virtual revolution

A Whiteheadian techno-optimism is typically Western and seems linked with its propensity for monotheism. It certainly makes sense from the perspective of creationism, since god's creation is understood demiurgically. When Plato systematized this pattern of thought, mechanism was unknown and an organic relation between the *demiurgos* and its cosmos was still conceivable. Nowadays, the question does not even occur anymore. If human logos is akin to the divine logos, *technè* is likely to be virtuous.

6.2.3.1. Personal computer (1984) and Internet (1991)

Since Gutenberg's first printing (1454), books have worked on communities and societies. They allowed the spread of Renaissance ideals and of the Reformation, which, in turn, encouraged a new form of collective consciousness (see the works of Herbert Marshall McLuhan, Elizabeth Lewisohn Eisenstein, and Jack Goody). Later, newspaper publishing was largely responsible for breaking the church's monopoly on existential issues and for fostering socialist reforms. Its heroic age dates back to the years 1850–1950 when the class consciousness summoned by the *Manifest der Kommunistischen Partei* (1848) slowly materialized.

When new media emerged (the BBC radio was founded in 1922 and regular television broadcasts began in 1934), they displaced the hegemony of printing and, again, modified collective consciousness.[137] Television got immensely popular in the aftermath of WW2 in the U.S., uplifting the moods of its valued customers. Whereas newspapers were instrumental in reforming class consciousness, radio, and especially television, immediately boosted a conservative worldview. Advertising became a real industry,with pure political and economical propaganda the rule.[138] Written material is no doubt less susceptible to rhetoric than speech and images.

In 1984, Apple released its first Macintosh personal computer. The multimedia universe, as its name indicates, depends upon the possibility to manage together text, audio, still images, animation, video, and interactive content forms, such as Wikipedia. The World Wide Web was born in 1991; the military ARPANET, its direct ancestor, was launched in 1969. Apparently a truly democratic device, the internet requires however some computer knowledge and access to the web through a provider, as well as, of course, a computer and some reliable electric power. When the "semantic web" (Web 3.0) is implemented in order to prevent the spread of pornography, etc., that relative democracy could be terminated and a tighter control on all traffic imposed.

Finally, let us mention cellular phones, which appeared in Europe in 1994 and quickly became an indispensable element in the life of denizens. More and more irrelevant information is being poured into our lives, especially since the merging of mobile phone and ultra-broadband internet access ("4G," 2008). Pinochet (1973), Thatcher (1979), and Reagan (1981) did not work for nothing.

6.2.3.2. RFID chips

RFIDs (acronym of "Radio-frequency identification") have been on the market since 1971; they constitute the spearhead of non-invasive control technologies. To simplify, there are basically two types of RFID tags. Passive RFID tags have no built-in power source and require an external electromagnetic field to initiate a signal transmission, usually no more than 10 meters. Active RFID tags contain a battery and can transmit signals once an external source, an "interrogator," has been successfully identified. Some are "read-only" chips, their data being set once and for all; others can be modified after implantation.

In order to keep the argument tight, the following schematization of the technical possibilities is proposed. We will peruse, on the one hand, passive nanochips that can be widely used to tag commodities; on the other, active microchips that are developed in order to help specialized institutions cope with some animal or some human beings. Nanochips could even be spread in the environment like dust. Microchips are implanted through surgery and should be soon localized by the cellular phone network.

6.2.3.3. Internet of things

The "internet of things" refers to the implementation of all available forms of tracking technologies, starting with RFID's, in order to obtain a virtual copy of the real world and to manage it totally. All items in our environment—including humans—could be tagged by a chip or caught in real time by sensors, cameras, computers, etc. The development of enhanced connectivity infrastructure and of ad-hoc programs and algorithms would allow total monitoring, management, and automation, removing the need for any, or much, human decisions. This concept is already at work in so-called smart cities, cars, and houses; it is part of the "connected culture" mythology. In short, this would be a fully fledged, built-in, paranoia.

The "internet of things" began as a research project by the Massachusetts Institute of Technology's Auto-ID Labs to help the Department of Defense track and control military stockpiling and inventory. Quite a relevant project in light of the now-forgotten conference given by then Secretary of Defense Donald Rumsfeld, who admitted on Sept 10, 2001, that "there is a $2 trillion hole in the Pentagon's accounting." Even a partial implementation of this program would constitute a major threat for democracy and for the world of life.

This question bounces back in §8.2.

6.3. How Does It Operate?

In 1929–30, Whitehead came very close to the heart of the problem faced by our societies when he identified atomism and conformism and especially raised the twin questions of the preservation of freedom in a consumer society and of the link between productivity and employment. He had all the tools to understand the stakes and take action; for some reason, he did neither. The question has since bounced back many times with the works of ecologists and environmentalists. Let us first differentiate these two streams of thought with the help of Lovejoy's seminal analysis, which contrasts chronological primitivism with cultural primitivism.[139] Then we will gradually focus on the reframing that propaganda made possible.

Chronological primitivism argues for an original and pristine condition, a Golden Age or an Age of Heroes. It was first expressed in mythological thought (Homer, Hesiod, Ovid), then reappeared, after all sorts of conceptual accidents (Rousseau, Schelling, Kierkegaard), in the middle of the 20th century, with the "ecological" movement (Carson, Meadows, Naess, etc.) that ended up bringing forth a *new green deal* in order to secure the revival of a capitalism in perdition. According to mainstream ecologists, to go back to that original epoch requires the expression of a luring idea that would exert its influence *from the top of society.* Society will be transformed by the expression of a new ideal in normative rules expressed in a legal corpus, preferably meta-national.

Cultural primitivism expresses the discontent with the current state of civilization and usually claims that a far simpler and less sophisticated life would constitute a better life. It was first tagged behind chrono-mythological primitivism (Cynicism, Skepticism, Stoicism, etc.). It then recurred, after the first warlike apocalypse of the century and its intellectual consequences (Spengler, Freud, Mumford), and then morphed into what can be called environmentalism (Ellul, Illich, Gorz). The point here is less to return to nature than to transform culture *from the bottom.* Global transformation is deemed useless; only local revolution will make the difference. This happens, very simply, when individuals decide to modify their habits in agreement with a new life standard. It is then hoped that these small scale events will "topple up."

The two streams are not always easy to distinguish in their consequences, but their guiding principles are clearly different. Chronological primitivism is positive or kataphatic; it institutes a uchronia that puts on stage a paradisiac epoch of sorts and suggests that one should seek rejuvenation on its shores. The hidden premise is a fusional tropism and an absence of real concern for contemporary matters. Cultural primitivism is negative or apophatic; it institutes a utopia that demands the reversal of the current "civilizational" trends in order to alleviate alienation without specifying, a priori, all the characteristics of this reversal (communitarianism and vegetarianism are however frequent imperatives). The explicit premise is a personal concern for the contemporary state of affairs, a renunciation of whatever seems seducing to most, and hence the enforcement of self-discipline and austerity. Technology is seen as intrinsically problematic as is wealth and sometimes property.

It is not difficult to understand why chronological primitivism has been progressively superseded by cultural primitivism. The development of scientific theories has made it difficult to support the idea of an Age of Heroes while technical progress has reinforced the unease that was already expressed at the time of bare tools and animal traction(cf. Cynicism and Epicurianism). For instance, contemporary ecology has historically been shaped by environmentalism. But an interesting shift has taken place, and now ecology has the best visibility. The shift has given an unexpected meaning and purpose to primitivist thinking. After having been a transformative force, ecology has become a hoax.

In sum, cultural primitivists are the only significant actors in the assessment of the Western disaster. The amazing thing is that all their works attack technoscientific capitalism while Whitehead remains atavistically confident in the power of technique to bend the altogether marginal problems created by capitalism. If we dig further, we thus have to acknowledge the relevance of Mumford (*Technics and Civilization,* 1934), Lovejoy (*Primitivism,* 1935), Heidegger ("Die Frage nach der Technik," 1949, in *Vorträge und Aufsätze,* 1954), Arendt (*The Origins of Totalitarianism,* 1951), Anders (*Nihilismus und Existenz,* 1946; *Die Antiquiertheit des Menschen,* 1956), Ellul (*La Technique,* 1954), Kohr (*The Breakdown of Nations,* 1957), Carson (*Silent Spring,* 1962), Schumacher (*Small is Beautiful,* 1973), Illich (*La Convivialité,* 1973) and Gorz (*Écologie et politique,* 1975). But the two decisive texts are most probably literary: Orwell's *Nineteen Eighty-Four* (1949) and Huxley's *Island* (1962).

In sum, three complementary heuristic tools need to be mobilized to obtain a better picture.

6.3.1. Massification

Massification is so to speak the finished product of the process of capitalistic deculturation. It involves the tight symbolic web of conformation and atomization. Communities are long dead in our political landscape, but so are societies. It seems now as if a pure fluid dynamics could be applied to clone-like denizens. If there is still freedom of speech, it certainly does not entail or even presuppose freedom of thought.[140]

6.3.2. Speculation

The accumulation of goods and capital that is the core of the process of total exploitation, and thus the engine of capitalism, necessarily leads to usury and speculation in resources, in goods, also in currencies, in bonds, in shares, and, eventually, in more and more abstruse derivative products. This leads to the financialization of economy, a virtual growth that can entail a real growth only if inflation is avoided. Here, private property means utmost greed, shameless cupidity.

6.3.3. Military Keynesianism

History teaches us that capitalism cannot survive independently of military Keynesianism. Why? For economic, social, and political reasons—all tied to the *imperium* of the inner party.[141]

There is first a tissue of economic reasons; military Keynesianism allows internal growth and fosters high-tech research and development. Weapons—of mass destruction or otherwise—need heavy investments and secrecy to be developed and thus flourish in a closed market. The sales of new weaponry are guaranteed in the homeland while lobbying seeks to obtain some market shares abroad. Since weapons systems are getting more and more sophisticated, it is furthermore possible to make sure they will never be turned against some nations. (The case of avionics stands out, with the explicit possibility of banning any aggressive actions against some forces with the "identification friend or foe" system).

Second, all the funds that are spent on socially useless programs prevent the distribution of wealth. Think for a second about the level of social care (education, health, culture) that could be obtained in the U.S. if all its troopers were upgraded into social workers. I do not talk about military personnel pretending to operate humanitarian missions in battledress, but of a genuine reallocation of resources.

Third, military Keynesianism guarantees international hegemony. This is what is politely called "gunboat diplomacy"; that is, the opening of markets for pillage. The opium wars constitute a good historical example, but all wars, without exception, qualify. What Clausewitz wrote is still valid provided one acknowledges that business imperatives have now entirely substituted for political intercourse: "war is simply a continuation of *economical* intercourse, with the addition of other means . . . War in itself does not suspend *economical* intercourse or change it into something entirely different. In essentials, that intercourse continues irrespective of the means it employs."[142]

Here, private property means security. In sum, industrial capitalism *qua* total exploitation benefits from the push of fascist, militarized capitalism and the pull of financial, speculative capitalism. Between the years 1944–1989 and 2001–2008, the Pentagon and Neo-Conservatism ruled the game. Between 1989–2001 and 2009–2012, Wall Street and Neoliberalism took over, with the latter as an economic policy agenda that began in Chile in 1973. Hence. I have two important last remarks. First, it is essential to carefully distinguish neoconservatism and neoliberalism and to notice that their respective agendas are contradictory. The former is made of fundamentalism, messianism, moralism, militarism, expansionism, and patriotism, while the latter embraces the perfect market, profitability, amoral market, globalization, deregulation, and entrepreneurial rationality. Second, neoliberalism and neoconservatism both share enough interest to work, *in fine*, hand in hand. The most recent amazing proof being probably the smooth transition between Bush and Obama. It is a screen that hides the agenda of the inner part, even to the outer party.

7. Actors, from Top to Bottom

Now, the actors of the capitalistic system deserve some special attention. Who runs the system? Who benefits from it (*cui bono*)? What does the exercise of power actually entail?

7.1. Who Runs Capitalism?

There is no easy answer to this question because of the limited horizon that defines everybody's social perspective (see section 4.2). At the same time, names are not difficult to identify. One should be especially aware of what Whitehead called the fallacy of misplaced concreteness. The pilots of the system are not big corporations or multinationals or even, as the story goes, a democratically elected parliament. The pilots are individuals who, at least at some point in their careers, have chosen to follow the path of greed rather the one of solidarity. When we will ask "why" (in section 7.3), we will not incriminate the will of a conglomerate (there is no Leviathan) but the decisions of individuals. This precision is important because if you choose to condemn such abstract entities, you pave the way for the devil's advocate, who will for sure claim that the responsibility and the freedom of choice that you seek in managerial matters does not really exist in so far as *There Is No Alternative*; the iron law of neoliberalism is as *natural* as gravitation is.

The general sketch is simple:

> Throughout recorded time, and probably since the end of the Neolithic Age, there have been three kinds of people in the world, the High, the Middle, and the Low. They have been subdivided in many ways, they have borne countless different names, and their relative numbers, as well as their attitude towards one another, have varied from age to age: but the essential structure of society has never altered. Even after enormous upheavals and seemingly irrevocable changes, the same pattern has always reasserted itself, just as a gyroscope will always return to equilibrium, however far it is pushed one way or the other. . . . The aims of these three groups are entirely irreconcilable. The aim of the High is to remain where they are. The aim of the Middle is to change places with the High. The aim of the Low, when they have an aim—for it is an abiding characteristic of the Low that they are too much crushed by drudgery to be more than intermittently conscious of anything outside their daily lives—is to abolish all distinctions and create a society in which all men shall be equal. (*Nineteen Eighty-Four* 231)

When an individual achieves class consciousness, the implications depend upon his or her actual social horizon. Proles are concerned about destroying the class dialectic; outer party members are only trying to climb the ladder and inner party members to maintain the status quo.

7.1.1. Inner Party

Orwell implicitly uses the idea of the social horizon to introduce the "first class:"

> a man named O'Brien, a member of the Inner Party and holder of some post so important and remote that Winston had only a dim idea of its nature. (*Nineteen Eighty-Four* 13)

In France, between the two World Wars, there was also the idea that the country was driven by two hundred families ("les deux cents familles"). This was an allusion to the pre-Revolution time when the old nobility of knightly origin ruled over the Kingdom. Some things never change, nor are they meant to. At the end of the nineteenth century, Ward McAllister was talking about America's social elite as the "Four Hundred." Scholars speak now about 6000 people,[143] but there is no real need to quantify. What would really matter would be to name these individuals or, failing that, to try to understand the meaning and significance of their behaviors. Psychopathy (or sociopathy, i.e., DSM-IV-TR's "Antisocial Personality Disorder") is likely to be the main nosological category applicable.

The inner party is where power is *exerted* for the sake of power. Its members usually do not seek the attention of the media.

7.1.2. Outer Party

The inner party, however, would be nothing without the outer party (and the thought police), with which it keeps conflicting relationships.

The outer party is the antechamber of the inner party; it is where promising members are selected or from where they arise. It is through them that the inner party exerts its power on the proles. But it is also the outer party that is subjected to the most pathological aspects of the worship of power. Proles are simply stupefied by poverty and frightened by everlasting wars; the outer party is the target of the mental destructiveness of the inner party. With that regard, it is worth remembering Orwell's definition of *doublethink*:

> It is only by reconciling contradictions that power can be retained indefinitely. ... The prevailing mental condition must be controlled insanity.[144]

It would be difficult to be clearer. The outer party members are caught in a thought patterning that is reminiscent of Bateson's double bind.[145] They are perhaps the most poignant victims of the systems. Proles are kept in gross ignorance of their condition. Having to cope with their misery on an everyday basis, they usually ignore their ignorance. On the contrary, outer party members sometimes share a glimpse of the reality of the system that enslaves them and the proles—but they cannot entertain that vision and need to work on their dutiful mindlessness.

The outer party is where power is sought for the sake of power. Its members usually occupy the front scene in the media circus. The appearance of power is still needed to complement its lack of reality.

7.2. On Whom Is It Imposed?

Orwell warns us that ambivalence reigns throughout.

7.2.1. Outer Party

The outer party is not only the antechamber of the inner party; it is also the only real threat to the inner party. Remember, "the aim of the Middle is to change places with the High"—hence another reason why they need to be closely monitored. As Orwell makes plain, this requires not only the manufacture of consent *but also the engineering of dissent*. This is the work done mostly by NGOs created by the inner party members in order to pilot dissent and make it innocuous. In contemporary parlance, false flag operations can be used both to obtain consent of the masses and also to lure politically borderline individuals to identify themselves during events following the pattern framed by W. Tarpley, that is, as technicians, moles, and patsies.

The inner and outer party members cannot enjoy or afford fully fledged rational thinking. They are stuck in double thought, the former by nature, the later by necessity. When their judgement is applicable, it is the product of a technical expertise that acts as a screen between the economical *qua* political ideology and the social facts.

7.2.2. Proles

Capitalism is imposed upon 99 percent of the population, which gets very little, if anything, from it. These are the "proles" in the Orwellian lexicon. Some of them have no doubt the vague desire to cultivate double-thought, but this would involve being "educated;" and most are simply confined in nothought. The desire for social change that the prole might have is indeed displaced by a desire for changes in commodities. Political freedom is equated with consumer choice and political citizenship with mass consumption. You exist only through your buying habits.

7.3. Why So?

We now understand better HOW capitalism works, but we still do not understand WHY the inner party members seek the subservience if not the enslavement of 99 percent of the world population.[146] We often read that the greed of the business class is insatiable, that, for them, more is never enough. Why so? Why such a haughtiness—what Greeks called "hubris"?

7.3.1. Power for the Sake of Power

Here also, Orwell offers the answer. Whereas most people, even nowadays, still think that the inner party is ruling over us for our own good—because there is no way people could manage their own lives by themselves—Orwell adamantly claims that the inner party actually seeks power entirely for its own sake while the outer party members are both mesmerized by the exercise of power and repelled by the effects they have to actually endure.[147]

Orwell replies here, probably purposively, to Huxley, whose *Brave New World* maintained that there is no other way than to let the most capable individuals (the "Alpha+" elite) rule over legions of more or less capable morons. According to Huxley's narrative, a society solely composed of Alphas has been proved indeed nothing less than suicidal.[148] Now, if the best minds cannot figure a way to live peacefully, neither would a society of betas and even less so a mixture of alphas, betas, etc. Power is, in other words, entirely benevolent and pragmatic. Orwell makes a strong case for the contrary.

Interestingly, Huxley wrote to Orwell right after the publication of *Nineteen Eighty-Four* in order to praise the book but also to underline that Orwellian totalitarianism is needlessly violent.[149] There was an incurable technophilia in Huxley.

7.3.2. Torture for the Sake of Power

The quest of power for the sake of power necessarily translates into the motto of totalitarianism: terror is an end in itself.[150] Terror is not how you rule but why you rule. O'Brien is very straightforward about this when he lists the four ignoble truths of totalitarianism: (i) power is not a means but an end; (ii) power is collective, it is power over human beings; (iii) power seeks total control of the mind in order to totally control matter (and the body); (iv)power necessarily consists in the capacity to impose suffering and, ultimately, to torture. Let us let Orwell speak for himself:

> 'How does one man assert his power over another, Winston?'
>
> Winston thought. 'By making him suffer,' he said.
>
> 'Exactly. By making him suffer. Obedience is not enough. Unless he is suffering, how can you be sure that he is obeying your will and not his own? Power is in inflicting pain and humiliation. Power is in tearing human minds to pieces and putting them together again in new shapes of your own choosing. Do you begin to see, then, what kind of world we are creating? It is the exact opposite of the stupid hedonistic Utopias that the old reformers imagined. A world of fear and treachery and torment, a world of trampling and being trampled upon, a world which will grow not less but *more* merciless as it refines itself. Progress in our world will be progress towards more pain. The old civilizations claimed that they were founded on love or justice. Ours is founded upon hatred. In our world there will

be no emotions except fear, rage, triumph, and self-abasement. Everything else we shall destroy—everything. Already we are breaking down the habits of thought which have survived from before the Revolution. We have cut the links between child and parent, and between man and man, and between man and woman. No one dares trust a wife or a child or a friend any longer. But in the future there will be no wives and no friends. Children will be taken from their mothers at birth, as one takes eggs from a hen. The sex instinct will be eradicated. Procreation will be an annual formality like the renewal of a ration card. We shall abolish the orgasm. Our neurologists are at work upon it now. There will be no loyalty, except loyalty towards the Party. There will be no love, except the love of Big Brother. There will be no laughter, except the laugh of triumph over a defeated enemy. There will be no art, no literature, no science. When we are omnipotent we shall have no more need of science. There will be no distinction between beauty and ugliness. There will be no curiosity, no enjoyment of the process of life. All competing pleasures will be destroyed. But always—do not forget this, Winston—always there will be the intoxication of power, constantly increasing and constantly growing subtler. Always, at every moment, there will be the thrill of victory, the sensation of trampling on an enemy who is helpless. If you want a picture of the future, imagine a boot stamping on a human face—for ever.'[151]

The argument is unanswerable. It echoes Jack London's:

This, then, is our answer. We have no words to waste on you. When you reach out your vaunted strong hands for our palaces and purpled ease, we will show you what strength is. In roar of shell and shrapnel and in whine of machine-guns will our answer be couched. We will grind you revolutionists down under our heel, and we shall walk upon your faces. The world is ours, we are its lords, and ours it shall remain. As for the host of labor, it has been in the dirt since history began, and I read history aright. And, in the dirt it shall remain so long as I and mine and those that come after us have the power. There is the word. It is the king of words—Power. Not God, not Mammon, but Power. Pour it over your tongue till it tingles with it. Power.[152]

Anyway, the "mega" or "filthy" rich do not retire after their first couple of millions, something that would be possible and fully rational. They do not *need* more property or more wealth. They seek *more* because their goal is to exert power over other human beings. Money does not bring them security, as is the case for the proles, but power. This abstract proposition could be understandable by the philosophically inclined mind. However, as soon as one acknowledges that this power *necessarily* amounts to the faculty to inflict suffering to others, one reaches the bottomless truth that all of us actually sense but that none of us wishes to consciously confront because the implications for our lives are too staggering. If the inner party not only lies to us but actively seeks our suffering, we are doomed. Women and children first.

Goya can help us to picture this, but some rationalization is in order.[153] How could this be specified with sobriety? The most immediate conceptual tool comes from theology: evil. *Radical* evil lies here. Kant probably saw it, and Arendt, *volens nolens*, dedramatized it. From a philosophical perspective, evil is only a form of power. Power, and the quest for power, are the sole relevant concepts. To flesh them out a bit, one needs to consider the resources of nosology and to acknowledge that the pathology that is the quest of power is worthy of the name sociopathy or perversion. All this is perhaps already too abstract for most readers, so let us try to exemplify what happens when one gets addicted to power.

In everyday life, it is impossible to avoid power games. Life, as Whitehead says, necessarily involves putting its own interest first; it is robbery (PR 105). The newborn has a social horizon that barely extends to include his or her mother. Total selfishness is the rule for survival at that stage. There are however two forms of power that are theoretically innocuous: (i) the *quest of power* that seeks to endow one individual with the curative potentialities required by therapy, especially psychotherapy, starting with shamanism; and (ii) the *dance of power* that takes place in a community where all individuals are co-developing cultural bounds.[154]

The individual who realizes that his or her social status allows him or her to inflict suffering, in whatever way, be it mild humiliation, instrumentalization, or infantilization, has taken the bait of power. Depending on the circumstances, that person will, or will not, start the long journey that leads to becoming a priest or priestess of power, as Orwell says. It is difficult to obtain a picture that would match all idiosyncrasies, but the main pattern is easy to visualize with the help of experience gained in psychotherapy.

If you aim at more power, you try to become able to inflict more suffering on living beings. A car or a watch do not suffer when misused, but a dog or a colleague certainly do. If you have few resources yourself, you will probably seek power only over animals and ill-treat them. Most scenarios involve domestic violence against children and women. But some individuals cannot quench their thirst for power that way either.

Raping women or men, undoubtedly a form of torture, could be the next step—but this is hardly the last one since the victim can still survive and usually keep up appearances; denial is one of the surest sign of PTSD. Then comes the epiphany of the need to torture itself, which can still accommodate rape and finally necessitates murder. The cycle is however not complete until the power seeker attacks the weakest human beings: sometimes elderly, often children, and eventually infants or even newborns.

The abduction, torture, rape, and murder of children is the ultimate form of the quest of power.

This is the truth of the inner party. It is the truth that Goya was trying to picture, that Sade made plain, and that Pasolini filmed. It is likely to be truth of the tormented childhoods of these individuals. It is the very reality that proles cannot confront for obvious emotional and rational reasons.

We do not claim however that there is a satanic initiation of sorts that secures membership in the inner party. This would amount to mixing up sociopathy with psychopathy. The most perverted human beings do not necessarily belong to the inner party—but they would certainly be at home there. So it is not surprising that Ayn Rand (1905–1982), the mouthpiece of U.S. neoliberalism, for whom a human being is only a savage who should live according to his/her impulses, and for whom selfishness truly is a virtue, went so far as to write positively in her *Journals* about William Hickman (1908–1928), who had been responsible for the kidnapping, the dismembering, and the murder of a 12-year-old girl.

Let us finally remark that the anthropological premises of classical economists perfectly match the sociopathic rationality of rulers and shakers, that is, they are egotistical, aggressive, lacking empathy, ruthlessly greedy, amoral due to a general lack of sense of responsibility, and they never really match the behavior of 99 per cent of the population. Most of us cannot be understood from the perspective of the "homo economicus."

8. Possible Outcomes—From Big Mother to Big Brother?

The perennial truth that is the quest for power has found new territories with the development of technoscience and especially with the subjugation of technoscience by the neoliberal economy. As soon as *Nineteen Eighty-Four* was published the question of the likely outcome of decadent democracies molded by technoscience took, for many, the form of an alternative: the World State or Oceania, *Nineteen Eighty-Four* or *Brave New World*. Huxley himself promptly raised that very question.[155] In light of recent historical and scientific developments, it seems likely that the West will get both worlds, one after the other. This means, of course, that the Orwellian nightmare will be preformatted with Huxleyan protocols. We will not obtain the shameless brutality that Huxley found outmoded; it will be unspeakably worse.

We have seen that to flesh out the present state of affairs and possible futures ("futuribles") without becoming entangled in long ideological discussions, it is advisable to consider the question from a pragmatic standpoint informed by the most recent technological advances. Interestingly enough, the pragmatic use of available technologies and current R&D developments is a methodology used by think tanks in order to bridle useless speculations and obtain heuristic tools. The implicit premise is Ellulian: everything that is technically possible is eventually necessarily implemented (see §5.3). The heuristic key will be RFID technology.

My thesis is that we are about to enter bigmotherhood and that, from there, Big Brother will disclose itself. Please note that the impending merging of bio and nano technologies with IT actually offers a far gloomier picture than the one I sketch here, but it is also more difficult to envision pragmatically in the context of this essay. In order to properly discuss these futuribles, it is necessary to first outline the 20th century utopias and dystopias.

This chapter has three sections. First, forms of utopias and dystopias are introduced with the help of a multi-layered comparison between Huxley and Orwell. Second, the concept of Big Mother is introduced. Third, the figure of Big Brother is so to speak rejuvenated. These last two sections benefit from the most recent analyses of U.S.-American imperial capitalism. It is in this country that one finds indeed the most significant proofs of the cultural collapse that is endangering not only all forms of civilization but the very existence of humankind. To speak of primary, or even secondary, anti-Americanism would be preposterous as U.S.-American citizens are the first victims of this state of affairs. This is one of the weapons used by the oligarchy to crush in the egg all forms of dissidence by destroying the very possibility of discussing any of these political issues. The sins of anti-Americanism, conspiracy, and anti-Semitism are usually threatening enough to keep intellectuals quiet. And those who have briefly and inadvertently sinned are asked to promptly repent because there will be consequences in this life, not the next one. Most of the time, these consequences are minor, however, simply because their arguments are totally ignored by other scholars and by the media.

8.1. Utopias and Dystopias

The concept of utopia is now commonly used to designate a political system that would bring meaning and happiness to all citizens but that, quite obviously, cannot be implemented in real life. Dystopias, on the contrary, embody political systems that would confer an absurd and miserable life to all and that, quite unfortunately, as time passes, are more and more likely. . . . How can we refine this discussion?

Lovejoy has shown the difference between uchronia and utopia (see §6.3) with the help of the concepts of chronological primitivism and cultural primitivism. The former refers to the political instrumentaliza-tion of the absolute truth about "primordial time," that is, a golden age of gods and heroes; the latter is a political instrumentalization of the relative truth about another "place." The contrast we require lies between utopia per se and dystopia. The former designates a cultural attractor likely to create a worst state; the latter a cultural destructor hoping for a rebirth. More's *Utopia* (1516) and Huxley's *Island* (1962) belong to another kind of narrative than Huxley's *Brave New World* (1932) and Orwell's *Nineteen Eighty-Four* (1949).

In order to screen the futuribles, we will put to work all the tools introduced so far. First, the conditions of possibility of authentic life can be correlated to the functors of Whitehead's creative advance. Direct democracy requires creativity *qua* individuation, not conformism, as well as efficacy *qua* solidarity, not atomism, and these together with vision *qua* culture, i.e., neither fear nor terror. Second, the use of technique and especially of technologies offer the decisive criterion between alternatives. As already stated, RFIDs will be on the hot seat.

8.1.1. Huxley, *Brave New World*, 1932

Huxley had a very inquisitive mind, curious about all new and past scientific discoveries and spiritual musings. Of special relevance for the understanding of *Brave New World* are his relations with his brother Julian, who kept him assiduously posted with recent developments in theoretical and applied biology.[156]

The story takes place in 26th century London, under the rule of the World State. Huxley's goal is to show the political consequences of consumerism, the "culture" of engineered abundance. Where do mass production and mass entertainment lead us? Certainly not in the direction of more democracy would be the first answer. Here springs the subsidiary question, which might actually be the main one: what is the most efficient form of government? Is it a totalitarian government and, in that case, what kind of totalitarianism would be, so to speak, better? Huxley had a staunch belief with that regard. Remember, he claimed that "government by clubs and firing squads, by artificial famine, mass imprisonment and mass deportation, is not merely inhumane (nobody cares much about that nowadays); it is demonstrably inefficient—and in an age of advanced technology, inefficiency is a sin against the Holy Ghost."[157]

The historical context in which Huxley writes is precisely the emergence of consumerism, as it was depicted above with the help of its two main sponsors: planed obsolescence and public relations (see §6.2.2). They are embedded in every part of his narrative—beginning with the dual meaning of his year-numbering system, "A.F." Huxley's story takes place in 632 A.F., i.e., the 632th year "After Ford" and/or "After Freud" (BNW 34). On the one hand, Huxley chooses to emphasize the importance of Ford's Taylorism. In a nutshell, Ford's idea is not only to improve the productivity of labor through standardization of product and automation (the "Model T" was produced by Ford Motor Company through Taylor's assembly line between 1908 and 1927). Ford also granted workers higher wages so they could afford to buy the product of their labor. On the other hand, Huxley acknowledges the tremendous importance of psychoanalysis on the management—and the creation—of human needs. The real hero is Bernays, who saw the commercial and political possibilities of a synergy between Freud's concepts and Pavlovian practice.

Let us now contrast the three functions of creative advance with the World State's motto "Community, Identity, Stability." Each term is then specified with three questions: What is the actual impact on the individual? Through what mechanism? For what purpose?

8.1.1.1. Creative individuation is downgraded to uniform identity

Identity is a principle of outstanding importance in *Brave New World*. Thanks to biological and emotional engineering, each citizen is confined within a very precise social circle or *Umwelt*; there is (almost) no elbowroom given to individual action. The most significant trait of Huxleyan conformism is recreational and promiscuous sex. There are no social boundaries between desire and its full realization. Here is an excerpt of his depiction of a "solidarity service:"

> Round they went, a circular procession of dancers, each with hands on the hips of the dancer preceding, round and round, shouting in unison, stamping to the rhythm of the music with their feet, beating it, beating it out with hands on the buttocks in front; twelve pairs of hands beating as one; as one,

twelve buttocks slabbily resounding. Twelve as one, twelve as one. "I hear Him, I hear Him coming." The music quickened; faster beat the feet, faster, faster fell the rhythmic hands. And all at once a great synthetic bass boomed out the words which announced the approaching atonement and final consummation of solidarity, the coming of the Twelve-in-One, the incarnation of the Greater Being. "Orgy-porgy," it sang, while the tom-toms continued to beat their feverish tattoo: "Orgy-porgy, Ford and fun, Kiss the girls and make them One. Boys at One with girls at peace; Orgy-porgy gives release." "Orgy-porgy," the dancers caught up the liturgical refrain, "Orgy-porgy, Ford and fun, kiss the girls . . ." And as they sang, the lights began slowly to fade—to fade and at the same time to grow warmer, richer, redder, until at last they were dancing in the crimson twilight of an Embryo Store. (BNW 75)

People are happy because they get what they want, and they never want what they can't get (BNW 200). How is this possible?

Each individual's conformal identity is achieved through a fully deterministic protocol that starts with contraception, dysgenics, and eugenics practices made possible by the use of artificial insemination and ectogenesis (incubators)[158] and that finishes with Pavlovian and hypnotic conditioning. In brief, sexual relations and reproduction have been severed once and for all. Artificial Insemination (AI), followed by bokanovskification in incubators, allowed the creation of ninety-six identical twins at a time (BNW 3ff.). Individuals are offered the horrible paradise of bio-mechanical progress.[159]

The end purpose of this individual engineering program is total and final infantilization. Nobody grows up anymore; the endless comfort of the womb rules.

8.1.1.2. Efficient solidarity is downgraded to fusional community

Community basically means social utility, pure utilitarianism: "Everyone belongs to everyone else" (BNW 38).

From the perspective of community, there is one high point: the strict social stratification in classes, from the Epsilon-Minus Semi-Moron to the Alpha-Plus. We are back to the logic of castes:

"Each process," explained the Human Element Manager, "is carried out, so far as possible, by a single Bokanovsky Group." And, in effect, eighty-three almost noseless black brachycephalic Deltas were cold-pressing. The fifty-six four-spindle chucking and turning machines were being manipulated by fifty-six aquiline and ginger Gammas. One hundred and seven heat-conditioned Epsilon Senegalese were working in the foundry. Thirty-three Delta females, long-headed, sandy, with narrow pelvises, and all within 20 millimetres of 1 metre 69 centimetres tall, were cutting screws. In the assembling room, the dynamos were being put together by two sets of Gamma-Plus dwarfs. The two low work-tables faced one another; between them crawled the conveyor with its load of separate parts; forty-seven blonde heads were confronted by forty-seven brown ones. Forty-seven snubs by forty-seven hooks; forty-seven receding by forty-seven prognathous chins. The completed mechanisms were inspected by eighteen identical curly auburn girls in Gamma green, packed in crates by thirty-four short-legged, left-handed male Delta-Minuses, and loaded into the waiting trucks and lorries by sixty-three blue-eyed, flaxen and freckled Epsilon Semi-Morons. (BNW 144)

The Bokanovsky process makes possible the highest social coherence insofar as castes are perfectly homogeneous in themselves and totally adapted to one another while the "human resources" match perfectly the production techniques. They are Borromean rings.

Why this multi-track social system? The real answer is stability, our next point—but one needs to underline here the brute consumerism of Huxley's vision. Nature has become obsolete; only retail goods are available. Commercial advertising and political propaganda have totally merged.

8.1.1.3. Visionary culture is only made of social and individually engineered stability

Stability is the *sine qua non* of civilization. In *Brave New World* total order is guaranteed by watertight structures. Even science has to be carefully monitored. Stability is the highest social virtue because it leads to lasting happiness. Individuals see their life's rhythm set by the absorption of all sorts of surrogates (passion-surrogate, pregnancy-surrogate, sex-hormone chewing-gum), the main one being soma, a cross between a hangover-free tranquillizer and a non-addictive opiate.

> Two thousand pharmacologists and bio-chemists were subsidized in A.F. 178. . . . Six years later it was being produced commercially. The perfect drug. . . . Euphoric, narcotic, pleasantly hallucinant. . . . All the advantages of Christianity and alcohol; none of their defects. . . . . Take a holiday from reality whenever you like, and come back without so much as a headache or a mythology. (BNW 47–48)

It is the universal drug, used to instantly erase mild discontent or negative ideations ("a gramme is better than a damn") but also to take a longer absence from interpersonal reality (a "soma-holiday"). Huxley likely refers here to amphetamines, whose pharmacological use was pioneered in 1927 by psychopharmacologist Gordon Alles. After generalization of the clinical use of morphine (1804), codeine (1832), and heroin (1874), the use of amphetamines (1927) fostered a cultural revolution of sorts. It was later said that "methedrine won the Battle of Britain."[160] The turning point will however come later, with the "chlorpromazine event"[161]—the first neuroleptic commercialized in France in 1952 (Largactil) and in the U.S. in 1954. This molecule brought together all the actors who have since secured their own wealth and the obliteration of the masses.

The general mechanism has already been alluded to. Eupaedia stands for social engineering through emotional-engineering, also known as hypnopaedia and Pavlovian subliminal conditioning.[162] To this purpose, there are numerous Bureaux of Propaganda and Colleges of Emotional Engineering (BNW 58).

Why? In order to foster blissful ignorance:

> our world is not the same as Othello's world. You can't make flivvers without steel—and you can't make tragedies without social instability. The world's stable now. People are happy; they get what they want, and they never want what they can't get. They're well off; they're safe; they're never ill; they're not afraid of death; they're blissfully ignorant of passion and old age; they're plagued with no mothers or fathers; they've got no wives, or children, or lovers to feel strongly about; they're so

conditioned that they practically can't help behaving as they ought to behave. And if anything should go wrong, there's soma. (BNW 200–01)

Power is exerted by the technocracy for our sake. And the World Controller seems indeed a quite benevolent figure.

In sum, "Community, Identity, Stability" amounts to watertight castes, mindless copulation, and blissful ignorance. Social engineering is so tight that the panopticon is faultless. There is basically *no need* for actual surveillance. The rare troublemakers, who are always Alpha +, are easily disposed of.

8.1.2. Orwell, *Nineteen Eighty-Four,* 1949

Huxley's Benthamian prison without walls takes quite a twist in Orwell. Although it is still possible to speak of a *panopticon*, I prefer, for the previously given reasons, to bind that concept with the early Huxley and to speak here of a *pancraticon*. According to Orwell, totalitarianism is indeed less a matter of total surveillance than of total subjugation. Invasive sousveillance can be preferred to intrusive surveillance.

The story takes place in 1984's London, the chief city of Airstrip One, itself the third most populous of the provinces of Oceania, one of the world's three superstates. In the essay section of his novel *1985*, Anthony Burgess states that Orwell got the idea for Big Brother from advertising billboards for educational correspondence courses from a company called Bennett's, current during World War II. The original posters showed Bennett himself, a kindly looking old man offering guidance and support to would-be students with the phrase "Let me be your father" attached. After Bennett's death his son took over the company, and the posters were replaced with pictures of the son, who looked imposing and stern in contrast to his father's kindly demeanor, with the text "Let me be your big brother." Speculation on the origin of "Big Brother" has also focused on Lord Kitchener, who among other things was prominently involved in British military recruitment in World War I.

In the same way that Hobbes' *Leviathan* (1651) constitutes the philosophical reply to the 17th century's political turmoil, *Nineteen Eighty-Four* matches the 20th century's fury.[163]

According to many readers, Orwell's goal seems to have been a depiction of the essence of Stalin's communism, as it was at work circa 1943–53.[164] But Orwell has repeatedly insisted on his political radicalism, and his biography amply testifies to his social and political commitments. So the first thing to do is to refuse, purely and simply, to identify Oceania with Stalinia. Furthermore, the assessment of Stalin's work at the head of the U.S.S.R. is quite disputed since Geoffrey Roberts, Domenico Losurdo, and Annie Lacroix-Riz have sought to rebalance the historical account.[165] War and shortage are no doubt important features of the narration, but they fit equally well other forms of imperialism.

Interestingly enough, the question of the most efficient political regime is equally present in Orwell:

> By comparison with that existing today, all the tyrannies of the past were half-hearted and inefficient. . . . Part of the reason for this was that in the past no government had the power to keep its citizens under constant surveillance. The invention of print, however, made it easier to manipulate public opinion, and the film and the radio carried the process further. With the development of television, and the technical advance which made it possible to receive and transmit simultaneously on the same instrument [telescreen], private life came to an end. . . . The possibility of enforcing not only complete obedience to the will of the State, but complete uniformity of opinion on all subjects, now existed for the first time.[166]

Now, Orwell's picture is different from Huxley in a number of ways that we will explore later. A couple of issues deserve to be highlighted straightaway. Huxley provides lengthy discussions of a technologically sophisticated world but displays a very shallow understanding of psychological matters. In a way, he really works towards a grasp of the amazing potentialities unleashed by 20th century science. To the contrary, Orwell relies upon simple technological devices but brings powerful psychological descriptions. The telescreen aside, borrowed from Chaplin's *Modern Times*, 1936, Orwell's technology is not in the least futuristic. Electric torture, for instance, was firmly aligned with the *Zeitgeist*.[167] The thought police, for its part, is clearly the heir of its recent counterparts in inverted totalitarian regimes.

Let us now adopt the same protocol and contrast the three functions of creative advance with Oceania's motto "War is Peace, Freedom is Slavery, Ignorance is Strength." Each term is then further specified with the same questions: What is the actual impact on the individual? Through what mechanism? For what purpose?

8.1.2.1. Creative individuation is now slavery

Doublethink embodies the very negation of creative individuation. It alone can prevent thought crime. As soon as Winston starts his diary, the veil falls:

> From the age of uniformity, from the age of solitude, from the age of Big Brother, from the age of doublethink—greetings! . . . Thoughtcrime does not entail death: thoughtcrime IS death. (*1984*, 32)

Thoughtcrime is death because it entails the destruction of the reality carved by the Party:

> All that was needed was an unending series of victories over your own memory. 'Reality control', they called it: in Newspeak, 'doublethink'. . . . To know and not to know, to be conscious of complete truthfulness while telling carefully constructed lies, to hold simultaneously two opinions which cancelled out, knowing them to be contradictory and believing in both of them, to use logic against logic, to repudiate morality while laying claim to it, to believe that democracy was impossible and that the Party was the guardian of democracy, to forget whatever it was necessary to forget, then to draw it back into memory again at the moment when it was needed, and then promptly to forget it again: and above all, to apply the same process to the process itself. That was the ultimate subtlety: consciously to induce unconsciousness, and then, once again, to become unconscious of the act of hypnosis you had just performed. Even to understand the word 'doublethink' involved the use of doublethink. (1984, 40–41)

Interestingly enough, doublethink is also called "crimestop," "blackwhite," and "protective stupidity" (*1984*, 241–42).

What is the mechanism that creates individuals ready to be enslaved? Orwell briefly evokes the eugenic potential of artificial insemination

(1984, 76),4 but this is not what concerns the inner party. Sexual relations are not bothersome because of the privacy they usually (but not necessarily) entail, but because during orgasm partners totally escape the power of the party. Orwell makes plain that female impotence (frigidity) has already been obtained amongst party members, while some work is still needed on the generalization of erectile dysfunction.

The immediate result of doublethink is a state of controlled insanity. The purpose of this borderline state and of anorgasmia is to secure the exercise of power for the sake of power. These are sure signs of the endless discomfort imposed by the unbalanced paternal rule.

8.1.2.2. Efficient solidarity is implemented by war and torture

Individual castration and impotence are of course not enough to mobilize them together; hate is needed. The collective dynamic depicted is akin to the symptoms identified by Le Bon, Trotter, and later by Bernays and Canetti, but Orwell is here also far more radical.[168] Le Bon's analysis boils down to three criteria: i) irresponsibility (and feeling of invincibility) of the massified individual, (ii) contagion of moods, and (iii) suggestibility. It reflects a negative understanding of hypnosis.[169]

The mutability of the past is the mechanism that allows the destruction of individual and collective memories and the destitution of all forms of desire. Individuals stand naked in front of the party's manipulative power:

> The mutability of the past is the central tenet of Ingsoc. Past events, it is argued, have no objective existence, but survive only in written records and in human memories. The past is whatever the records and the memories agree upon. And since the Party is in full control of all records and in equally full control of the minds of its members, it follows that the past is whatever the Party chooses to make it. It also follows that though the past is alterable, it never has been altered in any specific instance. For when it has been recreated in whatever shape is needed at the moment, then this new version is the past, and no different past can ever have existed. This holds good even when, as often happens, the same event has to be altered out of recognition several times in the course of a year.

> At all times the Party is in possession of absolute truth, and
> clearly the absolute can never have been different from what
> it is now. It will be seen that the control of the past depends
> above all on the training of memory. To make sure that all writ-
> ten records agree with the orthodoxy of the moment is merely
> a mechanical act. But it is also necessary to remember that
> events happened in the desired manner. And if it is necessary
> to rearrange one's memories or to tamper with written records,
> then it is necessary to forget that one has done so. The trick of
> doing this can be learned like any other mental technique. It
> is learned by the majority of Party members, and certainly by
> all who are intelligent as well as orthodox. In Oldspeak it is
> called, quite frankly, 'reality control'. In Newspeak it is called
> doublethink, though doublethink comprises much else as well.
> (*1984,* 243-42)

One day, Oceania is supposed to be at war with Eurasia; the next day it is
with Eastasia. Hence all records have to be rewritten, and all Party members have to doublethink this fact. The mutability of the past constitutes
a double destructuration. Individuals are broken down, and communities
are pulverized. There is a total breakdown of experience, synchronically
and diachronically. Atomization is introduced without personalities.

The purpose of war is essentially twofold. First, it retains the relative coherence of the outer party and the absolute atomicity of the
proles. Second, it keeps the economy running by providing raw materials (stolen), cheap labor (enslaved), and industrial outlets (armaments,
etc.). Orwell's denunciation of military Keynesianism is one of the best
passages of his novel (1984, 216 ff.). It deserves to be quoted at length:

> The primary aim of modern warfare (in accordance with the
> principles of doublethink, this aim is simultaneously recognized
> and not recognized by the directing brains of the Inner Party)
> is to use up the products of the machine without raising the
> general standard of living. Ever since the end of the nineteenth
> century, the problem of what to do with the surplus of
> consumption goods has been latent in industrial society. At
> present, when few human beings even have enough to eat, this
> problem is obviously not urgent, and it might not have become
> so, even if no artificial processes of destruction had been at

work. The world of today is a bare, hungry, dilapidated place compared with the world that existed before 1914, and still more so if compared with the imaginary future to which the people of that period looked forward. In the early twentieth century, the vision of a future society unbelievably rich, leisured, orderly, and efficient—a glittering antiseptic world of glass and steel and snow-white concrete—was part of the consciousness of nearly every literate person. Science and technology were developing at a prodigious speed, and it seemed natural to assume that they would go on developing. This failed to happen, partly because of the impoverishment caused by a long series of wars and revolutions, partly because scientific and technical progress depended on the empirical habit of thought, which could not survive in a strictly regimented society. As a whole the world is more primitive today than it was fifty years ago. Certain backward areas have advanced, and various devices, always in some way connected with warfare and police espionage, have been developed, but experiment and invention have largely stopped, and the ravages of the atomic war of the nineteen-fifties have never been fully repaired. Nevertheless the dangers inherent in the machine are still there. From the moment when the machine first made its appearance it was clear to all thinking people that the need for human drudgery, and therefore to a great extent for human inequality, had disappeared. If the machine were used deliberately for that end, hunger, overwork, dirt, illiteracy, and disease could be eliminated within a few generations. And in fact, without being used for any such purpose, but by a sort of automatic process— by producing wealth which it was sometimes impossible not to distribute—the machine did raise the living standards of the average human, being very greatly over a period of about fifty years at the end of the nineteenth and the beginning of the twentieth centuries. But it was also clear that an all-round increase in wealth threatened the destruction—indeed, in some sense was the destruction—of a hierarchical society. In a world in which everyone worked short hours, had enough to eat, lived in a house with a bathroom and a refrigerator, and possessed a motor-car or even an aeroplane, the most obvious and perhaps the most important form of inequality would already have disappeared. If it once became general, wealth would confer no distinction. It was possible, no doubt, to imagine a society in which wealth, in the sense of personal possessions and luxuries, should be evenly distributed, while power remained in the hands of a small privileged caste. But in practice such a society could not long remain stable. For if leisure and security were enjoyed by all alike, the great mass of human beings who are normally stupefied by poverty would become literate and would learn to think for themselves; and when once they had done this, they would sooner or later realize that the privileged minority had no function, and they would sweep it away. In the long run, a hierarchical society was only possible on a basis of poverty and ignorance. To return to the agricultural past, as some thinkers about the beginning of the twentieth century dreamed of doing, was not a practicable solution. It conflicted with the tendency towards mechanization which had become quasi-instinctive throughout almost the whole world, and moreover, any country which remained industrially backward was helpless in a military sense and was bound to be dominated, directly or indirectly, by its more advanced rivals. Nor was it a satisfactory solution to keep the masses in poverty by restricting the output of goods. This happened to a great extent during the final phase of capitalism, roughly between 1920 and 1940. The economy of many countries was allowed to stagnate, land went out of cultivation, capital equipment was not added to, great blocks of the population were prevented from working and kept half alive by State charity. But this, too, entailed military weakness, and since the privations it inflicted were obviously unnecessary, it made opposition inevitable. The problem was how to keep the wheels of industry turning without increasing the real wealth of the world. Goods must be produced, but they must not be distributed. And in practice the only way of achieving this was by continuous warfare. The essential act of war is destruction, not necessarily of human lives, but of the products of human labour. War is a way of shattering to pieces, or pouring into the stratosphere, or sinking in the depths of the sea, materials which might otherwise be used to make the masses too comfortable, and hence, in the long run, too intelligent. Even when weapons of war are not actually destroyed, their manufacture is still a convenient way of expending labour power without producing anything that can be consumed. A Floating Fortress, for example, has locked up in it the labour that would build several hundred cargo-ships. Ultimately it is scrapped as obsolete, never having brought any material benefit to anybody, and with further enormous labours another Floating Fortress is built. In principle the war effort is always so planned as to eat up any surplus that might exist after meeting the bare needs of the population. In practice the needs of the population are always underestimated, with the result that there is a chronic shortage of half the necessities of life; but this is looked on as an advantage. It is deliberate policy to keep even the favoured groups somewhere near the brink of hardship, because a general state of scarcity increases the importance of small privileges and thus magnifies the distinction between one group and another. By the standards of the early twentieth century, even a member of the Inner Party lives an austere, laborious kind of life. Nevertheless, the few luxuries that he does enjoy his large, well-appointed flat, the better texture of his clothes, the better quality of his food and drink and tobacco, his two or three servants, his private motor-car or helicopter—set him in a different world from a member of the Outer Party, and the members of the Outer Party have a similar advantage in comparison with the submerged masses whom we call 'the proles'. The social atmosphere is that of a besieged city, where the possession of a lump of horseflesh makes the difference between wealth and poverty. And at the same time the consciousness of being at war, and therefore in danger, makes the handing-over of all power to a small caste seem the natural, unavoidable condition of survival. War, it will be seen, accomplishes the necessary destruction, but accomplishes it in a psychologically acceptable way. In principle it would be quite simple to waste the surplus labour of the world by building temples and pyramids, by digging holes and filling them up again, or even by producing vast quantities of goods and then setting fire to them. But this would provide only the economic and not the emotional basis for a hierarchical society. What is concerned here is not the morale of masses, whose attitude is unimportant so long as they are kept steadily at work, but the morale of the Party itself. Even the humblest Party member is expected to be competent, industrious, and even intelligent within narrow limits, but it is also necessary that he should be a credulous and ignorant fanatic whose prevailing moods are fear, hatred, adulation, and orgiastic triumph. In other words it is necessary that he should have the mentality appropriate to a state of war. It does not matter whether the war is actually happening, and, since no decisive victory is possible, it does not matter whether the war is going well or badly. All that is needed is that a state of war should exist. The splitting of the intelligence which the Party requires of its members, and which is more easily achieved in an atmosphere of war, is now almost universal, but the higher up the ranks one goes, the more marked it becomes. It is precisely in the Inner Party that war hysteria and hatred of the enemy are strongest. In his capacity as an administrator, it is often necessary for a member of the Inner Party to know that this or that item of war news is untruthful, and he may often be aware that the entire war is spurious and is either not happening or is being waged for purposes quite other than the declared ones: but such knowledge is easily neutralized by the technique of doublethink. Meanwhile no Inner Party member wavers for an instant in his mystical belief that the war is real, and that it is bound to end victoriously, with Oceania the undisputed master of the entire world. (*1984*, 218-22)

The power of Orwell's vision is impressive. It is all the more so revealing of the human *psyche* that so few readers do actually realize its depth. Who could plunge his eyes in Saturn's gaze ventures himself in the margins of psychosis.

War is thus essential for the stabilization of society, but why should torture be preferred to more urbane ways of dealing with potential and actual dissent? The answer is given in (§7.3.2). The exercise of power necessarily involves the existence of a hierarchy in which higher levels make lower levels suffer. Interestingly, this issue allows an anarchic reading of Huxley; his dystopia involves a social structure carefully avoiding any power relation.

8.1.2.3. Visionary culture is ignorance

Whereas Huxley advocated the use of a sophisticated pharmaceutical molecule, Orwell resorts to Victory Gin, which is basically used as a powerful anesthetic.

He took down from the shelf a bottle of colourless liquid with a plain white label marked VICTORY GIN. It gave off a sickly, oily smell, as of Chinese rice-spirit. Winston poured out nearly a teacupful, nerved himself for a shock, and gulped it down like a dose of medicine. Instantly his face turned scarlet and the water ran out of his eyes. The stuff was like nitric acid, and moreover, in swallowing it one had the sensation of being hit on the back of the head with a rubber club. The next moment, however, the burning in his belly died down and the world began to look more cheerful. (*1984*, 7)

Two remarks are expedient: one, Orwell advocates the use of alcohol; two, he resorts to gin, not whiskey or brandy. Alcohol is a substance that has been developed alongside "civilization." Dependent upon agriculture and some, possibly rudimentary, form of technology, it tends to drug or stupefy its user.

What is a drug anyway? Independently of its possible efficacy on physical and mental pathologies, four criteria are required: (i) addiction, which means that one seeks to obtain everyday a certain dose of the drug and that the dose is likely to increase with the time (the addiction always has a physical as well as a mental side); (ii) health degradation (physical and mental corruption merge gradually); (iii) social and professional exclusion; and (iv) an economic transaction is involved (Burroughs[170]). So alcohol is a drug, and Gin is the lower-class drug.[171] But in this case the third criterion is fulfilled only in the late stages. On the other hand, coca leaf is not a drug since three, perhaps all four of the criteria are missing. Likewise, the ceremonial use of natural psychotropes, such as peyote, ayahuasca, and psilocybin, do not fulfill any of these criteria.

In Oceania, vision is ignorance. But in the case of the Inner and Outer Party, it is a peculiar ignorance, an ignorance one is fully aware of and yet voluntarily discards. The purpose of the resulting pendulation between dream and nightmare is to secure a mild psychosis to which the use of newspeak testifies. The conditioning mechanism is propaganda pure and simple, real-time media flow.

In conclusion, as Orwell himself claims, the three focal points of Ingsoc are: doublethink, the mutability of the past, and newspeak. Each requires the other two. Doublethink requires a continuous alteration of the past (1984, 242), that can be expressed only in newspeak, itself supporting doublethought. . . . The fundamental reason behind this is the necessity to destroy all standards of comparison (*1984*, 242). Orwell speaks:

> Doublethink means the power of holding two contradictory beliefs in one's mind simultaneously, and accepting both of them. The Party intellectual knows in which direction his memories must be altered; he therefore knows that he is playing tricks with reality; but by the exercise of doublethink he also satisfies himself that reality is not violated. The process has to be conscious, or it would not be carried out with sufficient precision, but it also has to be unconscious, or it would bring with it a feeling of falsity and hence of guilt. Doublethink lies at the very heart of Ingsoc, since the essential act of the Party is to use conscious deception while retaining the firmness of purpose that goes with complete honesty. To tell deliberate lies while genuinely believing in them, to forget any fact that has become inconvenient, and then, when it becomes necessary again, to draw it back from oblivion for just so long as it is needed, to deny the existence of objective reality and all the while to take account of the reality which one denies—all this is indispensably necessary. Even in using the word doublethink it is necessary to exercise doublethink. For by using the word one admits that one is tampering with reality; by a fresh act of doublethink one erases this knowledge; and so on indefinitely, with the lie always one leap ahead of the truth. Ultimately it is by means of doublethink that the Party has been able—and may, for all we know, continue to be able for thousands of years—to arrest the course of history. (*1984*, 244)

Slavery, War, and Ignorance are largely self-explanatory. Power is not exerted by the technocracy for the sake of the common good but for the sake of power.

A first contrast between Huxley and Orwell can thus be offered. Oceania and the World State are similar in the passivity and egoism of their respective denizens, but all the modalities of infantilizations do otherwise differ. For the former, it is essentially a matter of unconcern, and for the latter, of terror and humiliation. In Oceania, denizens are seduced into submission; conformity is cheerful. Love, lust, and mindless pleasure rule. It is a trivial culture that is obtained, with people drowned in a sea of irrelevance. Too much data and gossip is equivalent to no information. No one even wants to read books anymore. In the World State, denizens are frightened into submission. Conformity is here fearful; hate, anxiety, and pain rule everyone's behavior. It is a captive culture, where truth is meticulously concealed. No data, information, or gossip are available. The Inner Party has simply banned books.

8.1.3. Huxley, *Island,* 1962

Thirty years after the publication of *Brave New World*, Huxley published his last novel. He had not lost his interest in science, especially for eugenics and hypnosis, and he had retained a certain technophilia. Now, however, his standpoint is informed by a practical religiosity. Huxley had always been interested in religiosity, as one finds, for instance, in his *Perennial Philosophy* (1946) a typical argument for the unicity of the religious experience. Yet for a long time he believed that chemical mysticism was inauthentic.[172] In 1953, however, the psychiatrist Humphrey Fortescue Osmond (1917–2004), within the framework of his psychopharmacology research in schizophrenia, administered mescaline to him. One year later, Huxley published *The Doors of Perception*, which was called upon to become the manifesto of a new humanism.

It is my contention that the late Huxley implemented the program for which the Claremont Whiteheadians,beginning with John Cobb and David Griffin, have always argued. With Whitehead, they want to keep the advantages of modern science and to reenchant our decaying world.

Island takes place in the imaginary Kingdom of Pala, which Huxley apparently located first near the Andaman Islands and later in Bali (Indian Ocean).[173] The international state of affairs he describes is, however, clearly contemporary: consumerism, militarism, mass religion, oil-guzzling-contraptions, imperialism, etc.

To a significant extent, the spirit of *Brave New World* was embodied in the amphetamine-like "soma." Similarly, the spirit of *Island* rests in the spiritualizing "moksha." In this case, Huxley had in mind either mescaline or LSD, which was first synthesized by Albert Hofmann in

1938, and which led, in October 1955, to Ginsberg's reading of *Howl* at an experimental art gallery in San Francisco.

Huxley's last novel constitutes his spiritual will. It has, consciously or not, two main interlocutors: *Brave New World* and *Nineteen Eighty-Four*. It can be shown that *Island*'s main ideas take a stance opposite to the consumerist materialism of the former and the sadistic materialism of the latter. Both totalitarian pictures are built upon conformism, a fully stabilized one in *Brave New World* and a quasi-fluent one in *Nineteen Eighty-Four*. Both also exploit infantilization, each with a different ring. People are made to live through the immediacy of their desires in *Brave New World* while *Nineteen Eighty-Four* instills fears and terrors in order to silence party members. The main difference lies at the level of the type of so-called solidarity that is not fostered. In *Brave New World* the clones enjoy a fusional socialization and in *Nineteen Eighty-Four*, they are atomized.

To the point, again in three steps.

8.1.3.1. Creative individuation means liberation

According to our heuristic grid, the young Huxley was more faithful to Freud than to Ford when he centered his fake process of individuation on recreational sex while, for his part, Orwell transformed all party members into denizens affected by an engineered borderline personality disorder. In *Island*, the first condition of possibility of authentic existence is completely fulfilled, and Huxley chooses to underline it with one criterion: love—more precisely, free love.

Free love is possible because of the novative blend of science and Buddhism that characterizes the Kingdom of Pala. On the one hand, there is the use of contraception, deep freeze, and artificial insemination. On the other is the practice of *Maithuna* or the "yoga of love." *Maithuna* does not simply translate into *coitus reservatus*; it is part of an ecological worldview giving to human sexuality the metaphysical dimension it deserves. In the actual plot, however, the technoscientific dimension of human sexuality is far less underlined than its spiritual and self-developmental dimension. Huxley refers to the Oneida community, a U.S.-American utopia founded in 1848 and dissolved in 1881.

The purpose of this scientific Buddhism is plain: individual growth, that is, to become fully human (Isl 141, 202), something that entails experiencing for oneself the process nature of the chaosmos, to let oneself go in its web of connectedness, and to come back rejuvenated from this initiation.

8.1.3.2. Efficient solidarity is codependence

Community now means that everyone and everything belongs to everyone and everything else but not in a utilitarian way. Liberation does not happen outside of the communal tissue; there is a codependant liberation. Huxley speaks of "village communism" (Isl 89) in order to dismiss communism and capitalism together. Gregg's "Value of Voluntary Simplicity"[174] might be lurking here.

Through what mechanism is harmonious codependence secured? *Karuna* or compassion is not really a mechanism but rather an organic mode of tuning-in. If all members of the community care for their peers as well as all forms of life, a well-tempered community follows. Empathy and environmental concerns belong to the continuous spectrum of love: "Elementary ecology leads straight to elementary Buddhism" (Isl 212).

The vision behind this dialectic is unsurprisingly pantheistic. Huxley explicitly correlates happiness, freedom, and pantheism and opposes it to mass production, mass consumption, mass slaughter, and theism. Purity, family, and existential misery go hand in hand.

8.1.3.3. Visionary culture is gnostic: scientific and Buddhist

In the context of Buddhist science, the substance that is substituted for artificial soma and stuporous gin is moksha. It is a medicine imagined by Huxley after his mescaline and LSD experiences.

Moksha and liberation are supported by the widespread use of the various potentialities of hypnosis, such as hypnotherapy and meditation, and, above all, by a strong common sense informed by science. For instance, Pala runs an Agricultural Experimental Station and uses antibiotics and contraceptives.

The purpose is the implementation of a holistic culture of awareness, a gnosis of sorts. The goal is to provide the possibility for everyone to become a fully human being. Happiness here means awareness, spiritual growth, liberation, not the mechanical satisfaction of bodily desires.

Both Western science and Buddhist pragmatic culture contribute to awareness (i) through birth control to avoid a Malthusian explosion of misery (i.e., via contraception, artificial insemination, and the yoga of love), (ii) through holistic education to secure individuation and solidarity (on all fronts, verbal and nonverbal, with prevention and cure), and (iii) through hypnosis ("psychological facts of applied metaphysics" (Isl 76, 221) and spiritual exercises. The State also provides a potent drug—moksha—as a way of liberation from the prison of the self to an encounter with the Ultimate.

In conclusion, a second contrast between Huxley and Orwell can be offered (see also §8.3.3). The widest criterion of comparison between *Brave New World* (1932), *Nineteen Eighty-Four* (1949), and *Island* (1962) is technical and technological both an organizational matter and a matter of machines. Since Marx and Mumford, we furthermore know how much technoscience and capitalism go hand in hand. As a result three ambiguous political stages can be evoked.

The early Huxley depicts a quintessentially capitalistic society, insofar as everything is artificial and engineered, that is piloted by a communist ideal (the kingdom of heaven on earth). The late Huxley is far more pragmatic and contemporary when he contrasts the imperial capitalism of the so-called civilized West with the post-capitalism of Pala, where everything tends to be natural and spiritually driven. Orwell apparently stages a post-capitalistic society that has curiously kept all the main traits of its forefather, only coated by a strong government surviving through controlled insanity.

The psychology of the masses is treated accordingly. In *Brave New World*, Pavlov, Watson, and their kin provide the basic social framework. In *Nineteen Eighty-Four*, propaganda and schizophrenia rule. In *Island*, all revolves around arousing the mind and the personal journey towards Ithaca. Elements of psychopharmacology follow: (i) Soma's horrible paradise, vs. the use of mescaline in the reservation; (ii) Victory Gin's violently cheerful, stupor; and (iii) Moksha's road to enlightenment. Three diverging ways: to obliterate reality, to reveal it, to deepen to material quagmire. Totalitarianism always toys with curing all unacceptable emotions and tranquillizing the body. Only culture depends upon arousing the mind and the idea of perfectibility.[175] There are more or less crude and violent lies and illusions on the one hand, and the quest for truth on the other. Last but not least, all three pictures have a different economic setting: sheer abundance, war-time scarcity (unless gin is concerned), and simple comfort securing all the essentials.

Huxley as well as Orwell have insisted on the respective efficiency of their totalitarian program. Huxley had promptly raised the question of the coherence of Orwell's novel and of the low probability of a *1984* nightmare, whereas a *Brave New World* seemed so likely. Huxley maintained his basic dystopic claims: there is no need for Orwellian barbarity.[176] The only real Orwellian reply lies in the naïveté of Huxley when it comes to psychological issues.

One way of refining futuribles is through Bentham. In §5.2. we introduced the concept of pankatalepticon as the critical moment between the slow degeneration of the democratic ideal (direct and representative) and the modalities of the rise of totalitarianism (panopticon and pancraticon). Let us revisit the question.

8.2. Big Mother

The 20th century has seen a progressive transformation of the class struggle. Since the 1920s, the public relation business has allowed smooth forms of totalitarianism to take place, basically to sell more useless and expansive goods, but also to manage "democracy" through the engineering of consent *and* of dissent. Furthermore, since the 1940s, the military-industrial complex has asserted its rights on domestic and foreign policies. Buying weapons and building barracks secure the power of the oligarchy through what it gives, that is, the capacity to bully, to loot and to destroy at will, but also through what it takes away, that is, healthcare, education, social services. Since the 1990s, the so-called intelligence community has added its own blend of paranoia to this totalitarian landscape.

Tocqueville had foreseen the totalitarianism to come: massification entailing conformism (everyone is filled with the same desires), atomization (solitariness), and paranoia (war of all against all). The smallest social horizon is the rule, and the government's sole goal seems infantilization.[177]

According to Chomsky or Wolin, we live now in an *inverted* totalitarianism. Gross argues for a friendly fascism. Paye claims that the post-9/11 U.S. is also a post-constitutional one that gets away with political assassination, but also with torture, concentration camps, and imperial wars galore. Behind these scholarly analyses, there is one stubborn fact: the political climate is getting worse. Everyone feels it, as it is getting more and more palpable. Some are aware of it, and few understand the reasons for this substantial aggravation. A simple crash would be a huge burden (remember that in the U.S. the 1929 Crash ended only when the entire economy was mobilized by WW2). This, however, is not where we stand now with a global systemic crisis that is mainly fueled (no pun intended but appropriate) by resource scarcity and especially peak oil consequences, and that has to be envisioned in the context of climate change.

"Big Brother" is a well-known figure whose meaning and significance is however rarely understood. In order to suggest a straighforward contrast, the introduction of a "Big Sister" might have been advisable. But this would entail an Orwellian discussion of a reality that is not Orwellian. On the other hand, the "Big Mother" archetype has quite a history in clinical arguments. The generalized principle of bigmotherhood is nicely phrased by Keller, who, interestingly enough, writes in a completely different context:

> When lacking an empowering world, or an inner relation to ourselves, women can all too readily act out of the archetypal "dark side of the feminine," seeking power by working a web of emotional ensnarement of others—especially men and children.[178]

Whereas the authentic life requires individuation, solidarity, and culture, all forms of fascism— friendly or otherwise—provide only conformism, atomism, and infantilization.

In a nutshell, the immediate future that is prepared in labs and think tanks is a pankatalepticon. The world of opinion and propaganda in which we now live will be locked when nanochips will allow the collection and treatment, with real-time computing, of all data linked with our lives. This concept is the core vision of the "internet of things" (introduced in §6.2.3.3). The concept perfectly describes the bigmotherhood that RFID will allow, that is, a world in which privacy has vanished, a world of objectual transparency. There will be no escape from the smothering web. Neither denizens' actual location nor their thoughts will be left unmastered.[179]

8.2.1. The panoptic society

Where do we stand today? As its title suggests, the 2006 "Report on the Surveillance Society"[180] concluded that we already live in a technologically smothering society, our lives being completely transparent to technical devices. Moreover, this all-embracing surveillance has become largely invisible. Besides the cctv cameras and the airport-like security of some government buildings and shopping centers, monitoring takes place through built-in features of our everyday apparatuses. Homeland Security feeling up the genitals of air travelers and mildly embarrassed customers remains a limited practice—but by no means is this insignificant or harmless. Terror has replaced culture.

In its December 2010 study "Monitoring America," *The Washington Post* detailed the vast growth of U.S. domestic spying. It seems there were then 3,984 federal, state, and local organizations working on domestic counterterrorism (the number created since the 2001 attacks being 934). There is currently an inflation of military-grade technical devices. One can hardly mention all of these data-mining technologies: hand-held, wireless fingerprint and iris scanners; facial recognition programs;[181] infrared cameras allowing "Automatic Number Plate Recognition" mounted on hoods and moving robotically from left to right; facial recognition units toying with biometrics; and the "data shadow" of entire populations. The "Nationwide Suspicious Activity Reporting Initiative" is yet another of these libertycide measures and anti-terrorist legislations that deserves some attention, especially since the army is now ready to assume police missions while the police are getting militarized!

It is in this context that the Snowden affair broke out in 2013. Nobody can now pretend to ignore that all data that can be gathered are indeed gathered, 24/7.

8.2.2. The electrification of care chains and mental health

But aren't recent developments in pharmacology and psychosurgery equally problematic? Actually, the psychiatric care chains have been, so to speak, systematically electrified.

In the same way that the discovery of the electrical activity of muscles (Francesco Redi, 1666) has suscitated, as fast as technological progress allowed, experiments on animal electromyostimulation (Luigi Galvani, 1771), the discovery of the electrical activity of the brain (Hans Berger, 1924) has given rise to intracranial electrostimulation experiments (Walter Rudolf Hess, c. 1928). In the meantime, Pieter van Musschenbroek had invented the Leyden jar (1745) and Alessandro Volta, the electric battery (1800). Hence the weird experiments of Giovanni Aldini that inspired Mary Shelley's *Frankenstein or, The Modern Prometheus* (1818). These experiments are crucial because Aldini claimed that these electromyostimulations were actually electroneurostimulations.

As a counterpoint, three events are worth mentioning (i) Louis XIV's Great Confinement in the Hôpital Général (1656), that is only canceled with Pinel's arrival in the Salpêtrière in 1795; (ii) the emergence of the theory of functional location with Franz Joseph Gall's phrenology (1798), and Broca's (1861) and Wernicke's (1873) discoveries; and (iii) the electroconvulsive therapy of Ladislas J. Meduna (1934) and Ugo Cerletti (1937).

Since the use of RFID chips (1971) has already been sketched in §6.2.3.2, two new technologies deserve to be mentioned: brain gates (1952) and computer interfaces (2002). The former allow either an external stimulation of the brain, for instance to treat epilepsy, or the functional electrical stimulation to restore a deficient sense organ. The latter seeks to improve the interaction between the subject and its world by providing communication prosthetics and especially by seeking to give autonomy to patients.

Brain gates implants are almost history now. The reader will find in the Appendix the "Biocontrol" article that summarizes the visionary claims of the engineer Schafer. Published in 1956, this argument was studied by Vance Packard a year later.[182] Philip K. Dick is thus not the first to have probed the possibility of a brain piloted by a computer (*Ubik*,

1969). Interestingly, the stakes were already clear at the time. On the one hand, the techno-optimists were cheering this new step in the dehumanizing process. On the other hand, techno-pessimists were hoping for the mobilization of the citizenry.[183] It is moreover quizzical to note that Schafer's "socket mounted under the scalp" anticipates *The Matrix* (1999).

José Delgado creates his *stimoceiver* in 1952 and broadcasts his famous bullfight demonstration in 1963. He could stop a charging bull equipped with a *stimoceiver* implanted in the bull's caudate nucleus.

The first cochlear implant was activated in 1957 by André Djourno and Charles Eyriès, the first spinal cord stimulator in 1967, and the first electrostimulation of the visual cortex obtained in 1968. In 1999, Yang Dan and his team decoded neuronal (thalamic) firings to reproduce images seen by cats. In 2011, Alim-Louis Benabid inaugurates the Clinatec laboratory of the CEA-Minatec (Grenoble).

Computer (or neural) interfaces (2002–) constitute an important development. In 1998 Kevin Warwick , University of Reading, launched the "Cyborg 1.0" project by having an RFID implanted under his skin. His motto is "I want to be a cyborg."[184] In 2002, he launches the "Cyborg 2.0" project by going through surgery to have his left arm (the median nerve fibres) implanted with a one-hundred electrode array in order to control an electric wheelchair and an artificial hand. Vernor Vinge and Ray Kurzweil claim that we are approaching "the singularity," i.e., the point at which "intelligent" machines will exceed the human brain's capacities. The year 2045 seems likely. They also hope that the "brain in a vat" experiment will then be implemented. Literature does not evoke the mental age of the interested parties.

8.2.3. Pankatalepticon

Guattari and Deleuze (after Philip K. Dick, who is unfortunately absent from their bibliography[185]) pointed at the troubling resemblance that exists between the schizoid personality and the alleged android personality. In light of the previous paragraph, one could conclude indeed that the future of capitalism will be schizophrenic. The claim is apparently applicable but not adequate. The current trend is actually autistic. On the one hand, the so-called "elite" (0.1 percent of the first world) is born and lives more than ever totally cut off from the proles. On the other, the proles are themselves invited to live only vicariously, through and for the media.

Now, autism is defined by an early chronic dysfunctional communication that involves, willy-nilly, the parent in charge of the infant. Unless one argues for a purely deterministic etiology, it is impossible to neglect this fact. Then comes the interpretation, and of all theories the psychoanalytic ones are clearly the worst.[186] Political bigmotherhood provides an interesting expansion of controversial speculations that are as old as Kanner's paper ("Autistic disturbances of affective contact," 1943).

The shift from a surveillance (democratic) society that is quietly terrorizing its citizens—the panoptic dissociety—to a society that smothers, ensnares, and swallows its members simply needs the appropriate technology to be implemented. Conformism and atomism pave the way for bigmotherhood while infantilization, properly manipulated, sows the seeds of bigbrotherhood. The hypothesis is that as soon as information technology is fed with data coming from passive nanochips to constitute some form of "internet of things," the process will be completed. Huxley would claim that a political stabilization would follow, and it is no doubt the goal of the oligarchy. That is, to lock society before the collapse and uncontrolled decline takes place, i.e., before the positive feedback loops existing between all facets of the current global systemic crisis (depression of the real economy, financial bubbles, social unrest, peak resources starting with energy; collapsing ecology, explosive demography, discredited politics, religious extremisms, colonial wars, climate change, and the looming near-term human extinction) foster total chaos. Orwell would disagree.

8.3. Big Brother

Two trends support the idea of an unstable Huxleyian episode. On the one hand, technological developments should make active microchips as pervasive as passive nanochips while brain gates and other computer-brain interfaces become more common. However, the very absence of a cheap and reliable source of energy might impede such changes. On the other hand, the nature of the exercise of power, as disclosed by Orwell, requires a different relationship between the upper and the lower classes. The catalepsis secured by bigmotherhood could then topple into the full psychosis of the pancratikon.

8.3.1. 9/11 *qua* turning point

The controlled demolition industry was born with the 20th century, but it became visible only after World War II, when its services were badly needed to secure devastated European cities. In the early 1970s, America's TV-news industry began to capitalize on the strong visual appeal of "blasting down buildings" and, since then, no Westerner could really pretend not to recognize the implosion process. Most are aware of the *modus operandi* involved, i.e., the strategic placing of explosive material and the precise timing of its detonation so that a structure entirely collapses on itself, minimizing the physical damage to its immediate surroundings. Everything changed in 2001 when this scientifically savvy common sense was blown up with the three World Trade Center towers. Suddenly, there was no room for common sense anymore.

There is no need however to debate here the total incoherence of the official story. It will suffice to have a glimpse of the consequence of the event. Searches without warrants, telephone tapping and email bugging, body searches, house searches, surveillance of correspondence, and the use of undercover practices are now common. The writ of habeas corpus is basically revoked. Torture is allowed. Concentration camps are back. Suspects can simply disapear. Extra-judiciary executions by drones are standard, if not explicitly allowed, by the Patriot Act (2001). The apparent casualness of the U.S.-American denizens is, alas, not surprising.

8.3.2. Pancraticon

The other technology that is being developed will require a bit more time to spread—and some mythological narrative to make it acceptable. Its archetype is the "Digital Angel" chip that combines an implanted active microchip, just as a subcutaneous artificial pacemaker, with a Real Time Locating System. It already works in warehouses to localize equipment and stock. The immediate possibility of a geolocalized microchip is mind-blowing—and indeed neither Huxley nor Orwell envisioned it.

It would be possible, once all humans, or all humans worthy of being kept under control, are chipped, to localize them precisely at all times and to monitor all their activities.

The first steps in that direction have already been made by experts and corporations. We are insistently told that it would be wise to chip the elderly, who are so prone to health emergencies and who usually get somehow demented. It would make sense to chip children, who can equally get lost or go astray in our megapoles and who are sometimes abducted. It is equally urgent to chip criminals in order to monitor them closely and to avoid the social cost of imprisonment. And so forth and so on. The technology is available. It is simply waiting for a triggering event to be implemented in one of these fields, and from there, it will spread like a flashing cancer. Interestingly enough, supporters of warrant-less surveillance, including the Obama administration it seems, *already* argue that a person's movements in public are not protected by the Fourth Amendment and that an old-fashioned GPS tracking device can and should be used when "need" be. Furthermore, geolocation tracking devices are already embedded in smartphones.

The next steps have already been developed by surgeons and cognitive scientists, often under Darpa contracts (in France, research is fostered under the University of Grenoble's "Clinatec," which is part of the umbrella project "CEA-Minatec"). It is the old dream of the transhuman cyborg, the postmodern Golem, that is being fleshed out. An active microchip could be wired directly to the central nervous system in order to obtain a brain machine interface allowing humans to pilot external devices *and* IT to be implemented on the brain in order to monitor its activity.[187] Here also, the pretext can be medical, such as the use of deep brain stimulation to prevent epilepsy or alleviate Parkinson's disease or the dream of silicon-based immortality. (Cf. Kevin Warwick's multiple micro electrodes array.) Eventually, mental activity itself could be monitored.

In sum, the future is on the order of a *pancraticon*.[188] Transparency would be total, both objective and subjective. There would be no escape from the technocratic world and especially from the iron grip of the oligarchy. Please notice that technology would not be used simply to lure the appropriate behavior and to predetermine the adequate mental activity (this is Huxley's smooth totalitarianism)—but to impose behavior and mentation, thereby factually confronting what would remain of free processes. As Orwell taught us, power is not a matter of rationally organizing all social intercourse, but of crushing the will of *conscious* individuals. The art of torture does not exist to persuade into submission reluctant individuals or to murder those who refuse submission. It does not either seek to inflict abruptly a pain so unbearable that the individual loses consciousness. The priest of power imposes the highest possible pain that can be entertained without the loss of consciousness. A patient secured in a dissociative state is unacceptable.

8.3.3. Aldous Huxley and George Orwell on the political use of technoscience

Of all Huxley's (1894–1963) contemporaries, George Orwell (1903–1950) is arguably the most important fellow essayist, but he is also the one with whom there is probably the least intellectual kinship. Huxley made it plain he never understood Orwell's main intuition, that, according to the latter, "priests of power" cannot be satisfied with "dictatorship without tears." [189]

Most of Huxley's works are spread between *Brave New World* (1932) and *Island* (1962). In both books, technoscience constitutes the main background of the narrative, but with quite different outcomes. In *Brave New World*'s dystopia, it is the *mysterium tremendum et fascinans* that totally enslaves humans for their own good. In *Island*'s utopia, this *mysterium* is the very backbone of community life. Both narratives are organized around similar patterns involving a strong enthusiasm for technologies and techniques, broadly speaking, such as eugenics, hypnosis, birth control, and the use of psychotropic substances.

Orwell, for his part, finds only alienation in technoscience. In *Nineteen Eighty-Four* (1949), it is used only to discipline and punish through military Keynesianism, panoptic surveillance, and scientific electro-torture.

The specification of the main bone of contention—could or should political power be benevolent—will allow us to comprehend better Huxley's and Orwell's respective worldviews. The argument unfolds as follows: first the political contrast drawing a sharp line between Huxley and Orwell is specified. Second, this contrast is shown to be correlated with Huxley's technophilia, as it is the heir of La Boétie and Tocqueville, and with Orwell's technophobia, mainly summoned by the harsh reality of fascist totalitarianism. Third, we evoke the limited way in which Huxley can be said to have changed his reading of the relevance of his dystopia in the Sixties.

8.3.3.1. The political contrast

The fundamental contrast between Huxley and Orwell is—unsurprisingly—political. It boils down to the difference that exists between benevolent and malevolent political power, i.e., between power exercised for the common good and power exercised for the pathological enjoyment of the ruler(s).[190] This thesis is very easy to establish; it suffices to compare the key episodes of *Brave New World* and *Nineteen Eighty-Four*. On the one hand, the dialogue that takes place between Mustapha Mond and John the Savage makes obvious that the World State is ruling for the own good of its citizens, or at least claims to do so.[191] On the other hand, a key torture session of Winston deals with the question *why*. Why should the Ministry of Love "expend so much time and trouble" on him? O'Brien states explicitly on that occasion that "the Party seeks power entirely for its own sake."[192]

It sounds as if Orwell was precisely answering the question that bothered John the Savage. . . . Let us go through the details because it is difficult to overemphasize the importance of this dark contrast.

On the one hand, the dialogue between Mond and John constitutes a dispassionate plea for the World State's engineered stability:

> The world's stable now. People are happy; they get what they want, and they never want what they can't get. . . . And if anything should go wrong, there's soma.[193]

In other words, conformal identity and fusional community are not to be thought of as major drawbacks or as impediments to happiness. On the contrary, they grant it:

> We believe in happiness and stability. A society of Alphas couldn't fail to be unstable and miserable. Imagine a factory staffed by Alphas—that is to say by separate and unrelated individuals of good heredity and conditioned so as to be capable

(within limits) of making a free choice and assuming responsibilities. Imagine it![194]

A truly civilized society cannot afford old-fashioned citizens, (in the Greek democratic sense of the term, anymore. Even science has to be bridled for the sake of stability:

> "Sometimes," he added, "I rather regret the science. Happiness is a hard master—particularly other people's happiness. A much harder master, if one isn't conditioned to accept it unquestioningly, than truth." He sighed, fell silent again, then continued in a brisker tone, "Well, duty's duty. One can't consult one's own preference. I'm interested in truth, I like science. But truth's a menace, science is a public danger." [195]

We thus obtain the best possible world under the guise of a perfect clockwork society. This is nothing, after all, but the "primitive" ideal of community life in an environmentally friendly culture.[196]

On the other hand, stability is *also* the ideal cultivated by the Inner Party. The means are however quite different and the ethos of the "elite" is even more so. O'Brien speaks:

> "And now let us get back to the question of 'how' and 'why'. You understand well enough *how* the Party maintains itself in power. Now tell me *why* we cling to power. What is our motive? Why should we want power? Go on, speak," he added as Winston remained silent.
>
> Nevertheless Winston did not speak for another moment or two. A feeling of weariness had overwhelmed him. The faint, mad gleam of enthusiasm had come back into O'Brien's face. He knew in advance what O'Brien would say. That the Party did not seek power for its own ends, but only for the good of the majority. That it sought power because men in the mass were frail, cowardly creatures who could not endure liberty or face the truth, and must be ruled over and systematically deceived by others who were stronger than themselves. That the choice for mankind lay between freedom and happiness, and that, for the great bulk of mankind, happiness was better. That the party was the eternal guardian of the weak, a dedicated sect doing evil that good might come, sacrificing its own happiness to that of

others. . . . "You are ruling over us for our own good," he said feebly. "You believe that human beings are not fit to govern themselves, and therefore—"

He started and almost cried out. A pang of pain had shot through his body. O'Brien had pushed the lever of the dial up to thirty-five.

"That was stupid, Winston, stupid!" he said. "You should know better than to say a thing like that."

He pulled the lever back and continued: "Now I will tell you the answer to my question. It is this. The Party seeks power entirely for its own sake. We are not interested in the good of others; we are interested solely in power. Not wealth or luxury or long life or happiness: only power, pure power. What pure power means you will understand presently. We are different from all the oligarchies of the past, in that we know what we are doing. All the others, even those who resembled ourselves, were cowards and hypocrites. The German Nazis and the Russian Communists came very close to us in their methods, but they never had the courage to recognize their own motives. They pretended, perhaps they even believed, that they had seized power unwillingly and for a limited time, and that just round the corner there lay a paradise where human beings would be free and equal. We are not like that. We know that no one ever seizes power with the intention of relinquishing it. Power is not a means, it is an end. One does not establish a dictatorship in order to safeguard a revolution; one makes the revolution in order to establish the dictatorship. The object of persecution is persecution. The object of torture is torture. The object of power is power. Now do you begin to understand me?" [197]

This quote is self-explanatory. Power is sought for itself—full stop. The consequences are delineated *infra*. For the time being, let us underline that such "politics" *necessarily* involves pain, humiliation, and suffering; "a world of fear, treachery, torment."[198] In order to interpret this fundamental contrast with Huxley, it is wise to question the correlation that exists between technique and totalitarianism.

8.3.3.2. Technique and totalitarianism

In Huxley's and Orwell's works, the fundamental contrast between benevolent and malevolent power presupposes a strict correlation between technique and totalitarianism. Let us first define these terms. Whitehead has claimed that we should seek simplicity and distrust it. This is indeed the unavoidable burden of any scholarly discussion.[199]

The Ellulian concept of technique explicates to a great extent Gheorghiu's dramatic depiction of concentration camps under Nazi, American, and Soviet occupations of Central Europe. It could be defined in the following way: the systematic use of general categories to obtain maximum efficiency when dealing with events in some field of human activity or with individual human beings themselves.[200] This is typically of course what science does when it seeks to understand the world and how, consequently, technology grounds its efficacy.

Totalitarianism is the political system that imposes the single authority of the State over all aspects of public and private life. This is achieved through technique. Individual human beings are seen and, so to speak, taken care of through a screen that defines them as members of one or more given classes. Human beings are not considered in themselves, as unique individuals endowed with absolute value, but as mere bundles of data.

In sum, from the perspective of Ellul, technique and totalitarianism go hand in hand. This correlation actually involves two complementary arguments. On the one hand, since technique relies upon the categorization of individuals and ignores everything that cannot be categorized according to its own standards, it necessarily negates what makes individuals unique. Technique being intrinsically totalitarian, it pushes history in that direction. It not only makes totalitarianism possible, it makes it inevitable. On the other hand, totalitarianism cannot implement its agenda without the extensive use of appropriate techniques.

How are these processes embedded in, respectively, Huxley and Orwell? Some reference to the history of ideas will be handy in unravelling their respective conceptual threads.

On the one hand, Huxley's technophilia is plainly obvious. It has two main characteristics and two important historical anchors.

First, the creation of the best possible world requires the use of conformation techniques, and recent scientific advances are pushing politics towards a new form of totalitarianism. In other words, *Brave New World* lies at the junction of a top-down and a bottom-up process.

Second, Huxley's work is secured in the well-known arguments of La Boétie and Tocqueville, brought together with the musings of J. B. S. Haldane and Julian Huxley.

The import of La Boétie's *Discourse of Voluntary Servitude* (1574) is well-known. If tyrants want to establish their power, it is far more efficient to use opinion than force. Obedience, in other words, can be guaranteed if you enslave people's minds. Why would you regret liberty if you have never known it? Or, as Orwell would put it, if there is even no word to name it anymore? "The essential reason why men take orders willingly is that they are born serfs and are reared as such."[201] The use and abuse of opinion is of course not a new theme in Western philosophy, as Plato's corpus amply shows. In his *Tractatus theologico-politicus* (1677), Spinoza forcibly belabors the exact same point,[202] as does Hume's "Of the First Principles of Government" (1741).[203] So Huxley is in good company when he emphasizes that "a really efficient totalitarian state would be one in which the all-powerful executive of political bosses and their army of managers control a population of slaves who do not have to be coerced, because they love their servitude."[204] In sum, La Boétie offers the astrolabe, or final cause, of Huxleyan politics, that is, to give rise to and nurture people's love of their own servitude. But what about the plummet (or efficient cause)?[205]

For his part Tocqueville sets the tone of the discussion in his *De la démocratie en Amérique* (1835, 1840). The thesis is simple, namely, a democracy wherein conformism and atomism are structurally ingrained is likely to degenerate into a "friendly fascism" of sorts.[206] Please notice that his argument runs in the opposite direction as La Boétie's. We do not deal with a policy that molds the social tissue but with the corruption of the tissue itself. Ellul has also insisted on this, basically following the lead of Francis Bacon's *Nova Atlantis* (1624). Everything that is technically feasible will be actualized, and the social tissue will be modified accordingly.

Now, Tocqueville defines the form of the argument but not its content. Huxley is here mainly relying upon two contemporary scientists: J. B. S. Haldane and Huxley's own brother Julian.[207] It is in their works that we find Huxley's chief intuition: technoscience will inevitably transform the societies in which they dwell. The tone and content of *Brave New World*'s narrative clearly bears the mark of the biological science of his time. Eugenics is a constant theme in Huxley. In a nutshell, *Brave New World* fills La Boétie's intuition with the trends in contemporary biological science.

On the other hand, Orwell's technophobia is equally straightforward.

The same pattern is at work in Orwell. *Nineteen Eighty-Four* also lies at the junction of a top-down and a bottom-up process, but the result he obtains is completely different. For one thing, La Boétie is irrelevant. People are *not* meant to ignore their total servitude. For another, the technical possibilities are almost trivial. What really matters is the toxic climate they create and the crux of Orwell's argument—the scientific use of electro-torture—does *not* require the sophisticated apparatus sketched (sometimes clumsily) by Huxley.

Huxley's vision sprang from a La Boétian argument of sorts and was made operative by a scientific form of Tocqueville's striking anticipation. Orwell's correlation between technique and totalitarianism is bluntly anchored in the postwar descriptions of totalitarianism and on his understanding of Stalinism and of the impact of Nazi concentration camp policies on power games.[208] Orwell's vision is peculiar to him and was in all likelihood nourished by the accounts and reflections of camp survivors. Power is exerted *for the sake of power*. As Arendt will later claim, *terror is an end in itself*.

Orwell's vision can be boiled down to what could be called the four ignoble truths of totalitarianism. First, power is not a means but an end; second, power is collective, it is power over human beings; third, power seeks total control of the mind in order to totally control matter; and fourth, power *necessarily* consists in the capacity to inflict suffering and, ultimately, to torture.[209] As Huxley could have said, the *habeas corpus* is replaced by an *habeas mentem*.[210] In sum, Orwell offers a vision that updates Hobbes' *Leviathan* (1651) with Sade's *Cent Vingt Journées de*

Sodome (1785). By doing so, Orwell makes transparent the inherent, or nascent, psychopathy of the power seeker.

Three sources would need to be tracked to understand how Orwell's own borderline experiences have carved this vision. First is his life as a tramp in the years 1928–1931, as described in *Down and Out in Paris and London*, 1933. Second is his participation in the Spanish Civil War in 1936–1937 which is accounted for in *Homage to Catalonia*, 1938. And third is his understanding of the logic of concentration, which lies at the very core of the historical expression of Nazi totalitarianism. Since the present paper basically deals with the contrast between *Brave New World* and *Nineteen Eighty-Four*, it seems adequate to focus only on the third issue.

Some historical reminder is however needed. First, the gulag system (1930–1960) does not belong to the practice of concentration per se. Quite unfortunately, Arendt and many other Western scholars were obviously not interested in introducing a sharp distinction between the incriminated States.[211] Second, concentration camps per se were created during the Ten Years' War with Cuba (1868–1878). Animated with a "let rot and die" policy, they were soon used during the Second Anglo-Boer War (1899–1902) and the Philippine-American War (1899–1902).[212] What happened in Nazi Germany was in continuity with these "contingency plans." The concentration camps were created in 1933, that is, in the aftermath of the Reichstag arson (an event that is called in naval warfare a false flag operation), to house mainly communists and trade unionists, but also Gypsies, petty criminals, Jehovah's Witnesses, freemasons, and homosexuals. Jews were deported only if they belonged to one of these categories. The policy had changed however. It was no longer a matter of gathering individuals and letting them die because of poor hygiene, malnourishment, and ill-treatment—but of working the inmates to death while terrorizing and torturing them in the process. After the *Anschluss* (1938), this policy specifically targeted the Jews because of their Jewishness. When the Stalingrad moment came (1942), quick extermination became the goal.

Bruno Bettelheim was perhaps the first to publish an account of life in the camps. The purpose of the concentration camps, he claimed, was fourfold: (i) "to break the prisoners as individuals and to change them into docile masses," (ii) "to spread terror among the rest of the population," (iii) "to provide the Gestapo members with a training ground," and (iv) to create "an experimental laboratory" using human subjects.[213] As a result, prisoners would behave aggressively towards the so-called "unfit" prisoners, arrange their own clothing to imitate the guards' uniforms, reject the idea of intervention by foreign powers aimed at liberating them (before the outbreak of World War II), and even defend some elements of Nazi ideology.

Bettelheim was followed by Leo Löwenthal, who brought to the fore additional elements and insights relevant to our inquiry.[214] First, he explicitly linked fascist terror with "the pattern of modern economy,"[215] a thesis anticipated by Mumford.[216]) Second, he showed that the terror enforced in camps produced the atomization of the individual, who lived independently of his/her fellow human beings.[217] Third, he claimed that the terror furthermore dissociated the individual, who lived in a state of stupor, into a moral coma.[218]

Basically the same conclusions were also reached by Viktor Frankl, Virgil Gheorghiu, Victor Klemperer, and Hannah Arendt after the epoch-making Eichmann trial of 1961.[219]

The logic of torture is clearly a logic of power. It is never a matter of retrieving information. Insofar as data mining is concerned, it seeks to obliterate memories, to destroy evidence, and to dispose of the witness. It is always a matter of ruining the individual, of his/her own identity, culture, and social tissue. Only absentminded laypersons or ranting ideologues can believe that torture is justified by so-called asymmetrical threats. Additionally, if the purely pragmatic question of the reliability of data obtained during torture is raised, the answer is simply zero.[220]

8.3.3.3. The technological chiasma

In conclusion, technique broadly speaking and technoscience strictly speaking are put to work in completely different ways in *Brave New World* and *Nineteen Eighty-Four*. In both cases, the narrative relies heavily upon the Malthusian threat and the requirement of social stabilization while the unavoidability of industrialism, productivism, materialism, standardization (over-organization), and oil-guzzling militarism is accepted at face value.

Amongst the significant contrasts we have the following: the World State secures peace and abundance whereas the Inner Party purposely maintains a state of war, scarcity, and morbid austerity. The former exploits a shame culture in which you have to conceal your trespassings from the community's sight; the latter imposes a guilt culture that involves full confession to a priest of power. Accordingly, the penalty is exile or torture.

The bottom contrast is, as already claimed, the difference between the soft, so to speak benevolent, totalitarianism of *Brave New World* and the harsh, clearly malevolent one of *Nineteen Eighty-Four*. It is reflected in the specificity of the infantilization involved. On the one hand, denizens are treated liked spoiled brats expected to (unconsciously) love their servitude. On the other hand, they are akin to terrorized children who are asked to hate their servitude in a borderline manner.

We have claimed that the young Huxley shows clear signs of technophilia whereas Orwell is uncompromisingly pessimistic in that regard. Of tremendous importance is the fact that *Huxley never understood Orwell's meaning and significance*. The letter Huxley wrote to his fellow novelist after reading *Nineteen Eighty-Four* leaves no doubt about this:

> The philosophy of the ruling minority in *Nineteen Eighty-Four* is a sadism which has been carried to its logical conclusion by going beyond sex and denying it. Whether in actual fact the policy of the boot-on-the-face can go on indefinitely seems doubtful. My own belief is that the ruling oligarchy will find less arduous and wasteful ways of governing and of satisfying its lust for power, and these ways will resemble those which I described in *Brave New World*.... Within the next generation I believe that the world's rulers will discover that infant conditioning and narco-hypnosis are more efficient, as instruments of government, than clubs and prisons, and that the lust for power can be just as completely satisfied by suggesting people into loving their servitude as by flogging and kicking them into obedience. In other words, I feel that the nightmare of *Nineteen Eighty-Four* is destined to modulate into the nightmare of a world having more resemblance to that which I imagined

in Brave New World. The change will be brought about as a result of a felt need for increased efficiency. Meanwhile, of course, there may be a large scale biological and atomic war—in which case we shall have nightmares of other and scarcely imaginable kinds.[221]

There was obviously something in Huxley's education and life experience that prevented him from grasping Orwell's message. There are things, we are told, that a gentleman would not contemplate doing. Needless to say that his intelligence and wide culture cannot account for such a blunder.

By means of conclusion, it is interesting to question the likeliness of a late shift in Huxley's appraisal of the vices and virtues of technique. *Brave New World Revisited* (1958) showed a clear concern for the totalitarian potential of technoscience. Still, Huxley claimed that a scientific enslavement is better—say more comfortable—than the old-fashioned one! The West is after all the heir of the Enlightenment. Here's a statement he made in 1961 at San Francisco's California Medical School:

There will be, in the next generation or so, a pharmacological method of making people love their servitude, and producing dictatorship without tears, so to speak, producing a kind of painless concentration camp for entire societies, so that people will in fact have their liberties taken away from them, but will rather enjoy it, because they will be distracted from any desire to rebel by propaganda or brainwashing, or brainwashing enhanced by pharmacological methods. And this seems to be the final revolution.

Likewise in 1962:

It seems to me that the nature of the ultimate revolution with which we are now faced is precisely this, that we are in process of developing a whole series of techniques which will enable the controlling oligarchy, who have always existed and presumably always will exist, to get people actually to love their servitude. This seems to me the ultimate malevolent revolution... This is a problem which has interested me for many years and about which I wrote, 30 years ago, a fable *Brave New World* which is essentially the account of a society making use of all the devices at that time available and some of the devices which I imagined to be possible, making use of them in order to, first of all, to standardize the population, to iron out inconvenient human differences, to create, so to say, mass produced models of human beings arranged in some kind of a scientific caste system. Since then I have continued to be extremely interested in this problem and I have noticed with increasing dismay that a number of the predictions which were purely fantastic when I made them 30 years ago have come true or seem in process of coming true. A number of techniques about which I talked seem to be here already, and that there seems to be a general movement in the direction of this kind of ultimate revolution, this method of control by which people can be made to enjoy a state of affairs which by any decent standard they ought not to enjoy. I mean the enjoyment of servitude.[222]

The late Huxley seems thus keen to brush away *some* of the ambiguities of *Brave New World*, that navigated between disenchanted narrative knots factually arguing for the political use of technoscience and passages suggesting that life would lose its meaning in such a framework. It does not seem wise to privilege the heuristical thesis of a purely satirical work.

If we peruse the categories used earlier to contrast *Brave New World* and *Nineteen Eighty-Four* in order to screen *Island* (1962), we obtain the following. Interestingly enough, *Island* also accepts the Malthusian threat and the requirement of social stabilization: all three political systems are instances of "clockwork societies." But the status of technoscience and its contribution are here radically different. For one thing, technoscience is not piloted anymore by a blend of politics that is reminiscent of the "market economy," but by Buddhist spirituality. For another, it fosters an organic, nondualistic, social fabric instead of a materialistic, productivistic one. Furthermore, the insular kingdom, which has no army, is also characterized by peace and abundance, but the comparison with *Brave New World* stops here. A constitutional monarchy replaces the benevolent totalitarianism whereas individual growth and solidarity replace infantilization and unconscious servitude.

We could discuss other relevant contrasts such as the Moksha/Soma one, which exemplifies the difference between a natural entheogenic medicine enhancing awareness and a synthetic drug that induces total obliteration. Or the difference between hypnosis *qua* natural healing process and social engineering mated with hypnopedia, between true love and promiscuous sex, initiation and consumption, meaningful life and meaningless pleasure... There is no need to clarify all interpretational issues in the context of the present argument. Suffice it to say that the synergy *Island* depicts between technoscience and spirituality corresponds, *mutatis mutandis*, to the Whiteheadian interpretation of postmodern science that calls for a society rooted both in science and in Christian religiosity. (Sadly enough, some Whiteheadians have not yet realized this.)[223]

In conclusion, there is a long-lasting technophilia in Huxley that is completely foreign to Orwell's vision. As a matter of fact, Huxley's dystopia does provide a plausible picture of our future (the work on ectogenesis is only starting) while recent scientific advances (like cellular phones, internet, geolocalization and RFID technology[224]) make a Big Brother state perhaps more likely in the immediate future. One should certainly not forget that the global systemic crisis is only starting and will have devastating effects on all aspects of our lives.[225]

There is no need however to work out the odds because the respective arguments hold actually at two different levels. *In fine*, Huxley and Orwell provide indeed antagonistic perspectives on the stakes of power: Huxley sees the exercise of power as purely technocratic and, like it or not, happily envisions the complete fulfilment of La Boétie's nightmare. For his part, Orwell uncovers the very dynamics of power and demonstrates that, whatever the technological sophistication, the basics of politics ("101") will remain the same ("Room 101"). The exercise of power involves the capacity to impose suffering on human beings. There is no need of a very sophisticated argument to establish this. Only the suffering of the subordinate demonstrates the power of the superior (happiness can have various sources) and only torture secures that the suffering is real (more benign forms of torment allow the subordinate to *pretend* that s/he is not hurt).

III. Conclusion

Churchill's remark after Chamberlain returned from signing the Munich Agreement in 1938 is well known: "You were given the choice between war and dishonor. You chose dishonor and you will have war." Similarly, it seems that the choice between Huxley and Orwell is a red herring. One depicts the logic of technoscientific capitalism while the other unveils the pathology of the ruling class. Betting for Huxley in the hope to escape Orwell is shortsighted—unless, as Huxley might have hoped already in 1932, a perfectly formatted society would reform the very exercise of power. The question is not simply to get rid of the oligarchs but to destroy the possibility of the exercise of power by the fringe of sociopaths present in all societies. Traditional communities had tricks of their own to that effect; one fears that they are not adequate to post-modern societies.

Independently of the general philosophical standpoint that is adopted here—Whiteheadian optimism—there is however one reason to hope for a better world. All the crises that we have listed and all the facets of the capitalistic *modus operandi* can be subsumed under one single category: the political crisis. We are not confronted with multiple crises, each demanding a specific and highly expert answer. We have to deal with local exemplifications of the collapse of an ideological-political model of exploitation: "market democracy." In other words, if we could change the political system, all problems could come back within our reach. This does not mean of course that they would be solved instantly. Coping with climate change and managing nuclear waste, for instance, are likely to require hundreds if not thousands of years of effort to stabilize.

The main alternative trajectory is called degrowth and involves voluntary simplicity. Cuba, for instance, has shown a remarkable economic resilience after the collapse of the Soviet Union led her abruptly to embrace a post-carbon era. From the perspective of comparison between the Human Development Index and the Ecological Footprint, Cuba's achievements are indeed nothing less than amazing. Two final points deserve to be made from this perspective.

9. Politics and Radical Empiricism

9.1. Radical Philosophy

I have argued that the more you experience, the more you imagine and the more you think, the more you expand your horizon and the more you shift to the left of the political spectrum. So far, Western philosophy has largely committed itself to a metaphysics of feudalism.[226] It is about time to realize that philosophy *qua* philosophy is intrinsically radical—in all senses of the word.

Negatively, philosophy defines itself as the rejection of local expertise and dogmatism. This has been traditionally thematized with the concept of *doxa*: the philosopher endeavors to propose a global framework within which all limited standpoints receive their accountability. The philosopher is not a specialist, and Socrates is probably the first to have exemplified this in various ways. Neither the judge, general, poet, politician, nor hunter has any idea of the nature and scope of his or her knowledge. This definition seems fair enough to most philosophical schools. All refuse indeed to be seen as an expertise of sorts, and all claim to utter systematic judgments fair to all experience.

Positively, philosophy seeks an all-embracing perspective. When James speaks of a mosaic philosophy (ERE 42), he points out pluralism: there are individuals *and* relations. Since no experience should be ignored, the peculiarities of each and every experience are acknowledged. You cannot really hand pick some sections of a philosophical book. If a book is made to be consulted, it is not philosophy but expertise. Whitehead claimed that

> Education is the acquisition of the art of the utilisation of knowledge. This is an art very difficult to impart. Whenever a textbook is written of real educational worth, you may be quite

certain that some reviewer will say that it will be difficult to teach from it. Of course it will be difficult to teach from it. If it were easy, the book ought to be burned; for it cannot be educational. In education, as elsewhere, the broad primrose path leads to a nasty place. (AE 16)

This is a rather old-fashioned perspective. A philosophical treatise is a transfigurative tool, not a reference book.

Embracing all experiences goes hand in hand with the ideal of philosophy *qua* living wisdom or spiritual exercise. A living philosophy is the outgrowth rather than the outcome of a living philosopher. The process of individuation requires that the *cosmopolites*, the citizen of the world, emerge out of the innumerable links, made and in the making, that anchor him in a given spatio-temporal spot. *Experiential philosophy* cannot be taught, it can only be practiced or exercised. This is nothing but the etymological root of asceticism (*askêsis* or exercise). The role of philosophy is to create an *ekstasis,* that is, a standing outside one's self to give individual life perspective and meaning. Pierre Hadot has, for instance, reactualized the spiritual power of the philosophical exercises that have haunted the entire history of philosophy... until the second Renaissance, when the political emergency was, for Mersenne (1623), Descartes (1628), and Gassendi (1655), to crush the social and political reformism of the first Renaissance (say from Ficinus, 1482, to Andreae, 1619) and to provide a new, scientific foundation to Christian supernaturalism.[227] Philosophers ought not to forget that the First Renaissance was pagan and revolutionary.

9.2. Philosophical Expertise

How do experts, including philosophical experts, pretend to fulfill an ambitious philosophical program? Technique or "total expertise" is—like it or not—the trick used by experts in order to ignore the limits of their field. Although, by definition, expertise gives access only to a very limited segment of experience, the expert claims that this segment is actually the core of all experiences. Economists, for instance, instead of acknowledging that their understanding of a very limited and subsidiary dimension of experience *as it is lived* leaves a lot to be desired, claim not only that their expertise covers all aspects of life but also that it is adequate.[228]

Seeking the clarification of propositions (that common sense has most of the time no problem whatsoever to deal with) leads to a completely different philosophical ideal. The same holds for the definition of philosophy by the practice of thought-experiments and other armchair challenges. *Experimental philosophy* should be taught and leads indeed to the creation of more or less successful schools (where nobody of course ever reads Illich), academic degrees, awards, and grants. Philosophy is here far less adventurous. It is only a matter of acquiring by training the proper qualification in pedestrian affairs, such as decision aids, problem-solving tools, and other forms of expertise that are consensual enough not to see the flaws in market democracy yet adequate enough to smooth production processes and are thus valued by firms. Let us take an example of such a *useful* skill.

9.3. Brains in Political Vats

The "brain in a vat" thought experiment has become quite trendy. It was probably first imagined in 1954 by Philip K. Dick (1928–1982) in the context of one of his staggering science fiction novels (always outstandingly visionary but sometimes poorly written). Then it was theatricalized by Robert Nozick (1974) and especially by Daniel Dennett (1978), and later conceptualized by Hilary Putnam (1981) and by John L. Pollock (1986). When you boil it down, the question is: do we have an experience of *What is it Like to Be (in) a Vat?* In the eighties, scientists puzzled by the nature of computer processes used to claim "they're just like big brains." Nowadays, it is the other way around, and cognitivists argue that we will soon discover the exact mechanics of the brain because it is nothing else than a "big computer" and, of course, we know *exactly* how the computer works (compare Vico with Kevin Kelly[229]). Sadly enough, this is simply the behavioristic fallacy pushed to the hilt. But what is the use of envisaging absurd scenarios invoking *non-intuitive* experiences in order to be able to clarify features of our everyday, *intuitive*, experiences such as consciousness-zero? The usefulness of such a train of thought is obviously its uselessness. The intellectual gymnast shows strong evidence of her ability to analyze complex matters and to synthesize the imme-diate stakes (the ones that have not been filtered). The broad-sweeping judgment that is obtained might even sometimes pilot the Research and Development of a new commercial product or, more likely, of a new weaponry. And even if the discursive efforts lead to no application at all, they still serve the purpose of nurturing the image of the independent scholar pursuing totally objective scientific research with no pertinence, for instance, to the current global systemic crisis.

In a nutshell, philosophical training amounts (for only a small fee) to deliberate exercises in *doublethink*. If we dig further, we discover indeed the political relevance of this debate. Embracing all experiences also means adopting, *protego horribilis*, a left-ish political perspective—let us say a communist one to hammer the nail home: the experience of *hoi polloi*, the experiences of the multitude, the experience of the proles, the alienated, ostracized, tortured and assassinated *also* need to be taken into account.

There are actually two basic understandings of language involved in the feud. On the one hand, so-called continental philosophers are likely to use all the resources of their linguistic sphere and even to shame-lessly create new concepts which, according to Deleuze and Guattari, is supposed to be their *fatum*. Thinkers such as James and Whitehead furthermore acknowledge the necessity to satisfy common sense and to reconstruct the basic substantialism of everyday experience. On the other hand, so-called analytic philosophers seek to create an ideal language for philosophical analysis to avoid the use of ordinary language that is so prone to lead thought into contradictions and paradoxes (Russell and Wittgenstein). The parallelism with Orwell is striking:

> 'The Eleventh Edition is the definitive edition,' [Syme] said. 'We're getting the language into its final shape—the shape it's going to have when nobody speaks anything else.... You think, I dare say, that our chief job is inventing new words. But not a bit of it! We're destroying words—scores of them, hundreds of them, every day. We're cutting the language down to the bone.'... 'Don't you see that the whole aim of Newspeak is to narrow the range of thought? In the end we shall make thought-crime literally impossible, because there will be no words in which to express it.'[230]

From that perspective, the scenarios evoked earlier seek not only to provide orthodox judgements, they are likely to foster a language in which politics will be unthinkable.

The testimony of Victor Klemperer, published just before *Nineteen Eighty-Four*, shed some important light on the Newspeak cultural cleansing.[231] I have argued that there are, at the level of individuals, three conditions of possibility for authentic life (echoing the three functions of the late Whitehead's creative advance as well as Arendt's interpretation of classical Greece). These are (i) individuation (creativity, *archein*, action), (ii) solidarity (efficacy, *prattein*, work) and (iii) culture (vision, *theorein*, thought). In order to create themselves, individuals have to have some elbow room, some independence. However, such a spontaneity never occurs outside of a community providing support and interdependence, nor without the fine-tuning of a big narrative (*paideia* or *Bildung*). "Advanced" capitalist societies, which are the necessary precursor of totalitarianism (this is basically Arendt's argument), are characterized by the negation of these three conditions: conformism has replaced individuation, atomism, solidarity, and terror is now the common narrative.

When a philosophical school demands renunciation of common sense, it undermines solidarity. When it doubts sense-perception, it puts a damper on individuation. And when it claims scientificity by rejecting all forms of political concern, it paves the way to the unquestioned acceptance of a big narrative that is not worthy of that name anymore. Taken together, the three requirements seal the divorce between philosophy and life and lead the philosopher to compartmentalize his professional activities. With that regard, it is worth remembering Orwell's definition of *doublethink*:

> It is only by reconciling contradictions that power can be retained indefinitely.... The prevailing mental condition must be controlled insanity.[232]

To sum up. There can be conservative politicians, right-wing theologians, Nazi intellectuals, socialist psychoanalyst or crypto-fascist sociologists, but no conservative philosophers, right-wing philosophers, Nazi philosophers, socialist philosophers, or crypto-fascist philosophers. As soon as you accept all experiences and seek the ultimate generalities, you are *ipso facto* led to embrace a far left political stance. But do notice that this does not imply any extremism whatsoever. It simply means the radical will to see the actualization of the three conditions of possibility of authenticity: individuation, solidarity and culture. Accordingly, this "far left" does not belong either to historical liberalism or to the communist ideal or even to the *paideic* archetype. It is a place that remains to be invented for our time, a utopia that should no longer remain a uchronia.

10. The Pragmatics of Societal Change

"Those who make peaceful revolution impossible will make violent revolution inevitable." ~John Fitzgerald Kennedy[233]

We are stuck in an ill-fated ideology for ill-fated reasons. What the poets have chanted of the four ages can be said, but in reverse, of the age of technique. The Golden Age of technique dates back when technique was still piloted by science and art. This synergy ends, paradoxically, with the Second Renaissance and the so-called Age of Reason. The Silver Age is the time of the murder of God that may as well be depicted as the murder of Nature (1789–1793). The Bronze Age of technique is our age, the age of IT, the age of soulless propaganda and total exploitation. The Iron Age is the age of the totalitarianism to come. It will be the virtual age of doom, the age of the technoscientific creation of reality and of climate corruption.

Action must now be taken in order to reestablish the possibility of a meaningful life. One should not expect a philosophical essay—or any essay whatsoever—to propose a detailed new political system because it is never clear how ideas can be implemented in complex social tissues. A bundle of pragmatic measures that would act as a good, do however make sense.

The pragmatics of political change would involve three main types of measures that are, as far as I can tell, compatible with the constitution of most nations. In other words, a well-written constitution provides the general conditions of a meaningful political life. Laws then specify that basic orientation in ways that suit the most powerful social actors. Since they are interdependent, one could start from any of them but the main key is political, precisely for that reason.

10.1. At the Political Level

At the political level, three main actions ought to be taken: to terminate particracy, to politicize society, and to simplify laws and levels of power. These actions are essential because they constitute the only answer to the global systemic crisis. Unless we realize that the problem we have to confront is first and foremost political, no efficient, let alone constructive, move will be possible.

It is through particracy that the democratic interplay of actors is hijacked. Particracy—governance by one or more dominant political parties—bypasses the *separation of powers* imperative that is as old as the concept of direct democracy. Politicians nowadays do not represent their constituents but their own interests (usually) and their party's (always). Hence there cannot be any real independence between the executive, the legislative, and the judiciary. In sum, the termination of particracy means to divorce politics and economics. This, in turn, involves the politicization of the social tissue. If politics are divorced from economics and the revolving doors stop running, the old alliance of politics and the social tissue can be resuscitated. This means that people could accept the need to act as concerned citizens instead of worried customers. Only a tiny fraction of the population is currently involved in actual political decision-making. Additionally, more and more denizens are excluded from the vote or do not bother voting while those who do vote find it difficult to cast a vote in their own interest.[234] Bourdieu called this delusion "symbolic violence." Also, one should remember, with Plato and Thomas More that those who are begging for political responsibilities should be, *ipso facto*, denied any access to them, while citizens who would rather never obtain any decisional power should be put in the front line.

In order to make the shift possible, laws and levels of power must be simplified. In sum, it should be the end of expertise and the return of common sense.

At first, in times of crisis, it becomes especially obvious that the termination of particracy requires a divorce between politics and economics. We have seen the same scenario too often repeating itself. Proles vote for the extreme right in the hope that all the professional politicians will be removed definitively from the scene and that their interest will at last be taken care of. Here also the engineering of dissent obtains excellent results. The case of 20th century Germany provides a good idea of the methodology involved.

First, there is a major economical crisis, with unemployment rates as high as 30 percent, which supports the rise of new political demands and eventually suscitates a pre-insurrectional climate. At that stage, the crisis benefits the radical left. Before the rise of the Nazi party, the German communist party was indeed the most powerful of Europe, Soviet Russia excluded. But people seek salvation in solidarity only as long as their economic situation is more or less tenable.

Second, as soon as the proles are on the verge of toppling into misery—or when they so believe—they do not trust solidarity anymore but turn to selfishness and natural selection. It is at that point that the communist vote looses its attraction, thereby benefitting the fascist vote.

This existential proclivity is nevertheless not the sole thing responsible for the turnaround. Apparently subversive political structures are easy to create to orient people's fears. In the case of Germany, the inner party was keen to invest in the dissenting parties in order to secretly pilot them and to make sure that the oligarchy would not be threatened. It is from this perspective that the history of the Nazi party should be written. One discovers then a party created to hijack the worker's discontent to the profit of the business class. Nazism is actually the product of two main reversals or purges (one should really say *bleedings*) that could be introduced simply with the help of the name change that took place.

In 1919, the "Deutsche Arbeiterpartei" was created out of a previous small political group. It *was* the party of/for the workers ("Arbeiterpartei"). The initial program of the DAP (and later of the NSDAP) clearly competed with the communist party program .It was adamantly anti-capitalistic while, at the same time, equally anti-communistic.

In 1920, its name was changed into "Nationalsozialistische Deutsche Arbeiterpartei," initiating a right-turn that was still somehow in disguise: a "sozialistische" party could hardly be an imperialistic one.

After 1933, the NSDAP was known as the "Nationalsozialistische Partei," and the entire socialistic wing was soon destroyed. First, there was the Reichstag arson (1933) that was used to denounce, incarcerate, and murder communists. Then came the "Night of the Long Knives," during which Röhm and other high-ranking SA leaders were executed because of their socialistic views.

In sum, a major economic crisis that was meant to spring a communist revolution of sorts ended up fostering a fascist regime designed by German and Western capitalists to prevent such an uprising at all costs *and* to destroy the Soviet regime itself.

One last specification: from the perspective of the analysis developed here, the Nazi hounding of the Jewish communities is not totally irrational. First, there is indeed a purely racial element: a eugenics program (theorized in Great Britain and first put into practice in Switzerland, California, and Canada) seeking to preserve the purity of the German blood. Second, there is a social element, probably in part mystical, that basically uses the old pattern of the scapegoat. Third, there is a purely ideological element. In order to secure a fascist society, citizens have to be decultured, atomized, and conformized. Since Jews, perhaps more than other minorities, have kept—or successfully created, it does not matter here[235]—a strong identity over the centuries, they would not have been as easily massified as the other Germans, to whom the new mythology was served without the resistance, and sometimes with the help, of Christian communities. Fourth, there is the economic element. On the one hand, targeting wealthy Germans Jews was beneficial for every inner and outer party member seeking to improve or re-establish his local power. On the other hand, since international capitalism was supposed to be Jewish-dominated, it made sense to wage war upon its bases. From this twin perspective, the Jews were the victims of a class war.

All things considered it might be the case that eugenics is the main factor in Nazi ideology. But then the question bounces back, as the Nazi program stems from Anglo-Saxon upper class worries about the reproduction rate of the lower classes, which could soon outbreed them. This is plain in Galton's *Hereditary Genius* (1869). Why such a genocidal policy at that time? Was the Stalingrad debacle instrumental?

Second, the termination of particracy would open up the political field and thus require the factual involvement of citizens. On the other hand, if the end of particracy cannot be obtained by fiat, the repolitization of society should be enforced at the expense of the grip of the economic world. This would require time since a political consciousness is not easy to acquire. Some form of political education, together with a proper access to the relevant information, is indispensable to obtain a class consciousness and to open the door to a full awareness of the class struggle and of its whereabouts. The political dimension of schooling and media systems cannot be ignored any longer. This, in turn, requires the return of culture, individuation, and solidarity. It is because of conformism and atomism that denizens are so reluctant to discuss political issues while going into vivid details about their intimate lives. From the perspective of Greek democracy, this is a very topsy-turvy world indeed.

Third, the simplification of laws and of levels of power will be needed, the sooner the better. Rousseau, for one, underlined that if citizens do not know by heart the fundamental laws of their country, they do not live in a democracy. The current state of affairs in representative democracies prevents the empowerment of citizens. In order to obtain some idea as to how the intricate layers of international, European, national, and regional laws work, students spend five years in university with, as a result, only a very limited pragmatic knowledge. Additionally, there are far too many levels of power to guarantee a manageable participatory democracy. Should citizens be allowed to fulfill their political duties, common sense must be allowed to rule at the expense of expertise.

10.2. At the Social Level

To repeat: the problem we have to confront is above all political, and the most direct way to initiate adequate change is to put an end to particracy. However, we could also start at the social level by fostering communitarian degrowth. Here also, bottom-up processes take longer but are deeper than top-down policies. Anyway, degrowth would involve three moves, all of them involving the return of common sense at the expense of professional expertise and infantilization.

First, provide the conditions of possibility of conviviality and enforce technological simplicity. *Conviviality* is Illich's (1973) concept;. and it belongs to the long legacy of critiques of industrial society. Illich's legacy lies at the crossroads of three conceptual threads: the philosophical critique of industrialism, the history of the development of technoscience, and the matching political events.

Although Mumford (*Technics and Civilization*, 1934) is usually credited as the first ecological thinker of techno-capitalism, his work was preceded by important conceptual and artistic breakthroughs, including Tocqueville (*De la démocratie en Amérique*, 1835), Thoreau (*Walden*, 1854), Butler (*Note-Books*, 1863), Marx (*Das Kapital*, 1867), Spengler (*Der Untergang*, 1918), Lang (*Metropolis*, 1927), Freud (*Das Unbehagen*, 1929), Huxley (*Brave New World*, 1932), Chaplin (*Modern Times*, 1936), Anders (*Die Antiquiertheit des Menschen*, 1956).

The scientific thread is equally important. Watt made the steam engine operational in 1784 (see §6.2.1.), thereby launching the industrial revolution per se. After two full centuries of euphoria, Hubbert foresees the U.S. peak of conventional oil in 1956, which actually takes place in 1971. The Club of Rome is created in April 1968, and Meadows publishes its *Report* in 1972.

Politics moves along with the other dimensions of civilization and the contingencies of technoscience do of course have an impact on the political stakes. The lexicon of contemporary politics was carved out by Hayek in 1944 but put into practice only in 1973 when Pinochet overthrew the democratically elected president S. Allende. At the same time, the O.P.E.C. oil embargo of 1973–1974 shook economies worldwide. Heilbroner was probably the first, in 1974, to argue that, without cheap energy, representative democracy is doomed and that as soon as energy becomes scarce or too costly, totalitarianism will be unavoidable.

In sum, all relevant data were available half a century ago and by 1973 the approaching moment of truth became transparent in the works of Illich, Meadows, and Heilbroner.

Second, reframe society through public *education,* but not through private schooling.[236] Illich, for one, was critical of all forms of institutionalized education. His critique is still applicable, as one can see for instance in the work of N. Hirtt, who has recently shown how much schooling is determined only by the contingencies of the economy.[237] A real education would be *paideic*: it would seek to provide all citizens in the making with the right cultural tools. The goal would be to enforce common sense, not to transform everyone into an expert or, if impossible, into a consumer of expertise.

Third, relaunch social security, a feat that would not necessarily involve the abolition of private property.[238] Social security programs have always resulted from the conjunction of two factors: first, the existence of insistent demands from the lower classes for the improvement of their conditions of existence; second, the availability of resources to secure such measures. Usually, only the imminence of a revolt leads the upper classes to grant prophylactic reforms. The current social security system in Europe sprang from the Bolshevik revolution of 1917 and the actualization of the communist ideal in the Soviet Union. More precisely, it was set up after the Second World War, when most European citizens were politically aware and when the majority was shifting towards the left of the political spectrum. Also, the huge contribution the Soviet Union made to defeat Nazi Germany was obvious. When the Allies landed in Normandy on 6 June 1944, the Soviets were entering Poland, Czechoslovakia, and Prussia. The Nazis lost on the Eastern Front 10 million out of a total 13.5 million men killed, wounded, or taken prisoner during the entire war (the Red Army eventually claimed credit for 90 percent of all Germans killed). The human cost was equally horrendous. While the USA lost, during the entire war, 290,000 soldiers and no civilians, the Soviets lost as many as 10 million soldiers and 20 million civilians. So when the first French Institute of Public Opinion (IFOP) conducted opinion polls in Paris in September 1944, 61 percent understood that the Red Army defeated the Nazis while the USA and Great Britain, who did liberate France, received only, respectively, 29.3 percent and 11.5 percent.[239]

The point is this that De Gaulle was forced to adopt large parts of the National Council of Resistance (CNR)Program[240] in order to keep the presidency and to avoid a communist government. Let us be clear that it is one of two things: either the social security system is rebuilt because the storm is on our shores and the oligarchy wants to keep its privileges, or the social security system is rebuilt thanks to the implosion of the upper class. Additionally, the communist ideal should not be pictured as involving being stripped of all of one's assets but as being endowed with a life revenue. It is not difficult to see, although nowadays it has become counter-intuitive, that the current capitalist economy allows all advantages to the so-called investors and none to the workers. As soon as economy is centered upon life and not speculation, another world becomes possible indeed.

10.3. At the Economical Level

It should be clear by now that, more than ever, "politics is the shadow cast on society by big business."[241] Should one decide to propose reforms at the economic level, the first move will be to acknowledge that the real, local economy ("nuts and bolts") is the only meaningful one, and that it deserves some attention only insofar as it fosters life. This statement is really like kicking down an open door but, given the current doxa, these facts need to be hammered. The social ellipse and its organic environment should be managed by its political focus, not its economic focus. Hence the three following proposals: (i) a monetary reform that would involve the nationalization of central banks, the fostering of local exchange trading systems, and the encouragement of alternative systems such as the "bancor" (Keynes) or "melting money" (Jean Gesell); (ii) the degrowth of production and of consumption; and (iii) the relocalization of production and of consumption accordingly. To shorten the argument, we can focus on these three dimensions.

First, a monetary reform involving the nationalization of central banks is inevitable. The CNR Program (see §10.2.) underlined the absolute necessity of public management of the central bank would mean that States borrow money from their central bank, not from private banks. This is precisely what the Maastricht treatise prevents. States are obliged to borrow money from private banks and kindly requested to pay the price of this enslavement. As former French president Giscard d'Estaing claimed, socialism (nobody thinks of communism anymore) is now outlawed. Additionally, one should foster local exchange trading systems and alternative forms of money. The synergy between these top-down and bottom-up approaches should secure prompt changes.

Second, degrowth should become the motto of all economic actors. Production should be curved down for the same reasons consumption needs to be bridled. There is, first, a lack of resources (and especially of energy after peak oil) and the overwhelming pollution that industrial activities generate. But even if resources were not scarce and pollution not an issue, the inauthenticity of the consumer's life would remain untouched. In 1972, Meadows' crew could still argue for sustainability and controlled decline to obtain a just, peaceful, and equitable world; 40 years later, the overshoot and collapse scenario seems inevitable.[242] Unfortunately, Meadows refuses to utter any political claim and confines himself in contradictory claims. On the one hand, he correctly identifies the looming disaster, its chronology, roots, and consequences. On the other, he only very vaguely evokes the necessity of somehow changing our current political standpoint.

Third, to relocalize production and consumption will be inevitable, either because the lack of energy will make industrial agriculture and transportation impossible or because the real economy will be again in the service of life.

Now, the amazing fact is that, in the case of most countries, it would be possible to implement such changes without modifying their constitutions. So perhaps the very first move would be to realize that we should stick to our constitutions and to reconsider, in the case of European countries, the automatic implementation of European rules in domestic law. Of course, such a healthy dose of cultural relativism has its limits, and one could argue that some constitutions provide a better background for the pragmatics of political change, but such a Pandora's box cannot be opened here.

One last word. The story of the Titanic is well known. A true modern narrative full of technological expertise, hubris, and insanity, it is largely seen nowadays as a rather glamorous episode in oceanic conquest. Its modern meaning and significance, however, is deeper.

There were four turning points on that fateful night of April 14, 1912.[243] At 11:40 p.m., the lookout spotted an iceberg immediately ahead. Thirty-seven seconds later the starboard side of Titanic struck the iceberg below the waterline. Roundabout midnight, during a meeting in the captain's quarter, it became clear that, since five out of sixteen of the ship's watertight compartments were breached, the ship would sink in two hours. Indeed, at 02:20 a.m., the Titanic was lost. Seventy percent of the passengers disappeared but all were not equal in death: only 3 percent of first-class women were lost, whereas 54 percent of those in third class drowned.

The analogy with our current epoch is striking. In 1912, transatlantic ships were seen as largely unsinkable, just like Western capitalism in 2012. How far can we use the four turning points to understand the current global systemic crisis? The general pattern can be kept, but the actual chronology varies with the expertise, philosophers being always (humbly) far ahead of their times. Since the awareness of our likely future takes place differently according to discipline, it is wise to differentiate science, politics, and philosophy.

Who first spotted an iceberg immediately ahead, and when? The year 1968 is a good candidate, but cultural discontent had been growing since 1945, even as the euphoria of the Golden Sixties was spreading. The Club of Rome was created in April 1968; in May 1968. Students, and then workers, launched occupation protests against capitalism and consumerism. Without the betrayal of the unions and other corrupted entities, the voice of the people that was bought in 1945 by social security could have brought down the "market democracy." If we discriminate according to the expertise of the actors, three people stand out. In 1956, K. Hubbert foresaw the U.S.-American peak oil in 1971, thereby setting in motion the work of more or less obscure technocrats worldwide in order to understand the stakes and secure the status quo. As usual, the Pentagon's RAND Corporation was very keen to assess the impact on its combat readiness. In 1973, Pinochet seized power, giving a first instantiation of Hayek's neo-liberal program and heralding the end of the social security state. But as early as 1934, Mumford had clarified the issue of capitalistic management of technoscience and underlined the existential alienation of citizens. Even if social alienation could be disposed of, technoscience would still necessarily bring inauthenticity.

When did we strike the iceberg below the waterline? The year 1972 is key with publication of the conclusions of the Club of Rome. The Meadows Report did not mince its words in denouncing our nihilistic path and yet . . . nothing changed for another 40 years. The years

1973–1974 saw the oil embargo crippling Western economies. In 1974, Heilbroner claimed that peak oil, the collapse of the biosphere, and the consequent slowing growth, would require a highly authoritarian regime to monitor the transition to economic decline.[244] In 1973, Illich refreshed Tocqueville's (1835) and Mumford's analyses, urging Western societies to curb their consumerism. All the data were available then, and the collapse was modeled in Jay Forrester's *World Dynamics* (1971).

We are now roundabout midnight, in the captain's quarter. Although it is all too obvious that our ship will sink within two hours, there is still no awareness of it outside some restricted circles. Dedicated scholars know the odds, but they usually choose to ignore them with the facts that their own models disclose. The only exceptions are to be found at the two extremes of the spectrum: on the one hand, those who work for the oligarchy and prepare for the after-collapse in order to secure their masters' well-being; on the other hand, those who dare to speak at the expense of their professional lives. The landmarks here are the subprime crisis (2007) and the Fukushima disaster (2011). Also in 2007, Naomi Klein published *The Shock Doctrine: The Rise of Disaster Capitalism*, that explicates the *modus operandi* of international capitalism and links it with nefarious psychiatric experiments. Not many philosophers are actually seriously dealing with the Near-Term Human Extinction issue. Jean-Pierre Dupuy deserves a mention for his reasonable catastrophism (2002).[245]

Meadows seems to have kept the year 2050 as the likely date of the collapse. McPherson considers that 2038, or perhaps 2030, will see the extinction of the human race for purely climatic reasons. Recently, the World Bank has expressed similar concerns about 2025: the world is headed down a dangerous path with disruption of the food system possible within a decade as climate change undermines nations' ability to feed themselves.[246] Our incredibly complex civilization preserves the appearances of a very stable one; yet, because of its size and its technological complexity it is more fragile than ever. It is to be feared that only two consecutive years of bad harvest would guarantee social unrest worldwide.

When the Titanic sunk, the first-class passengers were, so to speak, as unaffected as one could be while the third class was decimated. The oligarchy expects the exact same scenario and is not overly worried it seems. The shift to a totalitarian regime in Western "democracies," the neocolonial wars, the unconcern for ecological matters, together with more peculiar measures, such as the opening of the Svalbard Global Seed Vault, "so that crop diversity can be conserved for the future,"[247] testify, however, to the changes to come.

Although all the parameters indicate an imminent and fast total collapse of our civilization,[248] with only probably a couple of million humans to survive under a strict totalitarian rule (hoped by the oligarchy) or absolute chaos (more likely given the circumstances), scholars have two duties: first, to make everyone aware of the conclusions they have reached; second, to provide actual tools, speculative or otherwise, to cope with the events; three, to preserve what is left of reason to hope that we will be more civilized in our decline than we were in our expansion.

Additionally, the future of complex systems is, by definition, unpredictable. Some scientists toy, for instance, with the idea that an algae such as the Emiliania huxleyi phytoplankton could evolve fast enough to cope with climate change. Nature might be more resilient than previously thought, and humans more inventive and adaptable. From a Whiteheadian perspective, the future is not written. If the global systemic crisis could be seen as what it is—first and foremost a political crisis—citizens would be empowered to foster a new habitus and, hopefully, to bring some form of relief to all those who will otherwise perish in the metamorphosis.

Appendix: "Biocontrol," *Times,* Oct. 15, 1956

A familiar horror of science fiction is the slave whose thoughts and actions are governed by an electronic gadget grafted into his brain. There might be some truth in this fiction, says Electrical Engineer Curtiss R. Schafer, who designs and develops electronic instruments for the Norden-Ketay Corp. of New York City. Electronics, he believes, could save a lot of work for the indoctrinators and thought-controllers of the future.

At last week's National Electronics Conference at Chicago, Schafer discussed recent improvements in scientific knowledge and control of the brain. After all, he pointed out, the brain is a digital computer whose functioning can be profoundly affected by electrical influences. The electroencephalograph (brainwave detector) shows electrical signals that ebb and flow in the brain. Perhaps these signals can be simulated, controlling the brain's sensations and thoughts.

Injected Signals

"The logical extension of electroencephalographic research," said Schafer, "may result in the formation of another hybrid science, biocontrol. The biophysicist has measured and recorded the electrical activity of the central nervous system, and shown that neural [nerve] currents control many of our mental and muscular activities. The electronic-control scientist has taught us that minute electrical signals, properly amplified, may be used for the control of airplanes, guided missiles and machine tools.

"It is quite logical to believe that these two sciences will merge. Biocontrol may be denned as the control of physical movements, mental processes, emotional reactions and apparent sensory perceptions... by

170

means of bioelectrical signals which are transmitted and injected into the central nervous system of the subject.

"Elementary forms of biocontrol have already been demonstrated... Direct current of the required waveform and intensity passed through [a man's] head... changes his sense of balance, and he leans to one side... Other experimenters have shown that rats and dogs may be made to feel hungry just after eating, or afraid when they had nothing to fear, simply by injecting the appropriate neural currents into the central nervous system of the animal."

Cheapest Machine

"The ultimate achievement of biocontrol," says Engineer Schafer, "may be the control of man himself.... Enslavement could be imposed upon the vanquished as a condition of peace, or through the threat of hydrogen bombing. Biocontrol could make this enslavement complete and final, for the controlled subjects would never be permitted to think as individuals. A few months after birth, a surgeon would equip each child with a socket mounted under the scalp and electrodes reaching selected areas of brain tissue. A year or two later, a miniature radio receiver and antenna would be plugged into the socket. From that time on, the child's sensory perceptions and muscular activity could be either modified or completely controlled by bioelectric signals radiated from state-controlled transmitters. The regular treatment for schizophrenia uses the same surgical techniques... The electrodes cause no discomfort, no damage to brain tissue and no interference with the functioning of the brain except when energized.

"The once-human being, thus controlled, would be the cheapest of machines to create and operate. The cost of building even a simple robot, like the Westinghouse mechanical man, is probably ten times that of bearing and raising a child to the age of 16."

Endnotes

1. This essay takes over some arguments made in my previous works, such as *Whitehead's Pancreativism: The Basics* (Frankfurt: Ontos Verlag, 2006) and *Whitehead's Pancreativism: Jamesian Applications* (Frankfurt: Ontos Verlag, 2011).

2. William James, *The Principles of Psychology* [1890], authorized edition in two vols., vol. 1 (New York: Dover Publications, 1950), 487:

> Our original sensible totals are, on the one hand, subdivided by discriminative attention, and, on the other, united with other totals,—either through the agency of our own movements, carrying our senses from one part of space to another, or because new objects come successively and replace those by which we were at first impressed. The "simple impression" of Hume, the "simple idea" of Locke are both abstractions, never realized in experience. Experience, from the very first, presents us with concreted objects, vaguely continuous with the rest of the world which envelops them in space and time, and potentially divisible into inward elements and parts. These objects we break asunder and reunite. We must treat them in both ways for our knowledge of them to grow; and it is hard to say, on the whole, which way preponderates. But since the elements with which the traditional associationism performs its constructions—"simple sensations," namely—are all products of discrimination carried to a high pitch, it seems as if we ought to discuss the subject of analytic attention and discrimination first. The noticing of any part whatever of our object is an act of discrimination.

3. With authors such as Auguste Comte (1830–1842), Ernest Renan (1863), Adolf von Harnack (1873), Alfred Loisy (1902), and Prosper Alfaric (1959).

4. See §4.2.3.1.

5. See, e.g., John J. McDermott, "Life Is in the Transitions: Radical Empiricism and Contemporary Concerns," in *Doctrine and Experience: Essays in American Philosophy*, ed. Vincent G. Potter (New York: Fordham University Press, 1988), 104-20; Charlene Haddock Seigfried, *Chaos and Context: A Study in William James* (Athens, Ohio: Ohio University Press, 1978); Eugene I. Taylor, *William James on Consciousness Beyond the Margins* (Princeton, New Jersey: Princeton University Press, 1983); Stéphane Madelrieux, *William James. L'attitude empiriste* (Paris: Presses universitaires de France, 2008).

6. Aldous Leonard Huxley, *Island. A Novel* (London: Chatto & Windus, 1962), 132.

7. An alternative formulation can be found in student's notes taken during Whitehead's classes: "You must survey all the sides of the universe, the variations in our value experience, we must look at all rare moments when we were near angels and near pigs, and the rare moments when our value notion is so indiscriminating that it is a mere throb of immediacy, a vague feeling as when we fall asleep." (Frederick Olson, *Alfred North Whitehead Lecture. Student Notes 1936–1937*, Unpublished, consult Harvard's Pusey: HUC 8923.368.3) The polar themes of clarity and vagueness are essential in Whitehead: cf. the well-known quote of Russell's from *Portraits from Memory and Other Essays* (New York: Simon and Schuster, 1956), 40: "You think the world is what it looks in fine weather at noon day; I think it is what it seems like in the early morning when one first wakes from deep sleep"—claimed Whitehead.

8. Hans Jonas, *The Phenomenon of Life: Toward a Philosophical Biology* (Chicago: University of Chicago Press, 1966); *Philosophical Essays: From Ancient Creed to Technological Man* (Chicago: University of Chicago Press, 1974), 224–36. With regard to our contention that Jonas was lured into that critique by his acquaintance with Whitehead (e.g., "in practice sense-perception is narrowed down to visual perception"—PR 36), see his *Wissenschaft als personliches Erlebnis* (Göttingen: Vandenhoeck & Ruprecht, 1987). Jonas' critique was also anticipated by Maine de Biran, Wilhelm Dilthey, and McLuhan (*The Gutenberg Galaxy: The Making of Typographic Man* [London, Routledge and Kegan Paul, 1962]), who quotes J. C. Carothers ("Culture, Psychiatry and the Written Word," *Psychiatry*, 22/4 (1959): 307–20).

9. See "Consciousness and Rationality from a Process Perspective" in *Process Approaches to Consciousness in Psychology, Neuroscience, and*

Philosophy of Mind, ed. Michel Weber and Anderson Weekes (Albany, New York: State University of New York Press, 2009), 345–84.

10. Bergson alludes to these messages when he speaks of "sensations de 'toucher intérieur' émanant de tous les points de l'organisme, et plus particulièrement des viscères." (*L'Énergie spirituelle*, 91; and *Oeuvres*, 883)

11. Articular capsule, periosteum, tendons, joints, and muscles house sensitive corpuscles and nerve endings similar to that of the skin. See Sir Charles Scott Sherrington's *The Integrative Action of the Nervous System* [1906] (Cambridge: Cambridge University Press, 1947), 132–33 and his *Man on his Nature. The Gifford Lectures, Edinburgh 1937–1938* (Cambridge: Cambridge University Press, 1940), 309.

12. See Eugene I. Taylor's reconstruction of James' 1896 Lowell Lectures in *William James on Exceptional Mental States: The 1896 Lowell Lectures* (New York: Charles Scribner's Sons, 1982).

13. We do not belong to a cosmos anymore—but neither do we live in a chaos. Hence Guattari's neologism.

14. Whitehead was more precise:

Speculative Philosophy is the endeavour to frame a coherent, logical, necessary system of general ideas in terms of which every element of our experience can be interpreted. By this notion of 'interpretation' I mean that everything of which we are conscious, as enjoyed, perceived, willed, or thought, shall have the character of a particular instance of the general scheme. Thus the philosophical scheme should be coherent, logical, and, in respect to its interpretation, applicable and adequate. Here 'applicable' means that some items of experience are thus interpretable, and 'adequate' means that there are no items incapable of such interpretation. (PR 3).

A rather long argument is needed to spell out this definition's meaning and significance: see my *Whitehead's Pancreativism. The Basics*.

15. Such as: eurocentrism (Africa, India and China don't exist), the Greek/French/German legacy, rationalism (the value of empiricism is denied), androcentrism, etc.

16. There are two adjacent territories. First, in the context of philosophical counseling, they involve purgation (spontaneity), structuration (maieutics) and recapitulation (paradox, lure): see my *L'Épreuve de la philosophie: Essai sur les fondements de la praxis philosophique* (Louvain-

la-Neuve: Éditions Chromatika, 2008). Second, interestingly enough, Jung's understanding of the meaning and significance of alchemy, obviously influenced by his own involvement in Freemasonry, can help identify the characteristics of the philosophical commitment. See my "Contact Made Vision: The Apocryphal Whitehead," in *Handbook of Whiteheadian Process Thought*, ed. Michel Weber and William Desmond, Jr. (Frankfurt/Lancaster: Ontos Verlag, Process Thought X1 & X2, 2008), 573–99.

17. On the development of "evolutionary epistemology," see Donald T. Campbell's "Evolutionary Epistemology" in *The Philosophy of Karl Popper*, ed. Paul Arthur Schilpp, The Library of Living Philosophers, XIV (La Salle, Illinois: Open Court, 1974), 413–51, and especially Milič Čapek's very suggestive works; e.g., *New Aspects of Time: Its Continuity and Novelties*, Selected Papers in the Philosophy of Science (Dordrecht-Boston-London: Kluwer Academic Publishers, 1991).

18. Quine's and Popper's views would need further specification.

19. Milič Čapek, *New Aspects of Time*, 112.

20. See James' "Remarks on Spencer's Definition of Mind as Correspondence," *Journal of Speculative Philosophy* XII, 1–18. Also worthy of mention: Ferdinand Canning Scot Schiller's (1864–1937) *Riddles of the Sphinx. A Study in the Philosophy of Evolution* (1891).

21. Charles Sanders Peirce, "The Architecture of Theories," *The Monist* (January 1891): 161–76; reprinted in *Values in a Universe of Chance: Selected Writings of Charles S. Peirce*, ed, with an Introduction and Notes by Philip P. Wiener (Garden City, New York: Doubleday Anchor Books, 1958), 148.

22. See *L'Évolution créatrice*, 1907, ch. IV.

23. WB viii, PU 321; cf. Ralph Barton Perry, *The Thought and Character of William James: As Revealed in Unpublished Correspondance and Notes, Together with his Published Writings; Volume I, Inheritance and Vocation; Volume II, Philosophy and Psychology* (Boston: Little, Brown, 1935), here vol. II, 700. "In its turn every philosophy will suffer a deposition. But the bundle of philosophic systems expresses a variety of general truths about the universe, awaiting co-ordination and assignment of their various spheres of validity" (PR 7).

24. See David Skrbina, *Panpsychism in the West* (Cambridge: Massachusetts Institute of Technology Press, 2005).

25. This difference is stressed by Griffin, e.g., in his *Founders of Constructive Postmodern Philosophy: Peirce, James, Bergson, Whitehead, and Hartshorne* (New York: State University of New York Press, 1993), 35 n17.

26. Marcus Peter Ford, *William James' Philosophy. A New Perspective* (Amherst: University of Massachusetts Press, 1982).

27. W. E. Cooper, "William James' Theory of Mind," *Journal of the History of Philosophy* 28 (4 October 1990): 571–93.

28. William James, "Confidences of a 'Psychical Researcher'" [1909], in EPR 361–75.

29. Cobb and Griffin proposed the concept of "panexperientialism" in 1977 to name Whitehead's attitude: cf. Cobb, John Boswell, Jr. and Griffin, eds., *Mind in Nature: Essays on the Interface of Science and Philosophy*, Washington, D. C., The University Press of America, 1977.

30. Cf. Ferdinand Tönnies' concepts in his *Gemeinschaft und Gesellschaft* [1887], ed. and trans. Charles P. Loomis (East Lansing: Michigan State University Press, 1957).

31. I have shown elsewhere that the best characterization of the late Whitehead should proceed from his basic intuition as it was spelled out in the proto-idea of creative advance. The creative advance requires private concrescence (creativity), public transition (efficacy) and divine fine-tuning (vision). Without the injection of the divine initial subjective aim into each event in the making, claims Whitehead, the interplay between contemporary creativity and past efficacy is likely to amount to the chaotic gearing of wild novelty with blind causation, of chance with necessity. (See, e.g., *Whitehead's Pancreativism: The Basics.*)

32. We are talking here of political issues, not adopting Whitehead's ontological lexicon.

33. Bergson, *Creative Evolution* [1907], authorized translation by Arthur Mitchell (New York: Henry Holt and Co., 1911), 53.

34. See relevant entries in the *Handbook of Whiteheadian Process Thought,* ed. Weber and Desmond (Frankfurt/Lancaster: Ontos Verlag, 2008).

35. Immanuel Kant, *Kritik der reinen Vernunft*, A444/B472.

36. "Le mouvement rétrograde du vrai" (Bergson, *La Pensée et le mouvant*, 15; and *Oeuvres*, 1264).

37. Hannah Arendt, *The Human Condition* [1958], 2nd edition, introduction by Margaret Canovan (Chicago: University of Chicago Press, 1958), 177; see 189.

38. To differentiate potentiality, virtuality, and actuality, see *Whitehead's Pancreativism: The Basics*, ch. VI.

39. Hannah Arendt, *The Human Condition*, 189.

40. See *Whitehead's Pancreativism: The Basics*, 226 ff.

41. J. Boydston, ed., *John Dewey: The Later Works, 1925–1953*, vol. 14 (Carbondale: Southern Illinois University Press), 224–30.

42. J. Boydston, ed., *John Dewey: The Later Works, 1925–1953*, 224–30.

43. Josef Pieper, *Muße und Kult* (München: Kösel-Verlag, 1948); *Leisure, the Basis of Culture*, trans. Alexander Dru, with an introduction by T. S. Eliot (London: Faber and Faber, 1952).

44. Hannah Arendt, *The Life of the Mind*, one-volume edition (San Diego/New York/London: Harcourt Brace Jovanovich), 1978.

45. See §1.1.

46. When Whitehead claims that "the future is merely real without being actual; whereas the past is a nexus of actualities" (PR 214), he endangers his own intuition: the future has, strictly speaking, no existence or reality whatsoever outside the expectations of a given concrescing (*i.e.*, contemporary) actual entity.

47. B. Russell, *Portraits from Memory*, 39.

48. Feeling is the term that James sometimes uses for pure experience (SPP 94, etc.), and that Whitehead chose to name the vectorial relations binding all events (PR 23, *et passim*).

49. SMW 136; Whitehead's definition of contiguity is in PR 307; cf. ERE 108.

50. When it mentions, for instance, two separate streams (PP 238), pluralism of experience (PP 488), "psychophysik" (*passim*).

51. Compare with the quote with these:

But that is exactly what is done when every individual morsel of the sensational stream takes up the adjacent morsels by coalescing with them. This is just what we mean by the stream's sensible continuity. No element *there* cuts itself off from any other element, as concepts cut themselves from concepts. No part *there* is so small as not to be a place of conflux. No part there is not really *next* its neighbors; which means that there is literally nothing between; which means again that no part goes exactly so far and no farther; that no part absolutely excludes another, but that they compenetrate and are cohesive; that if you tear out one, its roots bring out more with them. (PU 271)

In radical empiricism there is no bedding; it is as if the pieces clung together by their edges, the transitions experienced between them forming their cement. ... Experience itself, taken at large, can grow by its edges. That one moment of it proliferates into the next by transitions which, whether conjunctive or disjunctive, continue the experiential tissue, can not, I contend, be denied. Life is in the transitions as much as in the terms connected. (ERE 86–87; cf. 69)

52. See Francis J. McConnell, *Borden Parker Bowne: His Life and Philosophy* (New York: Abingdon Press, 1929), 277–78, cited by Randall E. Auxier, *Time, Will and Purpose: Living Ideas from the Philosophy of Josiah Royce* (Chicago and La Salle, Illinois: Open Court, 2010).

53. "I am fond of pointing out to my pupils that to be refuted in every century after you have written is the acme of triumph. I always make that remark in connection with Zeno. No one has ever touched Zeno without refuting him, and every century thinks it worth while to refute him." (ESP 114)

54. See §4.2.3.1.

55. See "The Art of Epochal Change" chapter in my *Jamesian Applications*.

56. Skrbina, *Panpsychism in the West.*

57. Wolfe Mays' "introduction" to Piaget's *Principles of Genetic Epistemology* points at the fact that the stages of learning are not quite linear but exhibit a dialectical pattern of a depassement. There is a kind of return through a re-appropriation at a higher level that contains what was not even present at the earlier stage (trans. Wolfe Mays [London: Routledge and Kegan Paul, 1972]).

58. From *koinos*, meaning "common," "public." I picked the concept in order to contrast Bateson's schismogenesis and later realized that Corné-lius Castoriadis made basically the same claim in *L'institution imaginaire de la société* (Paris: Éditions du Seuil, 1975); and (*The Imaginary Insti-*

tution of Society, trans. Kathleen Blamey [Cambridge, Massachusetts: MIT Press, 1987]).

59. For Bateson's term, see, e.g., "Culture Contact and Schismogenesis," *Man* XXXV (1935), 178-83; reprinted in Gregory Bateson, *Steps to an Ecology of Mind: Collected Essays in Anthropology, Psychiatry, Evolution, and Epistemology*, pref. Mark Engel (London: Intertext Books, 1972), 61–72.

60. "Knowing of Things Together," 1894/1895, reprinted in CER.

61. Cf. David Ray Griffin and Huston Smith, *Primordial Truth and Postmodern Theology* (Albany, New York: State University of New York Press, 1989).

62. For all biographical material, see ESP and Victor Augustus Lowe, *Alfred North Whitehead: The Man and His Work, Volume I: 1861–1910; Volume II: 1910–1947*, ed. J. B. Schneewind (Baltimore, Maryland and London: Johns Hopkins University Press, 1985 & 1990).

63. See ESP 12–13 and 200 ff. Cf. Lowe's *Alfred North Whitehead*, vol. I, 204 and 314.

64. James Bradley, "Transformations in Speculative Philosophy, 1914–1945," in *Cambridge History of Philosophy, 1870-1945*, ed. Tom Baldwin, (Cambridge: Cambridge University Press, 2003), 436-46, here 446. See §8.2.1 of my *Jamesian Applications*.

65. Guglielmo Ferrero, *Le Génie latin et le monde moderne* (Paris: Éditions Bernard Grasset, 1917).

66. Whitehead simplifies the historical facts more thoroughly perused in *Adventures of Ideas:* "In Europe, [slavery] was already a decaying institution, slowly withdrawing from slavery to serfdom, from serfdom to feudalism, from feudalism to aristocracy, from aristocracy to legal equality, from legal equality to careers effectively open to talent." (AI 20)

67. ESP 155 and 159; AI 28 nevertheless acknowledges the "enslavement of the indigenous American tribes."

68. Howard Zinn, *A People's History of the United States: 1492–Present* (New York: HarperCollins, 1980) 18.

69. Howard Zinn, *A People's History of the United States,* 143.

70. Charles Hartshorne equally proposes a soft mythology of the colonial times "From Colonial Beginnings to Philosophical Greatness," *The Monist* 48, N°3 (July 1964), 317–31; reprinted in *Creativity in American*

Philosophy (Albany, New York: State University of New York Press, 1984), 1–13.

71. Allison Heartz Johnson, *Whitehead's Philosophy of Civilization* (Boston: Beacon Press, 1962), 88.

72. "Of course, miracles do happen; but it is unwise to expect them" (ESP 58); "miracles are always possible" (ESP 60).

73. Josiah Royce, *The Philosophy of Loyalty* (New York: Macmillan, 1908). Later Whitehead will claim that "In its solitariness the spirit asks, What, in the way of value, is the attainment of life? And it can find no such value till it has merged its individual claim with that of the objective universe. Religion is world-loyalty." (RM 59)

74. See above citations of Howard Zinn, *A People's History of the United States: 1492–Present*.

75. See Alvin Finkel and Clement Leibovitz, *The Chamberlain-Hitler Collusion* (Rendelsham: Merlin Press, 1997)—but also, in chronological order: Albert E. Kahn and Michael Sayers, *The Great Conspiracy Against Russia* (London: Collet, 1946); James Stuart Martin, *All Honorable Men: The Story of the Men on Both Sides of the Atlantic Who Successfully Thwarted Plans to Dismantle the Nazi Cartel System* (Boston: Little, Brown, 1950); Gabriel Kolko, *The Limits of Power: The World and the United States Foreign Policy 1945–1954* (New York: Harper and Row, 1972); Charles Higham, *Trading with the Enemy: The Nazi-American Money Plot, 1933–1949* (New York: Delacorte Press, 1983); Harold James, *The German Slump: Politics and Economics, 1924–1936* (Oxford: Clarendon Press, 1986); Douglas Tottle, *Fraud, Famine and Fascism: The Ukrainian Genocide Myth from Hitler to Harvard* (Toronto: Progress Book, 1987); Thomas G. Paterson, *Contesting Castro: The US and the Triumph of the Cuban Revolution* (New York: Oxford University Press, 1994); Geoffrey Roberts, *The Soviet Union and the Origins of the Second World War: Russo-German Relations and the Road to War, 1933–1941* (New York: Saint Martin's Press, 1995); Frances Stonor Saunders, *Who Paid the Piper? The CIA and the Cultural Cold War* (London: Granta Books, 1999); Reinhold Billstein, Karola Fings, Anita Kugler, *Working for the Enemy: Ford, General Motors, and Forced Labor in Germany during the Second World War*, ed. and trans. Nicholas Levis (New York: Berghahn Books, 2000); Anne Morelli, *Principes élémentaires de la propagande de guerre, utilisables en cas de guerre froide, chaude ou tiède* (Bruxelles: Éditions Labor, 2001); Jacques R. Pauwels, *The Myth of the*

Good War: America in World War II, trans. from the Flemish [2000] by the author (Toronto: James Lorimer & Company, 2002); Lacroix-Riz, Annie, *Le Choix de la défaite: Les élites françaises dans les années 1930* (Paris: Éditions Armand Colin, 2006, nouvelle édition complétée et révisée, 2010).

76. Klemperer wrote in his August 16, 1936, *Tagebücher*'s entry:

> If one day the situation were reversed and the fate of the vanquished lay in my hands, then I would let all the ordinary folk go and even some of the leaders, who might perhaps after all have had honourable intentions and not known what they were doing. But I would have all the intellectuals strung up, and the professors three feet higher than the rest; they would be left hanging from the lamp posts for as long as was compatible with hygiene. (*Ich will Zeugnis ablegen bis zum letzten: Tagebücher 1933–1941* [Berlin: Aufbau Taschenbuch Verlag, 1999] 26; see Omer Bartov in *Germany's War and the Holocaust* [Ithaca: Cornell University Press, 2003], 201).

The original reads:

> Wenn es einmal anders käme und das Schicksal der Besiegten läge in meiner Hand, so ließe ich alles Volk laufen und sogar etliche von den Führern, die es vielleicht doch ehrlich gemeint haben könnten und nicht wußten, was sie taten. Aber die Intellektuellen ließe ich alle aufhängen, und die Professoren einen Meter höher als die andern; sie müßten an den Laternen hängen bleiben, solange es sich irgend mit der Hygiene vertrüge.

77. J. Cobb has remarked that Whiteheadians looking for a process political system of sorts, such as Daniel Day Williams, have actually turned to Reinhold Niebuhr's works ("The Political Implications of Whitehead's Philosophy," in *Process Philosophy and Social Thought*, ed. John B. Cobb, Jr. and W. Widick Schroeder (Chicago, Ill.: Center for Scientific Study of Religion, Studies in Religion and Society, 1981). For a recent synthetic account of the state of the art in the field, see the relevant entries in the *Handbook of Whiteheadian Process Thought*.

78. Letter quoted by Perry, *The Thought and Character of William James*, vol. II, 253.

79. Lord Arthur Ponsonby, *Falsehood in War-Time: Propaganda Lies of the First World War* (London: George Allen and Unwin, 1928). The same stories of alleged atrocities are used not only to spring war but

after the war has ended ("Vae victis"). A systematization of his analysis can be found in Anne Morelli's *Principes élémentaires de la propagande de guerre, utilisables en cas de guerre froide, chaude ou tiède* (Bruxelles: Éditions Labor, 2001).

80. From *Science in the Modern World:*

> This rapid outline of a thoroughgoing organic theory of nature enables us to understand the chief requisites of the doctrine of evolution. The main work, proceeding during this pause at the end of the nineteenth century, was the absorption of this doctrine as guiding the methodology of all branches of science. By a blindness which is almost judicial as being a penalty affixed to hasty, superficial thinking, many religious thinkers opposed the new doctrine; although, in truth, a thoroughgoing evolutionary philosophy is inconsistent with materialism. The aboriginal stuff, or material, from which a materialistic philosophy starts is incapable of evolution. (SMW 107)

81. The concept of *Umwelt* has been instrumental in the development of a zoo- or bio-semiotics and its phenomenological blend (Husserl, Heidegger, Goffman, Merleau-Ponty and Deleuze).

82. Aldous Leonard Huxley, *Brave New World* [1932], with an introduction by David Bradshaw (Hammersmith: HarperCollins, 1994), 203.

83. Marx, in his 1867 Preface to *Capital,* alluding to Perseus.

84. Jakob von Uexküll, *Streifzüge durch die Umwelten von Tieren und Menschen: Ein Bilderbuch unsichtbarer Welten* (Berlin: J. Springer, 1934).

85. William James, "Remarks on Spencer's *Definition of Mind as Correspondence*" [1878], reprinted in CER, 67.

86. It would be interesting to develop this concept along some of the lines suggested by Merleau-Ponty's "lived body" ("corps vécu") or "body itself" ("corps propre").

87. A parallel topology can be found in Edward T. Hall's proxemics. See his *The Hidden Dimension* (Garden City, New York: Doubleday, 1966); cf. *The Silent Language* (Garden City, New York: Doubleday, 1959).

88. What exactly was on Darwin's agenda? Did he really intend to argue for one single tree of life and hence for one single evolutionary scale of consciousness? Is that pyramidal concept furthermore worthy of the pragmatic standpoint? The fact is that the single illustration that enriches *On the Origin of Species* (in chap. 4) does not share the characteristics

of Haeckel's more well-known tree: it basically pictures human races as one of the currently most evolved organisms, not as the sole pinnacle of natural selection. Darwin's vision is dramatically different, as his notebooks make plain. In July 1837, shortly after his return from the renowned *Beagle* voyage (1831–1836), he drew a coral-like diagram and wrote that "the tree of life should perhaps be called the coral of life" (*B Notebook*, 25). Darwin's natural selection does *not* necessarily involve either anthropocentrism or progress.

89. Ben Stein, "In Class Warfare, Guess Which Class Is Winning," *The New York Times*, 26 Nov. 2006.

90. The original ethos might be clan-based segmentary social structures.

91. See also *infra* §6.2.1.

92. Claude Lévi-Strauss, *Race et histoire* (Paris: UNESCO, 1952).

93. Aristotle, *Politics*, 1313a34-b16.

Le despotisme, qui, de sa nature, est craintif, voit dans l'isolement des hommes le gage le plus certain de sa propre durée, et il met d'ordinaire tous ses soins à les isoler. Il n'est pas de vice du cœur humain qui lui agrée autant que l'égoïsme: un despote pardonne aisément aux gouvernés de ne point l'aimer, pourvu qu'ils ne s'aiment pas entre eux. Il ne leur demande pas de l'aider à conduire l'État; c'est assez qu'ils ne prétendent point à le diriger eux-mêmes. Il appelle esprits turbulents et inquiets ceux qui prétendent unir leurs efforts pour créer la prospérité commune, et, changeant le sens naturel des mots, il nomme bons citoyens ceux qui se renferment étroitement en eux-mêmes." (Alexis de Tocqueville, *La Démocratie en Amérique* [1835–1840], Paris: Robert Laffont, 1986), II, Second Part, Chap. IV.

94. See Roland Marchand (1933–1997), *Advertising the American Dream* (Berkeley: University of California Press, 1985.

95. Arendt would have written "solitariness" (*The Life of the Mind*, 185).

96. Translated by Henry Reeve (London: Saunders and Otley, 1835). "Une idée fausse, mais claire et précise, aura toujours plus de puissance dans le monde qu'une idée vraie, mais complexe." (*De la démocratie en Amérique*, 171)

97. E.g., Mark Townsend and Paul Harris, "Now the Pentagon tells Bush: climate change will destroy us," *The Observer*, Sunday 22 February 2004.

98. Democracy *per se* starts in Athens in 507 BCE with Clisthene's reformation and ends in 338 BCE with Athen surrendering to Macedonia. Between the birth of Pericles (495–429) and Aristotle's death (384–22) we have the acme of Greek civilization. Socrates (470–399) lived precisely at that time, between the end of the Greco-Persian Wars (498–79) and the end of the Peloponnesian War (431–04).

99. Vance Packard, *The Hidden Persuaders* (New York: David McKay, 1957).

100. Solon's (643–558) law against political apathy, passed in 594–93, is celebrated by Aristotle (*Constitution of Athens*, 8.5), also Plutarch (Solon, 20.1) and Pericles (quoted by Thucydides' *History of the Peloponnesian War*).

101. There is much to be gained by examining Howard Zinn's diagnosis (*A People's History of the United States: 1492–Present*) from the perspective of Bernays and Goebbels:

> If you tell a lie big enough and keep repeating it, people will eventually come to believe it. The lie can be maintained only for such time as the State can shield the people from the political, economic and/or military consequences of the lie. It thus becomes vitally important for the State to use all of its powers to repress dissent, for the truth is the mortal enemy of the lie, and thus by extension, the truth is the greatest enemy of the State. (The exact reference is, however, uncertain.)

102. The neologism is due to the collective "Pièces et Main d'œuvre" in *Terreur et possession: Enquête sur la police des populations à l'ère technologique* (Montreuil: Éditions L'Echappée, Négatif, 2008), 273. I do not use it here in the same way.

103. Bertram Gross, *Friendly Fascism: The New Face of Power in America* (New York: M. Evans & Co., 1980) and Sheldon S. Wolin, *Democracy Incorporated: Managed Democracy and the Specter of Inverted Totalitarianism* (Princeton: Princeton University Press, 2008).

104. For all this see Naomi Klein, *The Shock Doctrine: The Rise of Disaster Capitalism* (New York: ICM Books, 2007).

105. The neologism is from Bertrand de Jouvenel (1903–1987), who created the eponymous journal in 1974.

106. E.g., "On ne peut juger que de ce qui se voit; ce qui explique le jugement sur l'histoire: le fondement des civilisations c'est la technique

et non pas la philosophie ou la religion." (Jacques Ellul, *La Technique ou l'Enjeu du siècle* [1954], [Paris: Éditions Economica, 1990], 43)

107. Francis Bacon, *Nova Atlantis*, 1624.

108. Some pioneering work has been done by Pièces et Main d'œuvre, e.g., in *Rfid: la Police Totale Puces Intelligentes et Mouchardage Electronique* (Paris: Éditions de L'Échappée, 2008).

109. Jeremy Bentham, *"Panopticon:" or, the Inspection-House; containing the idea of a new principle of construction applicable to any sort of establishment, in which persons of any description are to be kept under inspection; and in Particular to Penitentiary-houses, Prisons, Houses of industry, Workhouses, Poor Houses, Manufacturies, Madhouses, Lazarettos, Hospitals, and Schools; with a plan of management adopted to the principle; in a series of letters, written in the year 1787, from Crechoff in White Russia, to a friend in England* (Dublin: Thomas Byrne, 1791).

110. Michel Foucault, *Surveiller et punir: Naissance de la prison* (Paris: NRF Éditions Gallimard, 1975).

111. The Rockefeller Foundation, *Scenarios for the Future of Technology and International Development*, 2010

112. The Rockefeller Foundation, *Scenarios for the Future of Technology*, 39.

113. This is Steve Mann's neologism. See Steve Mann, Jason Nolan and Barry Wellman, "Sousveillance: Inventing and Using Wearable Computing Devices for Data Collection in Surveillance Environments" in *Surveillance & Society* 1(3) (2003), 331–55; see also The Rockefeller Foundation, *Scenarios for the Future of Technology*, 27 and 31.

114. Richard Silberglitt, Philip S. Antón, David R. Howell, Anny Wong with Natalie Gassman, Brian A. Jackson, Eric Landree, Shari Lawrence Pfleeger, Elaine M. Newton, and Felicia Wu, *The Global Technology Revolution 2020: In-Depth Analyses Bio/Nano/Materials/Information Trends, Drivers, Barriers, and Social Implications* [Prepared for the National Intelligence Council; Approved for public release; distribution unlimited], Santa Monica, RAND—National Security Research Division, Technical Report, 2006.

115. Communication de la Commission des Communautés européennes au Parlement européen, au Conseil, au Comité économique et social européen et au Comité des régions: *L'identification par radiofréquence (RFID) en Europe: vers un cadre politique*, Bruxelles, le 15.3.2007. Voir

Secretariat of the European Group on Ethics in Science and New Technologies to the European Commission, *The Ethical aspects of ICT implants in the human body. Proceedings of the Roundtable Debate* [Amsterdam, 21 December 2004], publié en 2005. The group is composed of 15 members: 4 theologians (Emmanuel Agius, Peter Dabrock, Hille Haker, Günter Virt); 4 ethicists (Inez de Beaufort, Siobhan O'Sullivan, Laura Palazzani, Marie-Jo Thiel); 4 lawyers (Julian Kinderlerer, Paula Martinho da Silva, Linda Nielsen, Herman Nys); 2 M.D.s (Andrzej Gorski, Ritva Halila); 1 geneticist (Pere Puigdomènech Rosell).

116. Trotskyism is just a specular image of capitalism, but its logic is difficult to bypass (remember also Chomsky's "mafia principle"). James Connolly, for example, repeatedly underlined that the Irish will not get rid of the British yoke unless they establish a socialist Republic. If not, the military occupation will be simply replaced by a capitalistic one. This, he argued, is what happened with the USA: "Not a Republic as in the United States, where the power of the purse has established a new tyranny under the forms of freedom; where, one hundred years after the feet of the last British red-coat polluted the streets of Boston, British landlords and financiers impose upon American citizens a servitude compared with which the tax of pre-Revolution days were merely a trifle." (James Connolly, *Selected Writings*, ed. P. Berresford Ellis [1973] [London: Pluto Press, 1997])

117. James F. Eder, Jr., *On the Road to Tribal Extinction: Depopulation, Deculturation, and Adaptive Well-Being Among the Batak of the Philippines*, (Berkeley: University of California Press, 1987).

118. Jean-Pierre Berlan speaks of "ecocide" ("L'écocide, ou l'assassinat de la vie").

119. See S. Jay Olshansky *et al.*, "A potential decline in life expectancy in the US in the 21st century," *New England Journal of Medicine* 352, (2005), 1138-45; Claude Aubert, *Espérance de vie, la fin des illusions* (Paris: Éditions Terre vivante, 2006).

120. Jean-Pierre Berlan, "Les OGM, la faim et l'Académie des sciences," *L'Écologiste* N°7, Vol. 3 (June 2002), 41–47.

121. Jean-Pierre Dupuy, *Pour un catastrophisme éclairé: quand l'impossible est certain* (Paris: Éditions du Seuil, 2002). Cf. European Commission. Community Health and Consumer Protection, *Nanotechnologies: A Preliminary Risk Analysis*, www, 2004.

122. Jacques Ellul, *La Technique ou l'Enjeu du siècle*, 75–76, 86, 157, 216, 275, 357.

123. Vance Packard, *The Waste Makers* (New York: David McKay, 1960, 55 ff.

124. Les fameuses expériences de Pavlov (1849–1938) sur les réflexes conditionnés et conditionnels eurent lieu de 1890 à 1900. Le texte fondateur est de Marshall Hall: "On the Reflex Function of the Medulla Oblongata and the Medulla Spinalis," 1832.

125. Cf. John Broadus Watson, *Behaviorism* (London: Kegan Paul, 1928).

126. Herbart was a philosopher and a pedagogue; Weber and Helmoltz were professors of anatomy and physiology; Fechner was a physicist; Wundt was an M.D. Wundt created, in 1879, within the philosophy department of Leipzig's university, the first laboratory of experimental psychology: l'Institut für Experimentelle Psychologie.

127. Bruce Kuklick, *The Rise of American Philosophy: Cambridge, Massachusetts 1860–1930* (New Haven and London: Yale University Press, 1977), 475.

128. Edward Bernays, *Propaganda* (New York: Horace Liveright, 1928) and *The Engineering of Consent* (Norman: University of Oklahoma Press, 1947/1955).

129. From Fleet Admiral William Leahy, also chair of the Chiefs of Staff:

> It is my opinion that the use of this barbarous weapon at Hiroshima and Nagasaki was of no material assistance in our war against Japan. The Japanese were already defeated and ready to surrender because of the effective sea blockade and the successful bombing with conventional weapons... My own feeling was that in being the first to use it, we had adopted an ethical standard common to the barbarians of the Dark Ages. I was not taught to make wars in that fashion, and that wars cannot be won by destroying women and children. (William D. Leahy, *I Was There* (Whittlesey House 1950), 441)

For his part, Eisenhower wrote:

> [I]n [July] 1945...Secretary of War Stimson, visiting my headquarters in Germany, informed me that our government was preparing to drop an atomic bomb on Japan. I was one of those who felt that there were a number of cogent reasons to question the wisdom of such an act. ... the Secretary, upon giving me the news of the successful

bomb test in New Mexico, and of the plan for using it, asked for my reaction, apparently expecting a vigorous assent. During his recitation of the relevant facts, I had been conscious of a feeling of depression and so I voiced to him my grave misgivings, first on the basis of my belief that Japan was already defeated and that dropping the bomb was completely unnecessary, and secondly because I thought that our country should avoid shocking world opinion by the use of a weapon whose employment was, I thought, no longer mandatory as a measure to save American lives. It was my belief that Japan was, at that very moment, seeking some way to surrender with a minimum loss of 'face'. The Secretary was deeply perturbed by my attitude." (Dwight Eisenhower, *Mandate For Change. 1953–1956; The White House Years* [New York, Doubleday, 1963], 380) Cf. Gar Alperovitz, *The Decision to Use the Atomic Bomb* [New York: Vintage, 1996].)

130. Vance Packard, *The Waste Makers*, 235.

131. Quoted by Jeffrey Kaplan in "The Gospel of Consumption And the better future we left behind," *Orion Magazine*, May/June 2008.

132. Charles F. Kettering, "Keep the Consumer Dissatisfied," *Nation's Business*, 17, no. 1 (January 1929), 30–31, 79.

133. William Burroughs, *The Naked Lunch* [1959] (New York: Grove Press, 1991), xxxvi-xxxvii; cf. 186 ff.

134. Gary S. Cross, *Time and Money: The Making of Consumer Culture* (London: Routledge, 1993).

135. Spinoza, *Tractatus Theologico-Politicus*, 1670, Preface.

136. Aldous Leonard Huxley, *Brave New World* [1932], Foreword [1946].

137. The transition took place thanks to the influence of telegraphy upon the written press. The news has become decontextualized, overabundant, contradictory, futile, irrelevant, but entertaining. See Neil Postman's analysis in *Amusing Ourselves to Death: Public Discourse in the Age of Show Business* (New York, Penguin, 1985).

138. Propaganda and psychology as an academic discipline have had a common destiny, cf. the question of "The Committee on Public Information" or "Creel Committee," created by Woodrow Wilson in 1917.

139. Arthur O. Lovejoy and George Boas, *Primitivism and Related Ideas in Antiquity* [1935], with supplementary essays by W. F. Albright and P. E. Dumont (Baltimore and London: Johns Hopkins University Press, 1997).

140. Edward L. Bernays, Noam Chomsky, Jean Ovide Bourdeau, etc.

141. See also my recent Krakow keynote lecture, "Oldthinkers unbellyfeel Whiteheadian socialism," forthcoming in the proceedings of the International Whitehead Conference.

142. Carl Philip von Clausewitz (Hrsg. von Marie von Clausewitz), *Vom Kriege, Hinterlassenes Werk des Generals Carl von Clausewitz*, Bd. 1–3, (Berlin: Ferdinand Dümmler, 1832–1834), Book VIII.

143. David Rothkopf, *Superclass: The Global Power Elite and the World They Are Making* (New York: Farrar, Straus and Giroux & Little, Brown, 2008). When the Phantom Drophead Coupé debuted at the 2007 North American International Auto Show in Detroit, with a retail price of 630000€ excluded VAT, Rolls-Royce was allegedly targeting 85,000 potential consumers, 80,000 of them in the USA, 20,000 in Europe and 12,000 in Asia.

144. George Orwell, *Nineteen Eighty-Four*, 246.

145. G. Bateson, Don D. Jackson, Jay Haley, John H. Weakland, "Toward a Theory of Schizophrenia," *Behavioral Science* I (1956), 251–64.

146. "I understand HOW, I do not understand WHY." (*Nineteen Eighty-Four*, 91, 300)

147. "You are ruling over us for our own good. . . . The Party seeks power entirely for its own sake." (*Nineteen Eighty-Four*, 301)

148. "The Cyprus experiment was convincing." (*Brave New World*, 203).

149. See Huxley's October 1949 letter, reprinted in the Appendix of his *Brave New World Revisited* [1958] (New York: Harper & Row, Harper Perrenial Modern Classics, 2006). Huxley had actually been Orwell's French teacher at Eton in the years 1917–1921.

150. Arendt, *The Origins of Totalitarianism* (New York: Harcourt Brace, 1951; enlarged 1958).

151. Orwell, *Nineteen Eighty-Four*, 305-307.

152. Jack London, *The Iron Heel* (New York: Grosset & Dunlap, 1908), 96-97. William Steinhoff insists on the influence of London's *Iron Heel* and of H. G. Wells' *Island* on *Nineteen Eighty-Four* (*George Orwell and the Origins of 1984*, [East Lansing: University of Michigan Press, 1975]).

153. Goya, *Saturno devorando a un hijo*, 1819–1923.

154. The sexual practices around consensual humiliation and power exchange named by the compound acronym, BDSM (Bondage and Discipline, Dominance and Submission, and Sadism and Masochism) belong more to the pathology of power than to the game of power.

155. In *Brave New World Revisited*, 1958, quoted above.

156. Sir Julian Huxley, *What Dare I Think? The Challenge of Modern Science to Human Action and Belief,* Including the Henry LaBarre Jayne Foundation Lectures (Philadelphia) for 1931, (London: Chatto & Windus & Harper, 1931).

157. Aldous Huxley, Foreword, 1946, in *Brave New World* [1932], quoted in full at §6.2.2.3.

158. Incubators are already featured in Huxley's *Crome Yellow* (London: Chatto & Windus, 1921), 4; John Burdon Sanderson Haldane's *Daedalus or Science and the Future* ([1923] 3rd impr. (London: Kegan Paul, Trench, Trubner, 1924); Bertrand Russell's *The Scientific Outlook* (London: George Allen and Unwin, 1931); and Sir Julian Huxley's *What Dare I Think? The Challenge of Modern Science to Human Action and Belief.* Peter Firchow's "Science and Conscience in Huxley's Brave New World" (*Contemporary Literature*, Vol. 16, No. 3 [1975], 301–16) asks who influenced who. He remarks that Edwin Arthur Burtt, *The Metaphysical Foundations of Modern Physical Science: A Historical and Critical Essay* (New York: Harcourt, Brace, 1924); 2nd edition, revised (London: Routledge & Kegan Paul,1932) was Huxley's handbook at one point.

159. Cf. Peter Firchow, "Science and Conscience in Huxley's *Brave New World.*"

160. Cf. Pascal Nouvel, *Histoire des amphétamines* (Paris: Presses Universitaires de France, 2009).

161. Philippe Pignarre, *Les Malheurs des psys: Psychotropes et médicalisation du social* (Paris: Éditions La Découverte, 2006).

162. "Sleep-teaching" (*Brave New World*, 21, 24, 38, 91, 101, 234) or emotional-engineering (*Brave New World*, 58); "engineer into feeling" (*Brave New World*, 163): (subliminal) conditioning (*Brave New World*, 214) and scientific propaganda. Nonrationality of the "words without reason" (*Brave New World*, 24; cf. 23).

163. Bernard Crick, *George Orwell. A Life* (London: Secker and Warburg, 1980).

164. Stalin was General Secretary of the Communist Party from 1922 until his death in 1953 and Generalissimus of the Soviet Union from 1943 until 1953.

165. Geoffrey Roberts, *The Soviet Union and the Origins of the Second World War. Russo-German Relations and the Road to War, 1933–1941* (New York: Saint Martin's Press, 1995). Domenico Losurdo, *Stalin, Storia e critica di una leggenda nera* (Carocci: Milano, 2008).

166. George Orwell, *Nineteen Eighty-Four* [1949], 2003, 235.

167. Insulin shock therapy (1934), psychosurgery (1935), electroconvulsive therapy (1937).

168. Gustave Le Bon, *La Psychologie des foules* (Paris: Éditions Alcan, 1895); Wilfred Trotter, "Herd instinct and its bearing on the psychology of civilized man," *Sociological Review*, July 1908 and January 1909 (later included in his *Instincts of the Herd in Peace and War*, 1919); Edward L. Bernays, *Propaganda* (New York: Horace Liveright, 1928) and *The Engineering of Consent* [1947] (Norman: University of Oklahoma Press, 1955); Elias Canetti, *Masse und Macht* (Jena: Fischer, 1960).

169. Cf. Hippolyte Bernheim, *De la Suggestion dans l'état hypnotique et dans l'état de veille* (Paris: Octzave Doin, Éditeur, 1882).

170. William Burroughs, *The Naked Lunch* [1959] (New York: Grove Press, 1991); junk is the ideal product, the ultimate merchandise, xxxvii.

171. Zola's *Gin Palace* [*L'Assomoir*, 1877]; absinthe and laudanum are another matter altogether.

172. For instance, in his Epilogue to *The Devils of Loudun*, published in 1953, he is still critical of the religious potential of purposeful intoxications. This discussion finds an echo in Aldous Huxley's *Island*, 136–37.

173. See his 14 March 1956 letter to Humphry Osmond, and Peter Firchow's "Brave at Last: Huxley's Western and Eastern Utopias" (*Aldous Huxley Annual I*, 2004, 157–74).

174. Richard Bartlett Gregg, *The Value of Voluntary Simplicity* (Wallingford, Pennsylvania: Pendle Hill, A Quaker Center for Religious and Social Study, 1936).

175. "Perfectibilité": Rousseau and Condorcet.

176. Huxley, letter to Orwell, 21 October 1949 (the book itself was published 8 June), reprinted in Huxley, Aldous Leonard, *Brave New World Revisited,* New York, Harper & Row, 1958.

177. Alexis de Tocqueville:

Je veux imaginer sous quels traits nouveaux le despotisme pourrait se produire dans le monde: je vois une foule innombrable d'hommes semblables et égaux qui tournent sans repos sur eux-mêmes pour se procurer de petits et vulgaires plaisirs, dont ils emplissent leur âme. Chacun d'eux, retiré à l'écart, est comme étranger à la destinée de tous les autres: ses enfants et ses amis particuliers forment pour lui toute l'espèce humaine; quant au demeurant de ses concitoyens, il est à côté d'eux, mais il ne les voit pas; il les touche et ne les sent point; il n'existe qu'en lui-même et pour lui seul, et, s'il lui reste encore une famille, on peut dire du moins qu'il n'a plus de patrie. Au-dessus de ceux-là s'élève un pouvoir immense et tutélaire, qui se charge seul d'assurer leur jouissance et de veiller sur leur sort. Il est absolu, détaillé, régulier, prévoyant et doux. Il ressemblerait à la puissance paternelle si, comme elle, il avait pour objet de préparer les hommes à l'âge viril; mais il ne cherche, au contraire, qu'à les fixer irrévocablement dans l'enfance; il aime que les citoyens se réjouis-sent, pourvu qu'ils ne songent qu'à se réjouir. Il travaille volontiers à leur bonheur; mais il veut en être l'unique agent et le seul arbitre; il pourvoit à leur sécurité, prévoit et assure leurs besoins, facilite leurs plaisirs, conduit leurs principales affaires, dirige leur industrie, règle leurs successions, divise leurs héritages, que ne peut-il leur ôter entièrement le trouble de penser et la peine de vivre?" (*De la Démocratie en Amérique* [pt 2], 648.

178. Catherine Keller, *From a Broken Web: Separation, Sexism, and Self* (Boston: Beacon, 1986), 223.

179. Cf. Michel Schneider, *Big Mother. Psychopathologie de la vie politique* (Paris: Éditions Odile Jacob, 2002).

180. David Murakami Wood, ed., *A Report on the Surveillance Society. For the Information Commissioner by the Surveillance Studies Network*, September 2006, available online.

181. In September 2014, the FBI announced that its FRP is fully operational, with an NGI database containing over 100 million individual records linking a person's fingerprints, palm prints, iris scans and

facial-recognition data with personal information like their home address, age, legal status, etc.

182. Vance Packard, *The Hidden Persuaders* (New York: David McKay, Pocket Books, 1957), 239–40; French trans., *La persuasion clandestine* (Paris: Calmann-Lévy, 1989).

183. It is not easy to give a date of birth to the Luddites, that can after all be seen as the late legacy of Socrates, Cynics and Stoics, but Thoreau (*Walden*, 1854) seems to provide a likely date.

184. Warwick, Kevin, "I want to be a cyborg," *The Guardian*, 26 January 2000.

185. Emmanuel Carrère [d'Encausse]:

> Ressemblance troublante entre personnalité "androïde" et person-nalité "schizoïde," que Jung décrivait par l'économie permanente des sentiments. Un schizoïde pense plus qu'il ne ressent. Il a du monde et de son propre discours une compréhension purement intellectuelle, abstraite . . . Un schizoïde est capable de dire, plutôt que "J'ai besoin de speed pour soutenir une conversation:" "Je reçois des signaux venant d'organismes voisins. Mais je suis incapable de produire mes propres signaux avant d'avoir fait recharger mes batter-ies. *(Je suis vivant et vous êtes mort* [Paris: Éditions du Seuil, 1993], 163). See, for example, *Do Androids Dream of Electric Sheep?* (1968).

186. This is not the place to consider the incoherencies and inapplica-bility of psychoanalysis in general and Freud and Lacan in particular.

187. Cf. Kevin Warwick's multiple micro electrodes array.

188. Pièces et Main d'œuvre, *Terreur et possession: Enquête sur la police des populations à l'ère technologique* (Montreuil: Éditions L'Echappée, 2008).

189. Draft paper for *The Condemned Playground: Aldous Huxley and His Contemporaries,* Fifth International Aldous Huxley Symposium, Balliol College, Oxford, Sept. 1–4, 2013.

190. This contrast is akin to Aristotle's criterion structuring the typology of his *Politics* (III, vii; cf. IV, ii & *passim*): *who* exercises power and *for whom*?

191. Aldous Huxley, *Brave New World* [1932], antepenultimate chapter XVI.

192. George Orwell, *Nineteen Eighty-Four* [1949], introduction by

Thomas Pynchon (London: Penguin Books, [also ed. Penguin 1954], 2003), 301. See §7.3.

193. *Brave New World*, 200-201; the full quotation is to be found at §8.1.1.

194. *Brave New World*, 202-203; see also the quotation on "the Cyprus experiment was convincing," §4.2.1.

195. Aldous Huxley, *Brave New World*, 207. Mond continues: "Our Ford himself did a great deal to shift the emphasis from truth and beauty to comfort and happiness. Mass production demanded the shift. Universal happiness keeps the wheels steadily turning; truth and beauty can't" (208). "That's how I paid. By choosing to serve happiness. Other people's—not mine" (209).

196. "Société-horloge" vs thermodynamical societies ("société-vapeur")— Georges Charbonnier, *Entretiens avec Claude Lévi-Strauss* [1959] (Paris: Éditions Julliard et Librairie Plon, 1961). To speak of a "clockwork" society can either be derogatory or complimentary. When Lévi-Strauss speaks enthusiastically of the archaic communities as being truly democratic, he obviously embraces the latter meaning.

197. George Orwell, *Nineteen Eighty-Four*, 300–302

198. George Orwell, *Nineteen Eighty-Four*, 306

199. "Seek simplicity and distrust it." (*The Concept of Nature* [1920], [Cambridge, Cambridge University Press, 1964], 163).

200. Jacques Ellul, *Le système technicien* (Paris: Éditions Calmann-Lévy, 1977. Constantin Virgil Gheorghiu, *The Twenty-Fifth Hour* [1949], Trans. from the Romanian by Rita Eldon (New York: Alfred A Knopf, 1950).

201. "On ne regrette jamais ce que l'on a jamais eu. . . . La première raison pour laquelle les hommes servent volontairement, c'est qu'ils naissent serfs et qu'ils sont élevés comme tels." (Étienne de La Boétie, *Discours de la servitude volontaire* [1574]. Traduction en français moderne et postface de Séverine Auffret, Paris, Éditions Mille et une nuits, 1995, 17–19; I quote Harry Kurz's translation, p. 62)

202. "The supreme mystery of despotism, its prop and stay, is to keep men in a state of deception, and with the specious title of religion to cloak the fear by which they must be held in check, so that they will fight for their servitude as if for salvation." (Spinoza, *Tractatus theologico-politicus*,

Tr. by Samuel Shirley, 389)

203. David Hume, "Of the First Principles of Government":

Nothing appears more surprising to those, who consider human affairs with a philosophical eye, than the easiness with which the many are governed by the few; and the implicit submission, with which men resign their own sentiments and passions to those of their rulers. When we enquire by what means this wonder is effected, we shall find, that, as Force is always on the side of the governed, the governors have nothing to support them but opinion. It is therefore, on opinion only that government is founded; and this maxim extends to the most despotic and most military governments, as well as to the most free and most popular. The sultan of Egypt, or the emperor of Rome, might drive his harmless subjects, like brute beasts, against their sentiments and inclination: But he must, at least, have led his *mamalukes*, or *praetorian bands*, like men, by their opinion." (Essay V of *Essays, Moral and Political,* Edinburgh, 1741)

204. Aldous Huxley, "Foreword" [1946] in *Brave New World*, 1932, quoted in full §6.2.2.3. Interestingly enough, Orwell teases the same idea at one point:

By comparison with that existing today, all the tyrannies of the past were half-hearted and inefficient. The ruling groups were always infected to some extent by liberal ideas, and were content to leave loose ends everywhere, to regard only the overt act and to be uninterested in what their subjects were thinking. Even the Catholic Church of the Middle Ages was tolerant by modern standards. Part of the reason for this was that in the past no government had the power to keep its citizens under constant surveillance. The invention of print, however, made it easier to manipulate public opinion, and the film and the radio carried the process further. With the development of television, and the technical advance which made it possible to receive and transmit simultaneously on the same instrument [telescreen], private life came to an end. Every citizen, or at least every citizen important enough to be worth watching, could be kept for twenty-four hours a day under the eyes of the police and in the sound of official propaganda, with all other channels of communication closed. The possibility of enforcing not only complete obedience to the will of the State, but complete uniformity of opinion on all subjects, now existed for the first time." (*Nineteen Eighty-Four*, 235)

205. "Love is the plummet as well as the astrolabe of God's mysteries; . . . the teleological pull from in front. This teleological pull is a pull from the divine Ground of things." (Aldous Huxley, *The Perennial Philosophy*, [London: Chatto & Windus, 1947], 274, 276.)

206. Tocqueville actually speaks of "servitude" (656), "asservissement," "barbarie," "despotisme doux" (646). "Friendly fascism" is Bertram Gross' expression: cf. his *Friendly Fascism: The New Face of Power in America* (New York: M. Evans & Co., 1980)—that curiously does not quote Tocqueville.

207. John Burdon Sanderson Haldane, *Daedalus or Science and the Future* [A paper read to the heretics, Cambridge, on February 4th, 1923], 3rd impr. (London: Kegan Paul, Trench, Trubner, 1924); Sir Julian Huxley, *What Dare I Think? The Challenge of Modern Science to Human Action and Belief*, including the Henry LaBarre Jayne Foundation Lectures (Philadelphia) for 1931 (London: Chatto & Windus & Harper, 1931).

208. John Newsinger claims that "while [Orwell] certainly knew about and wholeheartedly condemned the mass murder of European Jews perpetrated by the Nazis, there is just no evidence to show that this was in any way central to his thinking." (*The Cambridge Companion to George Orwell*, ed. John Rodden, [Cambridge, Cambridge University Press, 2007], 123).

209. George Orwell, *Nineteen Eighty-Four*, 301 ff. See § 7.3.2. Cf. "Will you please remember, throughout our conversation, that I have it in my power to inflict pain on you at any moment and to whatever degree I choose? If you tell me any lies, or attempt to prevaricate in any way, or even fall below your usual level of intelligence, you will cry out with pain, instantly. Do you understand that?'" (281) See my *Whitehead's Pancreativism. Jamesian Applications* (Frankfurt/Paris: Ontos Verlag, 2011).

210. Aldous Huxley, *Brave New World Revisited* [1958], 114.

211. See, e.g., Geoffrey Roberts, *Stalin's Wars: From World War to Cold War, 1939–1953* (New Haven & London: Yale University Press, 2006); Domenico Losurdo, *Stalin, Storia e critica di una leggenda nera*, Milano: Carocci, 2008.

212. They were factually anticipated during the Indian wars (e.g., the Cherokee removal, 1836–39).

213. Bruno Bettelheim, "Individual and Mass Behavior in Extreme Situations," *Journal of Abnormal and Social Psychology* 38 (1943), 417–52, here 418–19.

214. Leo Löwenthal, "Terror's Atomization of Man," *Commentary* 1 (1945/1946), 1–8.

215. "I believe that [the fascist terror] is deeply rooted in the trends of modern civilization, and especially in the pattern of modern economy" (1). According to the axioms of neoliberalism, which are likely to have been written by Frank H. Knight (1885–1972), pure and perfect competition mainly requires atomicity of supply and demand (i.e., infinite buyers and sellers), homogenous products, market transparency (i.e., perfect information), zero entry and exit barriers, and perfect factor mobility.

216. Lewis Mumford, *Technics and Civilization* (New York: Harcourt Brace and Company, 1934).

217. Löwenthal:

> Essentially, the modern system of terror amounts to the atomization of the individual. We shudder at the tortures inflicted on the physical bodies of men; we should be no less appalled by its menace to the spirit of man.... The individual under terrorist conditions is never alone and always alone. He becomes numb and rigid not only in relation to his neighbor but also in relation to himself; fear robs him of the power of spontaneous emotional or mental reaction. Thinking becomes a stupid crime; it endangers his life. The inevitable consequence is that stupidity spreads as a contagious disease among the terrorized population. Human beings live in a state of stupor, in a moral coma" (2).

To specify this one should revisit the physiology of predation, which happens to throw light on the mechanism of (post-)traumatic stress: the keys are hyperarousal, constriction, fight/flight or freezing/dissociation, release/collapsus or helplessness, re-enactment.

218. Löwenthal:

> In a terrorist society, in which everything is most carefully planned, the plan for the individual is—to have none; to become and to remain a mere object, a bundle of conditioned reflexes which amply respond to a series of manipulated and calculated shocks. [...]In

a system that reduces life to a chain of disconnected reactions to shock, personal communication tends to lose all meaning (3).

219. Viktor Frankl, *Trotzdem Ja Zum Leben Sagen: Ein Psychologe erlebt das Konzentrationslager* (Vienna: Deuticke, 1946); Virgil Gheorghiu, *Twenty-Fifth Hour*, 1949; Victor Klemperer, *LTI-Lingua Tertii Imperii: Notizbuch eines Philologen* (Leipzig: Reclam Verlag, 1947); Hannah Arendt, *Eichmann in Jerusalem: A Report on the Banality of Evil* [1963], revised and enlarged ed. (Hardmondsworth: Penguin Books Ltd, 1977).

220. Cf., e.g., Françoise Sironi, *Bourreaux et victimes: Psychologie de la torture* (Paris: Odile Jacob, 1999).

221. Letter to George Orwell, 21 October, 1949, in Huxley, *Brave New World Revisited*, "P.S." section, 8 ff.

222. "The Ultimate Revolution," 20 March 1962, Berkeley Language Center—Speech Archive SA 0269 cf., e.g.: http://pulsemedia.org/2009/02/02/aldous-huxley-the-ultimate-revolution/.

223. See Griffin's constructive postmodernism, e.g., *The Reenchantment of Science: Postmodern Proposals* (Albany, New York: State University of New York Press, 1988). Cf. my *Whitehead's Pancreativism. Jamesian Applications*, §8.2.3.

224. To simplify, there are basically two types of RFID tags: passive RFID tags, which have no built-in power source and require an external electromagnetic field to initiate a signal transmission; and active RFID tags, which contain a battery and can transmit signals once an external source ("Interrogator") has been successfully identified. Some are "read-only" chips, others can be modified after implantation. In order to keep the argument tight, the following schematization of the technical possibilities could be proposed: to peruse, on the one hand, passive nanochips that can be widely used to tag commodities; on the other, active microchips that are developed in order to help specialized institutions to cope with some animal or some human beings. The thesis would be that we are about to enter bigmotherhood and that, from there, Big Brother will arise. Please note that the impending merging of bio and nano technologies with IT offers actually a far gloomier picture than the one I sketch here, but it is also more difficult to envision pragmatically in the context of this short essay. Some pioneering work has been done by a French group—Pièces et Main d'œuvre—e.g. in *Rfid: la Police Totale—Puces Intelligentes et Mouchardage Electronique* (Paris: Éditions de L'Échappée, 2008).

225. The expression "global systemic crisis" covers two main dimensions: on the one hand, the fact that all fields of human activity are now in a critical state and, on the other, the fact that all these dysfunctions are linked. The dematerialization of the economy fostered a global financial speculation; peak oil means the end of cheap energy and of all the petrol-derivative; the collapse of biosphere involves the exhaustion of vital resources (minerals, water, etc.), but also climate change (as it is linked with pollution), and the 6th mass extinction; social unrest (riots, famine, pandemics) are expected since the political vacuum is flabbergasting; wars and neocolonialism are already widespread while the demographic explosion (social Darwinism) remains threatening.

226. "See how largely philosophy has been committed to a metaphysics of feudalism. By this I mean it has thought of things in the world as occupying certain grades of value, or as having fixed degrees of truth, ranks of reality." (John Dewey, "Philosophy and Democracy," address delivered in November 1918, *University of California Chronicle* 21 [January 1919], 39-54; reprinted in *Characters and Events: Popular Essays in Social and Political Philosophy*, ed. Joseph Ratner, vol. 2 (New York: Henry Holt, 1929), 841–55, here 852.)

227. Cf., e.g., Hadot's *What Is Ancient Philosophy?* [1995], trans. Michael Chase (Cambridge: Harvard University Press, 2002). Hadot does not treat the question of the two Renaissances; my point here is twofold: one, it is important to discriminate the first Renaissance, which was close enough to worship nature, and the second Renaissance, which condemned the spirituality of immanence and re-established the hierarchical power in society and Church by linking it to a god understood as a Babylonian despot. Two, the turning point between the two schools is neither scientific nor philosophical but political: the new ideas had to be stopped when they started to lead more and more to communist utopias.

228. Technical totalitarianism is spelled out by Ellul with six characteristics: automatism of the technical choice, self-growth, unity, drive ("entraînement"), universalism, autonomy.

229. Kevin Kelly, *Out of Control: The New Biology of Machines, Social Systems, and the Economic World* (Boston: Addison Wesley, 1994).

230. George Orwell, *Nineteen Eighty-Four* [London, Martin Secker & Warburg, 1949], Introduction by Thomas Pynchon (London: Penguin Books, 2003), 59-60. Orwell mentions the famous *Encyclopaedia Britannica*'s XIth edition of 1910–11.

231. Victor Klemperer, *LTI—Lingua Tertii Imperii: Notizbuch eines Philologen* (Leipzig, Reclam Verlag, 1947).

232. George Orwell, *Nineteen Eighty-Four*, 246.

233. "Address on the First Anniversary of the Alliance for Progress," White House reception for diplomatic corps of the Latin American republics, 13 March 1962. Public Papers of the Presidents—John F. Kennedy (1962), 223.

234. Thomas Frank, *What's the Matter With Kansas? How Conservatives Won the Heart of America* (New York: Metropolitan Books, 2004).

235. Shlomo Sand, *The Invention of the Jewish People* [2008] (London: Verso Books, 2009).

236. Ivan Illich, *Deschooling Society*, 1971.

237. Nico Hirtt, L'École prostituée, l'offensive des entreprises sur l'enseignement (Bruxelles: Éditions Labor, "Espaces de Liberté," 2001).

238. Paul Tillich, *The Courage to Be* (New Haven: Yale University Press, 1952); R. D. Laing, *The Divided Self: An Existential Study in Sanity and Madness* (London: Tavistock Publications, 1960).

239. Frédéric Dabi, "1938–1944: Des accords de Munich à la libération de Paris ou l'aube des sondages d'opinion en France," *Revue politique et parlementaire*, 28 février 2012, http://www.revuepolitique.fr/1938-1944-laube-des-sondages-dopinion-en-france/. The question submitted to pollers was "Quelle est, selon vous, la nation qui a le plus contribué à la défaite de l'Allemagne?" In May 1945, in France, the results were 57 percent for the USSR and 20 percent for the USA. In June 2004, still in France, the picture was upside down: only 20 percent think that the USSR was the major cause of the Nazi's demise, while 58 percent now think that the USA did the job alone. This shift from historical consciousness to alienation matches the decomposition of the social tissue.

240. On March 15, 1944, the *Conseil National de la Résistance* (National Council of the Resistance) adopted a political blueprint for postwar France. Among the measures to be taken immediately after the liberation were the nationalization of energy, insurance companies and banks, and the creation of an ambitious social security program.

241 Robert Brett Westbrook, *John Dewey and American Democracy* (Ithaca, New York: Cornell University Press, 1991), 440.

242. Janine Delaunay, Donella H. Meadows, Dennis Meadows, Jorgen

Randers, and William W. Behrens III, *The Limits to Growth* (New York: Universe Books, 1972).

243. The narrative thread and the statistics can be found in the relevant Wikipedia entry.

244. Robert Heilbroner, *An Inquiry into the Human Prospect* (New York: W. W. Norton, 1974).

245. Jean-Pierre Dupuy, *Pour un catastrophisme éclairé: quand l'impossible est certain* (Paris: Éditions du Seuil, La couleur des idées, 2002).

246. Rachel Kyte, World Bank Group Vice President and special envoy for climate change, Crawford Fund 2014 annual conference in Parliament House, Canberra, Aug. 27 (see *Sydney Morning Herald*, 27 August 2014).

247. The group of investors includes The Bill and Melinda Gates Foundation, The Rockefeller Foundation, Monsanto Corporation, Syngenta Foundation, and the Government of Norway. Henry Kissinger used to claim that "if you control the oil you control the country; if you control the food you control the population."

248. On the climatic issue alone, scientific forecasts are getting worse year after year: "Late in 2007, the Intergovernmental Panel on Climate Change (IPCC) announced we were committed to warming the planet by about 1 °C by the end of this century. . . . In 2008, the Hadley Centre for Meteorological Research provided an update, indicating that, in the absence of complete economic collapse, we're committed to a global average temperature increase of 2 °C. . . . In September 2009, the United Nations Environment Programme concluded we're committed to an average planetary temperature increase of 3.5 °C by 2100. . . . In October 2009, Chris West of the University of Oxford's UK Climate Impacts Programme indicated we can kiss goodbye 2 °C as a target: four is the new two, and it's coming by mid-century. . . . In November 2009, the Global Carbon Project added to the increasingly miserable news by concluding that we're on a direct path to 6 °C by 2100. The Copenhagen Diagnosis chimed in a couple weeks later with a scenario of 7 °C by 2100. . . . The International Energy Agency added to the agony in November 2010 when, in its World Energy Outlook 2010, it concluded the average global temperature on the planet will increase by 3.5 °C in 2035. The United Nations followed up a month later with their latest and most dire assessment: 6.4 °C increase by 2050. In other words, human extinction looms within a generation." (Guy R. McPherson, *Walking Away from Empire: A Personal Journey* (Baltimore, Maryland: PublishAmerica, 2011), 60)

Bibliography & Abbreviations

1. Whitehead

AE   *The Aims of Education*, 1929 (Free Press, 1967).

AI   *Adventures of Ideas*, 1933 (Free Press, 1967).

CN   *The Concept of Nature*, 1920 (Cambridge, 1964).

ESP   *Essays in Science and Philosophy*, Philosophical Lib., 1947.

FR   *The Function of Reason*, 1929 (Beacon Press, 1958).

IM   Introduction to Mathematics (Williams & Norgate, 1911).

MTh   *Modes of Thought*, 1938 (Free Press, 1968).

OT   *The Organisation of Thought, Educational and Scientific* (Williams & Norgate, 1917).

PNK   *Principles of Natural Knowledge*, 1919/1925 (Dover, 1982).

PR   *Process and Reality*, 1929 (Free Press Corr. Edition, 1978).

R   *The Principle of Relativity*, Cambridge, 1922.

RM   *Religion in the Making*, Macmillan, 1926.

S   *Symbolism, Its Meaning and Effect*, Macmillan, 1927.

SMW   *Science and the Modern World*, 1925 (Free Press, 1967).

2. James

CER   *Collected Essays and Reviews*, Longmans, 1920.

EMS   *Exceptional Mental States*, Charles Scribner's Sons, 1982.

EP   *Essays in Philosophy*, Harvard U Press, 1978.

EPR   *Essays in Psychical Research*, Harvard U Press, 1986.

ERE   *Essays in Radical Empiricism*, 1912 (Bison Books, 1996).

ERM   *Essays in Religion and Morality*, Harvard U Press, 1982.

MS   *Memories and Studies*, Longmans, 1911.

MEN *Manuscripts, Essays and Notes*, Harvard U Press, 1988.

MTr *The Meaning of Truth*, Longmans, 1909.

P *Pragmatism*, 1907 (Longmans, 1916).

PP *The Principles of Psychology*, 1890 (Dover Pub., 1950).

PU *A Pluralistic Universe*, 1909 (Bison Books, 1996).

SPP *Some Problems of Philosophy*, 1911 (Bison Books, 1996).

TT *Talks to Teachers and Students*, Henry Holt, 1900.

VRE *The Varieties of Religious Experience*, Longmans, 1902.

WB *The Will to Believe*, Longmans, 1897.

3. Varia

Henri Bergson, *Oeuvres. Essai sur les données immédiates de la conscience. Matière et Mémoire. Le Rire. L'évolution créatrice. L'énergie spirituelle. Les deux sources de la morale et de la religion. La pensée et le mouvant*, annotate by André Robinet, introduction by Henri Gouhier (Paris: Presses Universitaires de France, Édition du Centenaire, 1959).

Herman E. Daly and John B. Cobb, Jr. (with contributions by Clifford W. Cobb), *For the Common Good: Redirecting the Economy Towards Community, the Environment and a Sustainable Future* (Boston: Beacon Press, 1989); 2nd ed. upd. and exp., 1994.

Philip Kindred Dick, *Five Great Novels. The Three Stigmata of Palmer Eldritch* [1964], *Martian Time Slip* [1964], *Do Androids Dream of Electric Sheep?* [1968], *Ubik* [1969], *A Scanner Darkly* [1977], (London: Gollanz, 2004).

Jacques Ellul, *The Technological Society* [1954], trans. John Wilkinson (New York, Alfred A. Knopf, 1964).

Aldous Leonard Huxley, *Brave New World* (London: Chatto and Windus, 1932); reprinted, with an introduction by David Bradshaw (Hammersmith: HarperCollins, 1994).

Aldous Leonard Huxley, *Island: A Novel* (London: Chatto & Windus, 1962).

Ivan Illich, *Tools for Conviviality* (New York: Harper and Row, 1973).

Naomi Klein, *The Shock Doctrine: The Rise of Disaster Capitalism* (New York: ICM Books, 2007).

George Orwell, *Nineteen Eighty-Four* (London: Martin Secker &

Warburg, 1949); reprinted with an introduction by Thomas Pynchon (London: Penguin Books, 2003).

John Perkins, *Confessions of an Economic Hit Man* (San Francisco: Berrett-Koehler, 2004).

Gore Vidal, *Dreaming War: Blood for Oil and the Cheney-Bush Junta* (New York: Thunder's Mouth Press/Nation Books, 2002).

Michel Weber, "On a Certain Blindness in Political Matters," *Cosmos and History*, www.cosmosandhistory.org, Vol. 7, N°2 (2011).

Michel Weber, *De quelle révolution avons-nous besoin?* (Paris: Éditions Sang de la Terre, 2013).

Howard Zinn, *A People's History of the United States: 1492–Present* (New York: HarperCollins, 1980).

Made in the USA
San Bernardino, CA
28 March 2016